ACTING HEIGHTENED TEXT

Acting Heightened Text: The Basics offers a foundational understanding of heightened text in drama, fused with a truthful, contemporary approach to acting.

Using detailed text analysis and dynamic rehearsal exercises, actors and students bring heightened language to life by cultivating a joyful curiosity. A three-step homework process focuses attention on demystifying the intricacies of verse and prose, conveying meaning, clarifying changes in action (subtle shifts and beat changes), playing actions, and utilizing tactics. An innovative technique called hooking sparks energy between partners, and focuses actors on responding to impulses to create a wide variety of textually-supported choices. The book includes up-to-date practical approaches to effective auditions, callbacks and rehearsals, specific tools for handling rhyming couplets, complex rhetorical arguments, and materials to support a lifelong pursuit of engaging with dramatic material with rigor and passion.

Acting Heightened Text: The Basics provides a wealth of resources for actors, directors, students, and teachers to navigate the demands and embrace the challenges within dramatic texts.

To support the learning process and enhance the understanding of the lessons from the book, please visit the Support Material, available at www.routledge.com/9781032695297. These include scenes and monologues for practice, real-life examples of students using these techniques, and detailed examples from the Try It! sections within each chapter, such as line-outs, action verbs, rhetorical maps, and hooking.

Catherine Weidner is a professional actor and director. She was the founding Program Director for The Shakespeare Theatre Academy for Classical Acting at the George Washington University and taught acting heightened text at DePaul University and Ithaca College.

The Basics Series

The Basics is a highly successful series of accessible guidebooks which provide an overview of the fundamental principles of a subject area in a jargon-free and undaunting format.

Intended for students approaching a subject for the first time, the books both introduce the essentials of a subject and provide an ideal springboard for further study. With over 50 titles spanning subjects from artificial intelligence (AI) to women's studies, *The Basics* are an ideal starting point for students seeking to understand a subject area.

Each text comes with recommendations for further study and gradually introduces the complexities and nuances within a subject.

SIKHISM
NIKKY-GUNINDER KAUR SINGH, ELEANOR NESBITT

TRANSACTIONAL ANALYSIS
MARK WIDDOWSON

POETRY
JEFFREY WAINWRIGHT

POLITICS AND RELIGION
JEFFREY HAYNES

SEMIOTICS (FIFTH EDITION)
DANIEL CHANDLER

EDUCATION (SECOND EDITION)
KAY WOOD

SPOKEN ENGLISH
MICHAEL MCCARTHY AND STEVE WALSH

BUSINESS START-UP
ALEXANDRINA PAUCEANU

ACTING HEIGHTENED TEXT
CATHERINE WEIDNER

For more information about this series, please visit: www.routledge.com/The-Basics/book-series/B

"Catherine Weidner's knowledge and expertise surrounding heightened text helped me to demystify the language, while simultaneously simplifying Shakespeare and acting into relatable terms: *do the work*. In theater, much is made of talent and instinct, but heightened text has a way revealing an actor's preparation, whether it be substantial or lacking. What *Acting Heightened Text: The Basics* provides is a toolbox for the modern actor, equipped with a variety of insights and immersions that invites the artist to delve into the work as deeply as they wish."

Kevin Bigley, *Writer/Actor*

"The best thing about *Acting Heightened Text: The Basics* is that it doesn't just apply to heightened text. There is no script that I work on that I don't clearly mark beats/shifts; or perhaps if my character uses language/vocabulary that I don't normally use, I will employ the line-out method to put the language into my own words. I use hooking to highlight the connective tissue between what I am saying and what another character has said. If there is an operative word that will help me land my action or intent more clearly, I mark it. Catherine Weidner taught me how to use tools that I continue to use today to ensure I truly understand what I am saying and that what I am intending to communicate is clear, whether it is considered heightened text or not."

KiKi Layne, *Actor/Producer,* If Beale Street Could Talk, The Old Guard

"*Acting Heightened Text: The Basic's* approach changed me as an artist for the better. What was once daunting and intimidating became approachable and exciting! I use many of Catherine's tools to this day when mining scripts for meaningful moments."

Taylor Misiak, *FX/Hulu's Dave*

"It's difficult to put into a few sentences what *Acting Heightened Text: The Basics* did for me. I studied Shakespeare for almost 15 years before I entered Catherine's class – yet what I learned under her tutelage put all that into a completely different light. Her approach has a way of making 500-year-old words and ideas so modern, so present and so immediate that you feel like they were written ten minutes ago. I wish upon wish I could take her class every couple months from now until forever."

Adam Wesley Brown, *Actor/Musician*, Once, Widows

"Catherine Weidner's teaching profoundly influenced how I understand and use language, particularly in how it can both reveal and conceal deeper meanings. The lessons in *Acting Heightened Text: The Basics* provided me with a valuable tool to recognize that a single word can have various meanings based on context, intent, and timing. This insight has greatly enriched my approach to my work, both past and present, allowing me to explore what lies beneath the surface of what's being said. It's a gift that continues to benefit me in my work."

Yaegel T. Welch, *Actor/Activist on Broadway, Television, and Film*

"I'm grateful to have learned the techniques in *Acting Heightened Text: The Basics.* Catherine's approach invited me to bring my full self without apology to my work. Shakespeare was intimidating at first, but these tools break it down in a way that felt easy and fun. I still use given circumstances, paraphrase, and operative words in my work today."

Celeste M. Cooper, *Member Steppenwolf Theatre Ensemble*

"Before I worked with Catherine Weidner, Shakespeare and heightened text felt a million miles away. *Acting Heightened Text* gives you the roadmap to walk closer to the part and enliven it in you, which is always the goal of the actor. When Shakespeare feels like a foreign language, her tools guide you to make it relatable, human and truthful in yourself."

Alexander Koch, *Actor/Writer*

ACTING HEIGHTENED TEXT
THE BASICS

Catherine Weidner

NEW YORK AND LONDON

Designed cover image: An *Othello, First Quarto* page
reprinted with permission of the British Library.

First published 2026
by Routledge
605 Third Avenue, New York, NY 10158

and by Routledge
4 Park Square, Milton Park, Abingdon, Oxon, OX14 4RN

Routledge is an imprint of the Taylor & Francis Group, an informa business

© 2026 Catherine Weidner

The right of Catherine Weidner to be identified as author of this work has been asserted in accordance with sections 77 and 78 of the Copyright, Designs and Patents Act 1988.

All rights reserved. No part of this book may be reprinted or reproduced or utilised in any form or by any electronic, mechanical, or other means, now known or hereafter invented, including photocopying and recording, or in any information storage or retrieval system, without permission in writing from the publishers.

Trademark notice: Product or corporate names may be trademarks or registered trademarks, and are used only for identification and explanation without intent to infringe.

ISBN: 978-1-032-69530-3 (hbk)
ISBN: 978-1-032-69529-7 (pbk)
ISBN: 978-1-032-69531-0 (ebk)

DOI: 10.4324/9781032695310

Typeset in Bembo
by codeMantra

Access the Support Material: www.routledge.com/9781032695297

*For Kevin, who knows what I mean,
no matter what I say.*

CONTENTS

	Rights and Permissions	xi
	Acknowledgments	xii
	Introduction	1
1	**Demystifying Verse**	10
2	**A Foundation of Meaning**	40
3	**Conveying the Ideas: Emphasis on Words, Thoughts, Ideas, and Images**	65
4	**Connecting to the Partner and the Situation**	88
5	**Hooking: Active Listening and Responding to Impulses**	114
6	**Playing Intentions, Actions, and Tactics**	143
7	**Advanced Skills: Prose, Rhetoric, and Rhyming Couplets**	155
8	**Helpful Advice for Callbacks, Rehearsal, and Performance**	185
	Support Material Available at: www.routledge.com/9781032695297	203
	Appendix 1: Geek-Out on Scansion/Iambic Pentameter Review Sheet	204
	Appendix 2: Verse Monologues for Practice (Iago, Portia, Leontes)	211

Appendix 3: Paraphrase of Emilia and Iago Scene	214
Glossary	218
Bibliography	225
Index	227

RIGHTS AND PERMISSIONS

Cover Image of an *Othello, First Quarto* page reprinted with permission of the British Library.

Excerpts from "Act I, Scene One" from A RAISIN IN THE SUN by Lorraine Hansberry, Copyright ©1958 by Robert Nemiroff, as an unpublished work. Copyright © 1959, 1966, 1984 by Robert Nemiroff. Copyright renewed 1986, 1987 by Robert Nemiroff. Used by permission of Random House, an imprint and division of Penguin Random House LLC. All rights reserved.

A Raisin in the Sun by Lorraine Hansberry, UK electronic rights: Permission granted for use by Joi Gresham, Lorraine Hansberry Literary Trust.

UK Print rights for *A Raisin in the Sun* by Lorraine Hansberry ©2021, Methuen Drama, an imprint of Bloomsbury Publishing Plc.

"Satisfied," from *Hamilton: An American Musical,* Words and Music by LIN-MANUEL MIRANDA © 2015 5000 BROADWAY MUSIC (ASCAP) All Rights Administered by WC MUSIC CORP. All Rights Reserved Used by Permission of ALFRED MUSIC.

Selections from Richard Wilbur's Introduction and Translation of Moliere's *The Misanthrope* are with permission of Dramatists Play Service/Broadway Licensing Global.

An excerpt from *Angels in America, Part One: Millennium Approaches* is printed with permission of Theatre Communications Group.

Drawings of Hooking Figures in Chapter 5 Copyright ©2024 by Leanna Yatcilla.

ACKNOWLEDGMENTS

A great many people are part of this book: my current and former students, treasured colleagues, mentors, teachers, directors, dramaturgs, and even my role models. This book represents an approach I've been developing in my teaching since graduate school, whether it was as an instructor in a year-long college course, a summer high-school program, a one-off workshop at a festival; while directing a production or leading a session at a conference. Teaching took root with each experience, and for me, built into a practice because of the questions, discoveries, risks and rewards that happen in the exploration of heightened text, particularly verse. The seeds were planted at Ithaca College by my undergraduate acting teachers Earl McCarroll and Arno Selco, and my directing teacher and mentor, Richard M. Clark, who taught me the importance of thoughtful, careful analysis of the text as the basis for specific, active choices for each moment. Further training at The Neighborhood Playhouse, The Second City, and Complicité challenged me to take risks and bring dynamic energy to the rehearsal process, whether as an actor, director, or teacher.

Big waves of discovery happened for me through a few extraordinary years interning at The Guthrie Theater and Theatre de la Jeune Lune while attending the University of Minnesota. My work grew with guidance from professors H. Wesley Balk, Michal Kobialka, Lou Bellamy, James Norwood, Glen Gadberry, Kent Neely, and dramaturgy and directing internships with Michael Lupu, Mark Bly, and Garland Wright. I was first introduced to the work of formidable directors Michael Kahn, Liviu Ciulei, Lucian Pintilie, Dominique Serrand and others, and I witnessed at-the-time-nascent directors Bartlett Sher and Charles Newell cutting their teeth on Shakespeare's History Plays. Ten years at The Shakespeare Theatre in Washington, DC afforded me a seat next to Michael Kahn, who has trained some of the greatest American actors working today. He expected students to bring a high level of preparation, a greater sense of the scope and size of the truth, and a dose each of humor, humanity and humility to their work with heightened text. I did my best to prepare students for Michael's classes, and this book represents the tangible steps any actor can take to be ready to work with this material. I draw inspiration from the work of directors Giorgio Strehler, Ariane Mnouchkine, Deborah Warner, and Simon McBurney, who bring a sense of immediacy to texts old and new.

Since those challenging, formative years, my teaching has taken shape with the support and inspiration of hundreds of academic and professional colleagues in voice, speech, text, movement, dramaturgy, directing, theatre history, and acting. Among them, immeasurable contributions to my teaching have come from James Magruder, Gary Logan, Ellen O'Brien, Edward Gero, Dody DiSanto, Isabelle Anderson, Christopher Bayes, Krista Scott, Gregg Henry, Wendy Dann, Paula Murray Cole, Kathleen Mulligan, Bill Langan, Dawn McAndrews, Brett Johnson, Theo Black, Leslie Jacobson, Phil Timberlake, Phyllis Griffin, Dexter Bullard, and Damon Kiely. Some of my former students graciously provided homework examples for this book, representing all three major institutions where I have taught: The Shakespeare Theatre Academy for Classical Acting at the George Washington University, DePaul University, and Ithaca College. Leanna Yatcilla, an artist and student in my Acting I course in my final year of teaching, drew imaginative, dynamic illustrations for the Hooking chapter.

Permission to use excerpts from contemporary texts was graciously provided by the authors through their representatives and licensing agencies. All other text examples are cited appropriately, or are within the public domain.

Though the content of this book owes thanks to so many people, its very existence is wholly because of my husband, partner, best friend, and editor, Kevin McGuire. To him, I am most grateful for everything he makes possible.

INTRODUCTION

When you want to travel somewhere, what's the first thing you would do? You'd look at a map. Whether it's a page in a road atlas or an app on a phone, a map helps you figure out how to get there. What roads should you take? Most of us know how to recognize the code that maps use: big, blue lines mean interstate highways, small red lines are state roads, black lines are less-traveled back roads, and dotted lines mean boundaries of states or countries. There's usually a Key or a Legend that explains what all the symbols mean. Alongside the lines are numbers to help in gauging the distance between points and little icons for places we can get food, fuel, or a place to rest. The map makes it easy, and for many of us, fun!

Acting heightened text is a similar kind of journey. The building blocks of language in the text provide us with information, and, if we pay attention to the signs, we can crack the code and navigate the path to conveying the deep and nuanced meaning of a play, letting the language lead us. Doing so requires learnable skills which take practice, and **this book is intended as a key to the map** to get you there. Heightened text skills can be applied to all text you might encounter as an actor, whether in a play, a musical, an opera, or any speech you need to make, even if you wouldn't consider the text to be heightened in any way.

DOI: 10.4324/9781032695310-1

A LITTLE BACKGROUND ON HEIGHTENED TEXT: WHAT DOES THAT EVEN MEAN?

Heightened text means that the language itself is in the driver's seat – whether in a play, a poem, or a song lyric. The words sound a little different than everyday speech, whether in verse or prose, and they are organized in ways that give them unique power to express feelings, ideas, and intentions. The unique components of heightened language convey meaning above and beyond how we usually talk.

Many actors think they need to speak heightened text with a British accent if they're in a Shakespeare play, or that there's a particular way to say classical or heightened text to make it sound better. However, Shakespeare isn't a style of acting, he's just a playwright, who wrote in a particular way at a time when plays were written mostly in iambic pentameter and prose. Today, his plays (and hundreds of other classical works) are produced in a myriad of periods and settings, including contemporary ones. Contemporary playwrights have their own vernacular language (reflecting the way people really talk), and this demands its own attention to detail, so that we can reflect the world in the most authentic way. The tools and skills I offer here apply to all dramatic works, whether the heightened text is immediate and incisive, like the plays of Tony Kushner, Jeremy O. Harris, Caryl Churchill, or Suzan-Lori Parks, or timeless and resonant, like Euripides' *Medea,* or Shakespeare's *Othello.* In this book, many examples are from plays available in the public domain, or when not, with express permission of the authors. Shakespeare is heavily featured because his plays have been the focus of my three decades of teaching and professional work. The techniques I developed used Shakespeare and his contemporaries as the material, though the skills are applicable to all dramatic texts.

WHAT THIS BOOK STRIVES TO ACHIEVE

This book focuses on demystifying heightened language to use it as the basis for conveying truthful behavior in imaginary circumstances as easily and readily as with a play written today. I approach style from the standpoint of entering the world that exists in the play (and the production), the same way you move in specific ways when you hear a particular kind of music or adapt to the road conditions and terrain when driving in unfamiliar places. This book strives to teach you how to prepare, what to look for, and what to do next that best serves the story. In acting that means doing the homework, digging into the text in profound ways to extract meaning, and then making choices based on those discoveries. I am striving to fill what I perceive as a gap between what actors working with heightened text bring to an audition or the rehearsal room, and what's possible: to help them prepare deeply and then put that preparation into effective and tangible use. Former students of mine who make use of these tools in rehearsal have found other actors leaning over to take a look at their working script, then pulling them aside at the end of the table reading to ask, "How did you do that?" The answer, invariably, is a version of "I just did the homework." For many actors, homework has only meant reading the play, highlighting their own lines, and memorizing them, along with whatever clues might have emerged as they do so. In this book, working step-by-step, you will learn how to focus on many other things in and about your lines: how they are structured, what they mean, which words need emphasis, what the character wants, how they plan to get it, what tactics the actor must employ to succeed, what the other character just said, and how you are going to respond to it. Ideally, every rehearsal turns into a joyful opportunity to share textually-based ideas and choices based on the given circumstances and informed by the world of the play.

The goal of this book is to offer actors, directors, students, teachers, and lifelong learners the knowledge and skills to overcome the challenges and reap the rewards that heightened text provides. Each chapter introduces a part of the process that merges the basics of acting and text analysis to take on the demands of plays written in verse and heightened prose. By demystifying the language, actors can make strong choices that are grounded in the text and then establish a compelling connection to a scene partner and the situation, listen and respond to what is happening in the moment, and fully inhabit the world of the play created by the playwright and director. Actors who can bring language to life have the flexibility to work within both period-specific and contemporary settings and are able to approach any text with confidence, readiness, and clarity.

HOW TO USE THIS BOOK

One of the ways to engage more effectively with this book is to read it aloud. That's how most of us learned to read when we were younger, by having someone else read aloud to us, until we were able to do it ourselves. Then we did so, to ourselves, silently. But when we read aloud, so many more senses are involved! If you are a visual or kinesthetic learner, or an auditory processor, you know that it helps your learning to hear, to speak, to see the words and to feel them coming alive in our mouths and bodies. Words are real, and ideas have power. Speaking the text aloud is how plays are meant to be experienced. A theatre isn't a library with everybody reading to themselves. (Some examples have a link to an audio file in the Support Materials to further enhance your learning.)

If you're in a course and using this as your textbook, great! If not, pretend you are! You might think of these eight chapters as eight intensive weeks of a class, and yourself as a student in the class. Try the examples in each section, teaming up with a partner whenever possible. View the appendixes as a treasure trove of resources to explore. Spend some time practicing on your own, using a pencil and paper, reading the whole play the selection is from, maybe going to see a production, or auditioning and then acting in one yourself.

Learning to work with heightened text takes time and practice, like learning to drive. Doing the work yourself is when the most effective learning takes place, and with heightened text, that process never ends (in a good way!). Experience helps you learn, and mistakes help you improve, if you commit to learning from them. You can't learn how to drive a car by reading a book. Eventually, you need to get behind the wheel to experience it for yourself: make some wrong turns, get lost, and learn how to respond when something unexpected happens. Acting heightened text is like that, too. A book can teach you how to scan metrical verse, but once you do it aloud for yourself and see the value of uncovering thousands of clues, you'll gain confidence and skill. If you bring a growth mindset, (the concept that intelligence and ability can be developed through effort, popularized by Stanford psychologist Carol Dweck), you will learn through challenges, focus, feedback, and practice.

Skill with heightened text didn't come easily for me, but neither did learning to tie my shoelaces or driving a stick shift, but I learned how through practice! When I was a college student, I expressed to my teacher that I had difficulty with scansion, that I found it confusing and tedious. I told them that I could hear the rhythm, but when I marked up my script, it was all backwards. They listened, nodded their head, and handed me their single Pelican edition of Shakespeare's *Richard II,* one of the few plays written entirely in verse. I read the whole play aloud and scanned every single line with my pencil and eraser in my hand, cramming the unstressed and stressed marks within the tiny spaces on the printed page. It felt like the equivalent of the 70 hours of driving behind the wheel before I was allowed to get my driver's license. I understood (and embraced) all of the rules and most of the exceptions, even though at the time I had no idea what they were called (there's a fancy name for everything, to be sure). Think of this book as a driving manual for heightened text, it can do a lot, but it can't do everything – you've got to get out there and try, open your mouth and speak, get up on your feet and respond.

WHAT LIES AHEAD

Here's a brief overview of the landscape before you, though you'll have to read the book to dig deeper and learn what it all means and how these skills can support your process.

There are three basic steps to the process of demystifying heightened text written in verse: **scansion,** *paraphrase*, and **operative words**.

STEP ONE: SCANSION

Scansion is tracking the number and weight of syllables, like the ten alternating weak [˘] and strong [/] syllables in a line of iambic pentameter in this regular line from Shakespeare's *Measure for Measure:* (Please read it aloud.)

The duke is very strangely gone from hence.

Having a numerical structure provides order, whether in music, architecture, or golf. When we **scan**, we look closely at the rhythm of the syllables, noting them with little marks above the syllables that indicate their **rhythmic weight**: light [˘] or heavy [/], and discovering how they align with the **meter** (which means how many syllables there are), adding up to ten syllables. Here is how this line scans:

> ˘   / ˘ / ˘   /   ˘   /   ˘   /
> **The duke is very strangely gone from hence.**

Meter in heightened text is similar to what's called a time signature in music. In music, there are a certain number of beats per measure that might be divided up into whole notes, quarter notes, triplets, etc. **Metric feet | ˘ / |** in **verse** work essentially the same way. Knowing how the meter plays out is a critical step, even in a "regular" line like this one:

> ˘   / ˘ / ˘   /   ˘   /   ˘   /
> |The duke | is ve|ry stran|gely gone| from hence|.

Why scan? Because there is information for the actor within the scansion, just as for the musician there is information within the measures full of notes. This information includes feelings, actions, thoughts, and responses – things actors need in order to **make choices** based on the **given circumstances** of the story, something we will encounter later in the homework.

STEP TWO: PARAPHRASING

The second step whether it's verse or prose is *paraphrasing* the line to ensure we know what it means. We put it into our own words, exploring what images or metaphors are being used, looking up words we are curious about in a dictionary, and learning about any historical or mythological references. Here's a paraphrase of our example:

> The duke is very strangely gone from hence.
>
> *The man in charge, uncharacteristically, and for no known reason, left Vienna.*

We must know what the words mean and what ideas are being expressed, in order to convey that meaning to an audience. Part of the paraphrase step is **being curious**, looking up words we don't know, or words we think we know in a dictionary, and using other resources to help us understand references made in the text. In this passage, I chose to look up these words: duke, very, strangely, gone and hence, even though I was relatively sure I knew what they meant. This led to discoveries that enhanced my understanding. An actor's understanding supports the audience's understanding.

STEP THREE: OPERATIVE WORDS

The third step of the homework is to find the **operative words** and underline them: what words we emphasize with a little more energy to make the meaning clear.

> The duke is very strangely gone from hence.

We emphasize operative words in our everyday communication. If we aren't being understood, we double down and speak those words with stronger emphasis. Perhaps we re-phrase things until we receive a signal that the message is conveyed. The same thing happens in heightened text. Often a character says the same thing in different ways, when it's clear their message isn't getting across. Operative words provide clues not only for the character who's speaking, but for the ones who are listening. How a character utters their words matters. Every choice has to be activated, manifested physically and vocally, resulting in dynamic acting that proceeds **moment-to-moment**, as if it's happening for the first time on stage.

NEXT STEPS: CONNECTING THE HOMEWORK TO SCRIPT ANALYSIS AND ACTING TECHNIQUE

I've given you a quick preview of the three steps of homework for demystifying and preparing a passage of heightened text. After the text homework reveals so much, this new understanding needs to be applied in rehearsal. This is when the **basic skills of script analysis and acting** come into play: finding the **given circumstances**,

identifying the changes in a scene whether they are big ones (**beats**) or subtle ones (**shifts**), and playing the **intentions, actions,** and **tactics**.

Using Lucio's line from *Measure for Measure* above, here's what might emerge from our **script analysis** of the scene to support the **acting choices**:

- **Given circumstance**s: The Duke is absent for unknown reasons. Lord Angelo is now in charge and enforcing laws long dormant. Claudio has been arrested and has asked his friend Lucio to reach out to Claudio's sister, Isabella, to intercede with Angelo, and ask for mercy on his behalf. Isabella is about to take her vows as a nun. Lucio is a bit of a rogue himself.
- **Intention**: to convince Isabella to go see Lord Angelo and urge him to free Claudio
- **Actions**: to move her, to push her, to direct her
- **Tactics**: to shock her, to ignite her, to inspire her

"FINISHING THE HAT": ADVANCED SKILLS AND ADVICE FOR THE JOURNEY

Inspired by Sondheim's lyric from *Sunday in the Park with George*, the later chapters of this book focus on developing advanced skills for **working with heightened prose** and **rhyming couplets** and introduce the process of **"hooking,"** which builds on the **discoveries** made in the homework but requires **engagement with scene partners**. We use a different lens if we are working with heightened **prose** and employ a technique called a **line-out** to help us give shape to the text and uncover its clues without the benefit of scansion. Working with **rhyming couplets** leans into how operative words interact with the rhyming words. **Hooking** provides the connectivity between what one character says and how another character responds. It's where the rubber meets the road in acting heightened text, but it cannot be effective without the work that comes before – as Hamlet says "the readiness is all." By building these skills, you will bring more to the table, and more of what you bring will be focused and grounded in specifics. Some final words provide guidance for navigating heightened text in audition and callback situations, as well as considerations for how to manage expectations of the profession with a positive mindset. My hope is that you will find that embracing a process of focusing on what other characters are saying and doing creates a profound sense of generosity in your acting.

LET'S BEGIN!

This book helps you find buried treasure within heightened language and bring it to life in your acting through tangible steps you take on your own and in rehearsal with others. You can use these tools with any text and, as you get comfortable using them, change the order in which you do them to serve your needs. The words in heightened text will never disappoint you; they tell a particular story with passion and specificity.

Knowing how to begin, figuring out what to do next, and embracing the process of homework as a source of discovery are the pathways to confidently and capably inhabiting heightened text. The lessons in this book present skills that take time and practice. When a process has value, a substitute or shortcut will not bring the same result. Enjoy the journey and the destination will be all the more worthwhile.

DEMYSTIFYING VERSE

DECODING THE TREASURE MAP OF HEIGHTENED TEXT

Think about a time in elementary school when you were asked to memorize a poem or a speech. More than likely, the focus was simply to be able to repeat it, "by rote" that is, knowing it without really understanding it, the way some of us learned addition, subtraction, or multiplication, memorizing the equations without really comprehending the concepts of basic arithmetic. Just like with other structured systems like maps and recipes, there are letters, numbers, special symbols, and patterns that help us on our way to understanding, and consequently, delivering a richer, more detailed performance. If we learn a song, we hear the notes, and sing along, even if we have no idea how to read the weird squiggles and lines that we see on sheet music. Once we understand how the system works, however, we can enjoy the process, and delight in its nuances, like solving a puzzle. With heightened text, a little bit of information demystifies the process and unlocks the fun, creativity, and understanding that comes with learning how to act heightened text of all kinds, whether it's song lyrics by Stephen Sondheim, Michael R. Jackson, or Lynn Ahrens, or plays by William Shakespeare, Sarah Kane, August Wilson, or Ike Holter. Heightened text is like a buried treasure, and this book is the map that gets you there. Once you discover the treasure, though, what do you plan to do with it? This book fills the gap for actors who don't know what to do first, or

DOI: 10.4324/9781032695310-2

what to do next, and so on, from homework that really serves you well, to interacting with scene partners and directors in rehearsal, all the way up to the closing performance. These tools and techniques help actors cross a threshold into taking responsibility for every moment with a textually supported choice, brought to life by dynamic listening skills and shrewd awareness of the intricacies of the words.

The only special equipment we need for this work is a pencil, some paper, and curiosity. We are investigating and solving little puzzles with every line of text we encounter. For some people, poetry is like broccoli: we may have a negative experience with it in our past and never want to try it again. Let's begin by taking a deep breath and shaking off those memories, both of the poetry (and the broccoli). If you have only pleasant memories, take a deep breath anyway.

If you felt bored and frustrated when *Romeo and Juliet* or *Julius Caesar* was being taught in English class, if it seemed like a foreign language with no connection at all to what was happening in your life at that moment, we are about to step through that fog and find that connection, plug into our imaginations and make the text come alive. The power of the spoken word is matched by the compelling themes of the plays written in verse and heightened prose. It's more than regular text. It's higher! It's too much meaning, emotion, or higher stakes for plain old language.

Song lyrics are poetry, sung to music, making it another form of heightened text. Whatever kind of music you listen to, whether it's heavy metal, rap, hip-hop, roots, pop, rock, power ballads, opera, or jazz standards, the lyrics tell the story. The music gives the story tone, feeling, and mood. The basic elements of music are present in all these genres and styles: notes on a scale, in a particular key, and marked to represent their rhythm and length. These components develop a melody or a theme, and the variations are distinct and appreciated. Heightened text doesn't have to be written in verse or sung. The "heightened" part can be what's at stake. When you have something important to say, for example, a speech at a friend's wedding, or an address to a group of people, your words carry weight to convey a message to that particular audience. Actors need to hone several skills in navigating verse to sound like real people actually talking. These skills include three basic steps of homework introduced over the next few chapters, followed by more advanced skills as we gain confidence through practice. Though the risk isn't the same as, say, whitewater rafting, even with heightened text, it helps to learn the basics and follow the rules in order to understand how to harness the power of the language.

DECODING THE BUILDING BLOCKS OF VERSE: RHYTHM AND METER

Think about the first heightened text you ever encountered. It might have been nursery rhymes – which are fancy rhyming poems, often songs, written for young children. Poetry is called "verse" and is a form of heightened text: something written in a different way than the way we usually talk, speak, or write, which is called "prose." Verse has more structure than prose, and the rules about verse can be simple or complex, but every kind of verse has specific rules, just like any game you might play.

Nursery rhymes are written in verse with rules about **rhythm** (how it sounds) and **meter** (the length of the line measured in syllables). For nursery rhymes, we know there's a **rhythm** to each line that is exactly the same, like "da dum da dee da dum, da dum da dee da dum." The ending word of each line usually rhymes with the ending word of the previous line or in alternating lines. This makes them easy for children to remember and enjoy, as in this popular example from the 1800s by Sarah Hale:

> Mary had a little lamb,
> Its fleece was white as snow.
> And everywhere that Mary went,
> The lamb was sure to go.

The **meter** of verse is how many **syllables** are in each line, which usually stays the same throughout the text or has a regular pattern and some variations. Verse can be rhymed (like most nursery rhymes), blank (not rhyming, like much of Shakespeare), or free (like Gwendolyn Brooks) – describing how it employs both rhythm and meter (or not). To begin, we will focus on blank, non-rhyming dramatic verse, and cover rhyming couplets in a later chapter.

The first kind of poetry many young people learn to write themselves is Haiku. It's an ancient Japanese poetic form that contains three lines of text, follows a simple theme, and has a very specific metrical structure that most people call "5-7-5," representing the number of syllables per line. The first line has 5 syllables, the second line has 7 syllables, and then the final line contains 5 syllables. Young people easily grasp this structure, count out the syllables on their fingers, and compose delightful Haiku poems following those rules, conveying their idea simply and sparsely. The only rule to follow is the number of syllables per line.

Here's a classic Haiku example by Japanese poet Murakami Kijo (1865–1938):

First autumn morning	5 syllables
the mirror I stare into	7 syllables
shows my father's face.	5 syllables

If you read it aloud a couple of times, you might instinctively pause slightly at the end of the verse lines (even though there's no punctuation) and lift the ending word of the first and second lines, as if to extend the anticipation of what comes next. This delivery heightens the language enough to convey the realization of the speaker – it's a new day, but he's seeing the past, seeing time go by, and becoming his father. The use of only one-syllable and two-syllable words seems to give the poem a slow, even pace. This simple blank verse poem (not rhyming) communicates the effectiveness of heightened text, how knowing its structure and decoding the signs is a valuable skill for actors.

So as Haiku is a syllable structure of 5/7/5, iambic pentameter (the dramatic verse we'll be exploring the most in this book) has a built-in meter of 10.

The structure of ten is embedded into our world with our phone numbers. Try saying aloud this made-up telephone number: 555-724-3279. Telephone numbers are ten numbers, but not always ten syllables. In this example, the number "seven" is two syllables if you elongated it in both instances and said "sev-en," but in the context (and pace) of saying a telephone number, we smush the word, or **elide** it, into one quicker syllable "sev'n" in order to make it efficient every time we say it. The apostrophe ['] takes the place of the syllable we no longer say aloud, similar to the way use contractions like [don't] instead of "I do not." And there are exceptions to the ten-number rule, too. We add a +1 to the front of the 10-digit telephone number, or a +011 if we're out of the country, and it's still a phone number. Exceptions have rules, too, in phone numbers and in verse structure.

Now that we've covered the **meter** of our phone number, let's make sure we get the **rhythm** of it by finding out what parts are **unstressed** and which are **stressed**, even though it's not exactly iambic pentameter. Try it, but this time saying the little words that represent the scansion instead of the numbers, adding some emphasis to those <u>underlined</u> and in **bold**:

[da-da- DUM	da-da- DUM	da-DUM-da-DUM]
5 5 **5** -	7 2 **4** -	3 **2** 7 **9**

We recognize this as a phone number when we hear it, because of the variations in the rhythm between light and heavy, and the inflection pattern, emphasizing the final number of each of the first two sets of three sounds, pausing slightly, and then a faster tempo and alternating emphasis on the final set of four sounds. There's a set of 3, then another set of 3 and then a set of 4, and it adds up to 10. We demystified the code of the Haiku and the phone number!

We shift our focus now to demystifying Shakespeare's verse, written in **Iambic Pentameter**, the most common form of English poetry since the 1400s. This is a measure of rhythm (that's the **iambic** part) and just like in Haiku, how many syllables there are (that's the **pentameter** part), but it also adds a rule about how those syllables are organized, dividing them into **feet**, which means small measured units that make up the verse line, just like in the phone number. We don't need to emphasize the division of feet, but they help us keep time, like the minute marks on a clock face. We mark them through a process called **scansion,** which tracks the rhythm of the line and helps us land on the meaning. Doing your scansion when a text is in verse is like the "You are here" point on a map, it gives you the lay of the land, the arrangement, that things are in a particular place for a reason. As we mark the syllables with [˘] and [/] – indicating weak and strong, written just above the syllable, we determine its rhythm and look carefully at something to understand more about it, to look at all of its parts, like a CT scan (a "CAT scan") can look inside the human body. Scansion is an important first step that identifies the rhythm that makes the line move, in the same way you keep time with your foot or clap along with beats in music.

Two alternating syllables, one weak, marked [˘] and one strong, marked [/], are considered **a foot of verse** | ˘ / |. Since there are 5 metric feet, the Greek prefix **"penta-"** is used to measure the meter. You can choose any pair of words that suits you to describe these two kinds of syllables: weak/strong, light/heavy, little/big, or unstressed/stressed. When we speak this way, even in conversation, we often alternate light and strong syllables, naturally putting less stress on the first syllable and more stress on the second, as in the word "enough."

> Enough with calling other people names!
> *Scanned, it would look like this on our homework:*
> ˘ / ˘ / ˘ / ˘ /
> Enough with calling other people names!

That doesn't sound like a nursery rhyme, it sounds like how people really talk! Iambic pentameter often mirrors ordinary speech patterns.

The simplest explanation for iambic pentameter requires a little math:

> 2 × 5 =10, which represents:
> 2 syllables in an iambic metrical foot | ˘ / |
> x
> 5 feet = 10 syllables per verse line

To get a feel for how this might sound, let's try out what a meaningless line of iambic pentameter would sound like if we marked the **iambs** (with a light and then a heavy mark above each syllable) and did that five times (for the pentameter). Read this aloud, emphasizing the strong syllables:

> ˘ / ˘ / ˘ / ˘ / ˘ /
> |da-dum| |da-dum| |da-dum| |da dum| |da dum|

But iambic pentameter doesn't have to sound like that, beaten out and repeated line after line. The alternating of weak and strong syllables is an accurate reflection of the way we speak every day. It's the organizing of alternating stress into the specific meter that makes it verse. Imagine if we had to make each of our conversational thoughts exactly ten syllables:

> I haven't done a single thing all day.
> Well, every now and then you need a rest.

It would be a fun game, to make every line we speak have to be in iambic pentameter (some improvisation groups incorporate this into their live shows!), but fortunately, we don't have to hold to this rule in everyday situations.

Let's practice the **Iamb** aloud, the basic regular pattern (unstressed-stressed) of [˘ /]: weak, then strong, as in these words spoken the regular way

˘ /	˘ /	˘ /
Christine	enough	terrain
Chris-TINE	e-NOUGH	ter-RAIN

The most common variation to an iamb is the natural **Trochee** (stressed-unstressed) or [/ ˘], which is a reversed Iamb, strong then weak, as in these three words spoken the regular way:

/ ˘	/ ˘	/ ˘
Ryan	weather	kettle
RY-an	WEA-ther	KET-tle

Scansion can seem easier if we focus on any **multisyllabic words** within the line (words that have more than one syllable) and mark which syllables are either unstressed or stressed, regardless of where they fall as feet within the line. **Monosyllabic words** (one-syllable words) are the harder words to decipher for stress, since their weight depends on the rest of the line.

To get a little perspective about scanning multisyllabic words, say these six multisyllabic iambic words aloud **the opposite way** than we did above:

/ ˇ	/ ˇ	/ ˇ
Christine	enough	terrain
CHRIS-tine	EE-nough	TER-rain

And look what happens when we take what are the naturally occurring trochees, but scanning and saying them as if they were iambic:

ˇ /	ˇ /	ˇ /
Ryan	weather	kettle
ry-AN	wea-THER	ket-TLE

The reversed scansion doesn't work, the words don't make sense pronounced this way. Or as my father used to say: "That dog don't hunt." There is no right or wrong in scansion. There is scansion that works or doesn't work, scansion that is helpful or is not helpful. If you think you've got some challenging scansion, try saying the problematic word or phrase the other way, and always within the context of the whole line. Some words mean one thing scanned as an iamb, and another thing entirely when scanned as a trochee, like the following:

> u /
> **object** (a verb, expressing disapproval)
> "I object!"
>
> / u
> **object** (a noun, a thing that can be seen or touched)
> "It's a valuable object."
>
> u / u
> **objective** (a noun, a purpose or goal)
> "My objective is to win."

Words "scan" regardless of whether or not they are part of a metered sentence or thought. The way we actually say the word is what matters most, so that its meaning is clear. How that weight of stress falls within a line of iambic pentameter is the puzzle we need to solve when doing our scansion, so it can be the foundation of everything we do next.

It's important to reinforce that reading aloud is the most effective way to reveal the scansion, and as one of my former teachers used to say, "sound like a normal person," instead of with a forced rhythm or hyper-awareness of it as iambic pentameter (or in whatever meter it's written). When I encounter a new piece of text, the first thing I do is read it aloud: twice. I put my pencil down and just read it. Just reading it aloud a couple of times helps to get more senses involved, not just eyesight, but sound, and even touch, by having the words make contact in my mouth. Also, plays (and lyrics) are meant to be heard, so saying text aloud helps us remember to share it from the outset. Saying text aloud also helps us learn it, in the same way that we can remember songs from years ago because we sang along every time we heard them. We became part of the song through singing it, without having to try to memorize it. If you are a visual learner, or an auditory processor, this tool (and ones in future chapters) are going to be very helpful in what used to be time spent memorizing your lines. Following the steps in this book will allow you rarely, if ever, to have to sit down and memorize anything again. Having a process to employ, and following the steps every time, with practice, will help you investigate and learn the text at the same time.

As a final rationale for the importance of scansion, take your hand and place it over your heart. Feel that? An iamb is the heartbeat of humanity: da-dum, da-dum, da-dum. It is the rhythm of life, our pulse.

Here's even better news: this alternating light and strong stress is how we speak every day, just (thankfully) not organized into tens. Alternating stress is the way that we talk. This is the way we talk. Say those two sentences aloud: "Alternating stress is the way that we talk," "This is the way we talk." Now try to make every single syllable stressed, almost as if it's written in ALL CAPS in a text message. "THIS IS THE WAY WE TALK." Nobody wants to hear that, talk like that, or worse, be talked to like that. We only talk that way for emphasis, and usually in times of extreme frustration or anger, when every single syllable is important, in times of extreme emotion, or to a misbehaving dog. Understanding, appreciating, and embracing scansion demystifies the rules of the game, and is the first step in the homework process of acting heightened text.

> ### TRY IT! SCAN A LINE OF IAMBIC PENTAMETER
>
> Let's start with this iambic pentameter line of Lucio's from Act I, scene iv of *Measure for Measure*:
>
> **The duke is very strangely gone from hence.**
>
> Begin by reading any new text aloud twice:
>
> **The duke is very strangely gone from hence.**
>
> Repeat it again, without adding any forced rhythm, not even thinking about scansion:
>
> **The duke is very strangely gone from hence.**
>
> Decide where to put the unstressed [˘] and stressed [/] marks above the text, or copy the line on another piece of paper and make your marks.

How'd you do? Here's how I chose to mark it:

> ˘   / ˘ / ˘   / ˘   /   ˘   /
> **The duke is very strangely gone from hence.**

This is an example of what we call a **regular line**. It has no variations in iambic (alternating light and strong) or pentameter (ten total syllables). It scans as alternating unstressed and stressed for the whole line from start to finish with no breaks. It makes sense especially if we don't think about it as scansion or as iambic pentameter. (If we say it with the annoying "da-DUM" rhythm to point up that it's iambic pentameter, it certainly doesn't make it any clearer, and serves as a reminder that alternating light and strong stress is the way we normally speak anyway.)

Let's double-check the scansion by looking closely at the feet (just for a moment) by placing vertical lines in between each iambic foot:

> ˘ / ˘ / ˘ / ˘ / ˘ /
> **The duke | is ve- | -ry strange- | -ly gone | from hence.**

There are mostly monosyllabic words and two multi syllabic words (very, strangely), and it doesn't matter that they cross the foot markings (the straight-up-and-down lines I inserted in the line of text). We can notice how the foot markings might break up a word, but it doesn't have any impact on how we say or scan it. The line's two multi syllabic words: "very" and "strangely" – and they both scan as strong-light as independent words, which seems like the opposite of iambic, but fortunately, they are not in the same feet:

> / ˘ / ˘
> **very strangely**

Try to say them **as if** they were scanned the opposite way, [˘ /]: [ve-REE] and [strange-LEE] – and the words don't make sense. **The way they are scanned within the line is what works best, even if they are broken up across feet of verse.** We don't have to change the way we pronounce a word to make it scan, unless there's some special reason to do so. Sometimes, clapping the back of your hand into your other hand on the strong stresses is helpful, or tapping the eraser end of a pencil on the desk in front of you helps identify the strong stresses. It's helpful to try saying the syllables another way to help see if it's simply regular, or if there are variations. There's little to be gained from pounding out the weaker syllables, but finding the strong stresses is important to see if there are any variations at all. Counting out the syllables on the fingertips on the tabletop is another way to check for pentameter. There should be ten syllables most of the time. I lay my hands flat out on a surface in front of me and say the line aloud as I tap out each syllable from the pinky finger of my left hand across each finger and thumb to the pinky finger of my right:

> 1 2 3 4 5 6 7   8   9 10
> The duke is very strangely gone from hence.

Between those two physical methods of determining if a line is regular (especially helpful for kinesthetic learners), we can move quite efficiently through the text, trusting the regular lines and noting the irregular ones, gaining confidence through practice. Noticing that a line is regular is like a straight stretch of highway: you know what you have to do. If a line is irregular, it's like a turn in the road, and you need to maneuver a little to stay on track. The irregularity is there for a dramatic reason, same as the regularity. Regular lines can save you time, like restaurants that have a prep cook who comes in every morning just to chop onions, because they use them in almost every recipe. I enjoy finding out that a speech is mostly regular, and I also relish a speech full of irregular lines – it's more of a puzzle to figure out what is happening in the verse, and then why. What's the secret ingredient that makes this moment so special? Or what is the regular verse hiding?

Here is an example of a longer thought from another play, *Richard III* – three whole lines of verse that are entirely regular, with no variations in either the Iambic rhythm or the Pentameter. Read this excerpt aloud twice, and experience the pace and connectivity of the Queen's denial of Richard's accusation of her influence in the imprisonment of Clarence:

> **I never did incense his Majesty**
> **Against the Duke of Clarence, but have been**
> **An earnest advocate to plead for him.** – Queen Elizabeth, *Richard III*,
> Act I, Scene iii

Elizabeth doesn't miss a beat after being called out by Richard. Every syllable is accounted for and in place. A regular line starts weak and ends strong and has exactly ten syllables. It's the gold standard for a character telling the truth, or for the same character lying through their teeth. Here's how the scansion would look:

˘ / ˘ / ˘ / ˘ / ˘ /
I never did incense his Majesty
˘ / ˘ / ˘ / ˘ / ˘ /
Against the Duke of Clarence, but have been
˘ / ˘ / ˘ / ˘ / ˘ /
An earnest advocate to plead for him.

With no variations in the verse, Elizabeth speaks this line after swearing an oath to God that she is telling the truth. As an actor, noticing this during the scansion phase of the homework makes a more specific choice of playing ease and self-righteousness in this compelling rebuttal. Knowing the scansion grounds the acting choice in how the character is speaking, above and beyond the words they are speaking.

FOLLOWING, BENDING, AND BREAKING THE RULES OF SCANSION

Now that we understand why rules about scansion in verse exist, we can see why writers created circumstances in which the rules can be bent or broken. For the most part, playwrights and lyricists follow the rules, since they are there for a reason. Complex rules like tax laws get broken all the time and can have serious consequences to the perpetrator. Going the wrong way on a one-way street is wholly irresponsible, and the results can be tragic and widespread. In instances with heightened text, thankfully, no one is going to get hurt by an irregular line.

Sometimes, there are variations and exceptions to the rhythm or the meter, and a reason or rationale always exists for these changes and additions. The rationale might be as simple as the author choosing a particular word to get the idea across and not concerning themselves with holding to ten syllables. Volumes of books by noted scholars explore these variations, and different editions of texts provide detailed analysis, if this is of greater interest to you. In many cases, we may never be able to learn the author's reason behind these variations, but as actors we must make choices based on these discoveries.

Each variation in Iambic Pentameter has been given its own name, which makes it easier for us to label them when we find them in our text, like road signs on the side of the road to help get us to our destination. We'll go through these exceptions one by one in the next section of text. Just noticing that a line has a variation, or is irregular, is the most important thing, so that we can determine if we need to do anything. It's like seeing a traffic light turn yellow: we must decide whether to slow down or speed up to proceed safely. Spotting these signs at the very beginning of the homework process matters. An actor playing Hamlet might discover that he's "all over the place" with scansion and that might manifest itself in the acting choices as having multiple focus points, or pacing back and forth, working out what to say or do next.

TRY IT! SCAN IRREGULAR LINES (VARIATIONS FROM IAMBIC AND AN EXTRA SYLLABLE)

Here are a few lines for practicing identifying variations in the scansion process, applying what you've learned about regular iambic pentameter. Be sure to read each line aloud twice before you start marking above the text, using a pencil in case there are changes in your choices as you continue. (We will set aside the impact of punctuation for now.)

To be, or not to be, that is the question:
Whether 'tis nobler in the mind to suffer
The slings and arrows of outrageous fortune,
Or to take arms against a sea of troubles,
And by opposing, end them. To die, to sleep... – Hamlet, *Hamlet*,
Act III, scene i

The first line clearly isn't regular iambic or pentameter. Here's how it might scan, with my observations as comments *in italics*:

| ˘ / ˘ / ˘ / ˘ ˘ / ˘ | *It has 11 syllables and ends weak, not strong.* |
| **To be, or not to be, that is the question** | *The last two feet do not seem to be iambic.* |

In this line, the fourth foot is reversed [/ ˘], as a choice, to emphasize "that" is the question. This reversed iamb is called a Trochee [TROH-kee]. The fourth foot scans strong, then weak. An easy variation, and there's nothing wrong with it, but it is different. In text, this trochee is being marked as a choice, since there's nothing wrong with scanning it as regular, because "that is" the question, after all. Hamlet wants to reiterate the question, without naming it. (We'll get to more on that in Chapter 2.) But why are there 11 syllables? And why is the final syllable unstressed? This variation in the fifth foot is called a **weak ending.** A weak ending used to be called a "feminine ending" because at some time in history women were seen as weaker than men (imagine!) or had qualities that were lighter than male qualities such as strength, which translated into these terms, as with word endings like "-ette" to indicate gender. These terms have shifted to express that words and musical phrases have "weak endings," which means that the final syllable has the lighter cadence or weaker stress (leaving the gender generalization aside). But in a line of iambic pentameter, the weak ending means there is an extra, eleventh syllable and that it is a weak one, tacked on to the fifth foot that begins regular: [da-DUH-da]. We mark a weak ending with a little *w* at the end, in *italics* to notice it.

If there seem to be 11 syllables in the line, look at the end of the line, and if it ends weak, it's likely a **weak ending**. If the line seems to end with strong stress, look within the line for other possible puzzle solutions.

Hypothetically, Shakespeare might have chosen to write it as a regular line, but it wouldn't convey the same level of complexity, or pose it as a dilemma, as with **this imagined revision:**

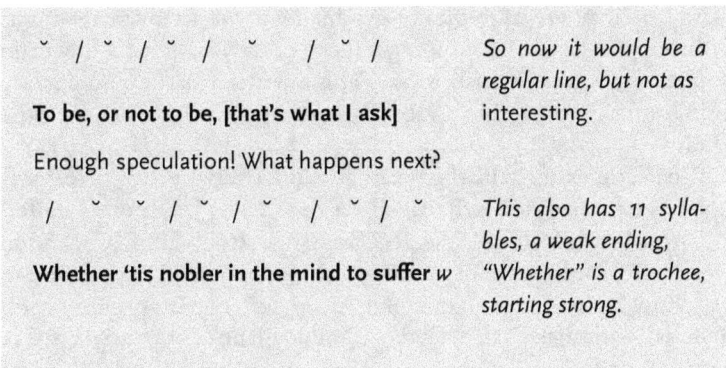

The word "whether" at the beginning of the line is clearly a trochee [/ ˘], but this time it's a **fixed** or **forced trochee**, because that's the way the word is pronounced. We wouldn't say "weth-ER." In contrast to the way we chose to use a trochee in "that is the question" in the previous line, in this instance, the trochee is fixed in scanning "whether" as [/ ˘] – and then the line also has a weak ending with the extra unstressed 11th syllable. Lots of multisyllabic words become fixed or forced trochees depending on where they land within a verse line. This is a very common variation in verse plays, and little analysis is needed, like taking a left turn rather than a right turn at a stop sign.

As the speech continues, we see two more weak ending lines and another internal variation. Let's break these down one at a time to make sure we understand what the scansion is doing within each line.

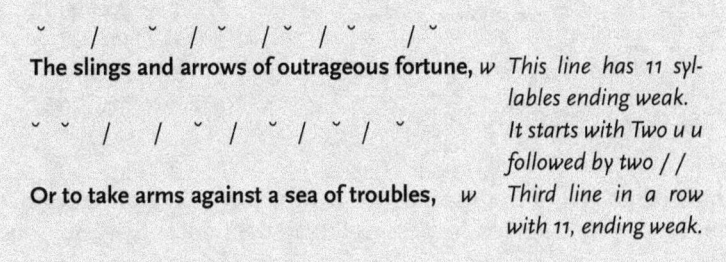

A foot with **two weak syllables [˘ ˘] is called "pyrrhic"** – usually two short monosyllabic words or the unstressed ending of a word followed by a short word, and almost always setting up a strong stress in the next foot. A pyrrhic foot is rarely if ever two syllables in one word. You may see examples of pyrrhic feet when a character wants to move things along, skipping a beat or two to get to the main points of what they wish to say. This variation name references a military term, "a pyrrhic victory," essentially a lot of work for little reward.

What comes next in this example, just after the two weak syllables, is **two stressed syllables in a foot [/ /], which is called a "spondee."** Both syllables receive equal, strong emphasis, and in most cases, these are short monosyllabic words that form a phrase, like "too far" or expressions like "deep six" or compound words such as "handshake" or "heyday." Think of how you might speak harshly to someone, with equal emphasis on both words, pleading "Don't go!" Spondees are like an iambic pentameter version of typing in ALL CAPS, except instead of yelling, it's about strong stress. They are rare in verse poems and plays, and in most cases, they are preceded by a pyrrhic foot or a trochee foot of verse, in order to create space for all that emphasis.

Let's review these last two variations we just encountered:

A **pyrrhic foot** [˘ ˘] makes both syllables unstressed or weak – mostly in cross-over of feet (or quick little syllables leading to a trochee or a spondee.

A **spondee foot** [/ /] stresses BOTH WORDS – equal emphasis (though not necessarily yelling) is required on both syllables.

To end our use of this *Hamlet* example, we have this line (which continues into the rest of the speech – hence the dash):

˘ / ˘ / ˘ / ˘ ˘ / ˘ /	A strange foot in the middle of the line but the line ends with a strong stress.
And by opposing, end them. To die, to sleep--	

In this final line of our excerpt, we have two regular feet to begin, a third foot that looks like a weak ending in the middle of a line, "-ing end them" another [da-DUH-da], followed by internal punctuation, and then two regular iambic feet, ending with a strong stress. The line is 11 syllables long, but it isn't a weak ending of the line. The line ends with a strong stress on "sleep." What could possibly be happening here?

This uncommon variation, making up only 2% of the lines in all of Shakespeare's plays, is a poetic textual phenomenon called the **epic caesura,** which can be marked as EC, a weak ending foot [˘ / ˘] **located anywhere but at the end of a line** and **must be followed by any form of punctuation** (, ; : . ? ! ... --) [comma, semi-colon, colon, period, question mark, exclamation point, ellipsis, or dash]. In poetry and music, a pause within a thought or between thoughts is called a caesura. The additional suspension of the pause through punctuation, to sustain the idea, is called an "epic caesura" or in layperson's terms: a big pause.

The term "epic caesura" was believed to be from the myth that Julius Caesar came into the world via the first C-section, and the poetic term seemed to be based on the creation of an opening, concurring with this event. But Caesar's mother lived a long healthy life following his natural birth. The term for Caesarian section comes from the Latin word "caedere" meaning "to cut." The poetic term "epic caesura" indicates a mid-line pause, resulting from an unstressed syllable followed by some form of punctuation. It's not as graphic a lineage as believing it was named after the great Roman emperor, but it makes sense to indicate a cut (or break) in the middle of a line.

We **mark the epic caesura** with a little [^{EC}], placed in the space that it creates, by hand, or using superscript. This reinforces the length of the pause, whether it be the briefest moment for a comma, or longer for a full stop. The feet are marked in this version with [|] symbols to make them abundantly clear. (The punctuation section in the next chapter will clarify what each mark signifies, and how it impacts scansion, meaning, and acting choices.)

1	2 (EC)	3 (Trochee)	4	5	
˘ /	˘ /	˘ /	/ ˘	˘ /	11 syllables, but ends strong
And by	opposing, ^{EC}	end them?	To die,	to sleep --	*Two variations and three regular feet*

Sometimes, a line of iambic pentameter has **more than 11 syllables**, but clearly the line ends in a strong stress when it's spoken aloud:

> **And cleave the <u>general</u> ear with horrid speech.**
>
> If we assigned every syllable and foot regular iambic weight, it would look like this:
>
> ˘   /   ˘   /   ˘   /   ˘   /   ˘   /   ˘   *It's 11 syllables and ends weak now,*
> **And cleave the general ear with horrid speech.**   *but the last few feet don't scan well.*

The first and second feet seem fine, and though "general" certainly could be 3 syllables, the rest of the line is decidedly off, and the 4th and 5th foot scansion makes no sense at all.

What do we do now? We look to an interior foot to see if there's an epic caesura, but there isn't any punctuation, which is a requirement for that variation. In this case, one of the words might require an **elision**, using fewer syllables intentionally to say a word, as we discussed earlier.

If we smush the word [general] to two syllables, essentially eliminating the [er] in the middle, it makes the word [gen'ral] and the rest of the line scans easily, and we are restored to 5 feet, ten syllables. This is called an **elision,** when we omit, elide, merge (or smush) syllables together when saying a word aloud. In everyday speech, we do this all the time. The shop down the road is called the "gen'ral store," rather than "gen-er-al store." We elide or smush a syllable for ease and understanding, taking the line down to 10 syllables and restoring it to being regular:

> ˘   /   ˘   /   ˘   /   ˘   /   ˘   /
> And cleave the **gen'ral** ear with horrid speech.   *Using an apostrophe to mark the elision*
>
> OR
>
> ˘   /   ˘   /   ˘   /   ˘   /   ˘   /
> And cleave the **general** ear with horrid speech.   *Using a strikeout through the elision*

Proper names are often either **elided** or **lengthened** to make the pentameter regular. We might see the same name elided in one line and lengthened in another. "Cassio" could be elided to 2 syllables [CASS-yo] or "Iago" lengthened to 3 syllables [ee-AH-go], depending on the needs of the meter in each line:

	˘ / ˘ / ˘ / ˘ / ˘ / ˘	
"Cassio" elided:	I will in **Cassio's** lodging lose this napkin	w

	/ ˘ ˘ / ˘ / ˘ / ˘ /˘	
"Iago" lengthened:	Now do I see 'tis true; look here, **Iago**	w

In many instances, names like Romeo, Juliet, Julia, or Bassanio are elided or lengthened throughout the play. The actor can use moments like this to make a more specific choice, which is the ultimate goal of our work in heightened text. The important thing to remember once we elide something in a word is not to draw further attention to it, especially to common ones such as "to't" for "to it," or "e'er" for "ever." If these elide into one stressed syllable, we hit it with strength, but if the purpose of the elision is to further weaken the syllable, we keep it light. See what the elision does to the rest of the word and the line, and act accordingly now that the line is down to a manageable number of syllables. In Shakespeare and other early modern playwrights, certain words are elongated for the benefit of scansion, for example, "marriage" might be pronounced as three syllables, sounded as [MARE-ee-EDGE], whereas today we pronounce it as a two-syllable word [MARE-idge]. Using these elongated forms can seem antiquated today, and the choice can be made to modernize these pronunciations (rather than have them stand out as pretentious or dated), in the same way productions choose contemporary settings, regional dialects, and modern dress styles.

> **REVIEWING EXCEPTIONS TO IAMBIC FEET**
>
> - When you find 11 syllables in a line, read it aloud and pay attention to the ending syllable. Is it unstressed? It's a **weak ending**, and can be marked [w].
> - If you think the last syllable should be stressed, the line could require an **elision**. Adjust the scansion of the word that can be shortened, using an apostrophe [gen'ral], or crossing out the elided syllable [gen[e]ral] and then adjust the scansion of the rest of the line as needed.
> - If you don't think an elision helps, then look for an **epic caesura** in an earlier foot, which requires that punctuation be present at the end of the three-syllable foot [ˇ / ˇ], and mark with an [EC] at that point in the line.
>
> That's scansion. That's it. There are **4 kinds of metric feet**, and we even found a passage from *Hamlet* that expresses all four variations in rhythm in just a few lines:
>
> - **Iamb [ˇ /]** weak followed by strong;
> - **Trochee [/ ˇ]** strong followed by weak, either as a choice, fixed, (or forced);
> - **pyrrhic [ˇ ˇ]** two weak syllables in the same foot – usually two monosyllabic words setting up a trochee or a spondee in the next foot (rarely two syllables within one word), sometimes the unstressed end of one word coupled with the unstressed beginning of the next word;
> - **Spondee [/ /]** Strong stress followed by another strong stress, usually two monosyllabic words in a foot.

Regarding meter, the most common variation from **pentameter** (5 feet = 10 syllables) is the use of 11 syllables in a line such as the **weak ending** or the **epic caesura**. In some cases, an **elision** is needed, which restores the line to ten syllables. Look to the next section of this chapter, and in the Appendix for other rare exceptions to these extra syllables (or just to "geek out" about scansion) beyond 11 syllables in a line.

What can we glean from this use of the writer's variations, both in stress and length of line in terms of acting choices? Clearly, Hamlet is not himself. He is questioning his very existence and purpose: having an existential crisis. He is also very much alone, and does not need to perform or speak properly to anyone else but his own thoughts. Though the character may not make conscious decisions to manage his words in a particular way, (as he might when faced with his mother and his uncle), the playwright has provided clues to the psychology of the character's motivations or his emotional state in the tiniest variations away from the plotted structure of the iambic verse. Volumes have been written about these intricacies, and are worth reading, but for our purposes, we note the changes and mark them, like signposts on the road of our journey.

VARIATIONS TO THE PENTAMETER (MORE THAN 5 FEET OF VERSE IN A LINE)

Now that we have covered changes to the Iambic part of the line (including adding an extra syllable to a foot), let's cover when there are **more than 5 feet of verse**. In our previous examples using *Hamlet,* there are still 5 feet of verse, indicating pentameter, but one of those five feet contained an extra syllable – spilling over a bit into a weak ending, or in the middle of the line with an epic caesura, but not adding whole feet.

Sometimes, the line of verse has **six metric feet**, that is, **hexameter**, instead of pentameter. It capably holds twelve syllables that might be mostly iambic and holds those variations capably. These are often called "Alexandrine" lines, apparently named after Alexander the Great, and are the form for most classical French poetry, written entirely in six-foot lines, and ending strong, similar to pentameter. Often Alexandrine lines have an internal pause caused by punctuation. When they appear amid lines of pentameter, they represent one more regular foot, or two more syllables, and can be marked with an [@] symbol (for "Alexandrine") or a [+2] at the end of the line (if the variation is at the end), but can also be constructed in other ways, such as sharing the 12-syllables or the 6-feet, which we mark accordingly, using lines from *Othello,* as below:

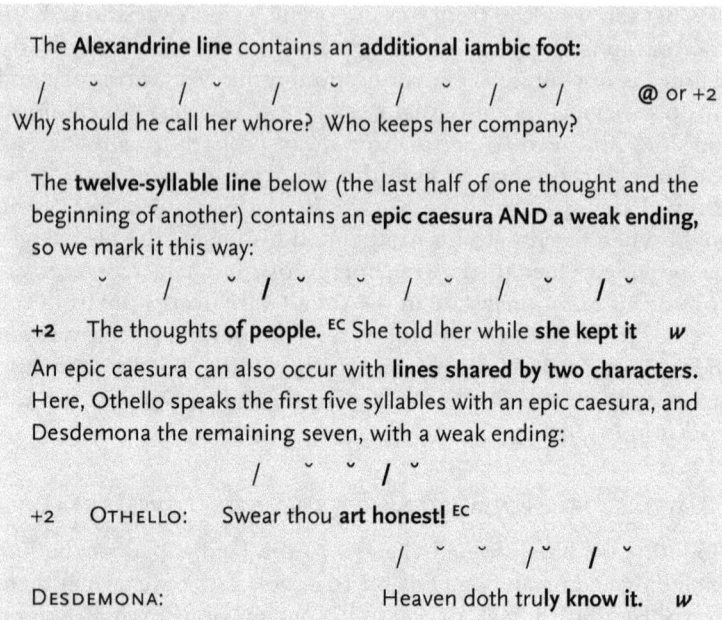

This final example reveals another way that the playwright is bending or breaking the rules of scansion for a dramatic reason. Othello yells at his wife to swear she's telling the truth, using an extra syllable, and she responds instantly, doing the same. Shakespeare even altered the formatting to reflect the immediacy of the moment, though some published editions, including the Folio, do not express these lines divided across the page as indicated above.

BENDING THE RULES: SHARED LINES AND SHORT LINES

Sometimes, **a line of verse may have less than ten syllables or fewer than five feet**. In these instances, we have to discern if the verse is shared by another character, who picks up their cue, as we would say, and shares the line's metrical integrity. These are called "**shared lines**" and they are formatted in most versions in ways that indicate the energy continuing, as we saw above:

		/ ˇ ˇ / ˇ EC
+2	OTHELLO:	Swear thou art honest!
		/ ˇ ˇ / ˇ / ˇ
	DESDEMONA:	Heaven doth truly know it. *w*

In a **shared line**, the characters share the scansion. The entire line of verse, though spoken by two characters, is 12 syllables, with 2 feet (5 syllables) in the first half (a trochee and an epic caesura) spoken angrily by Othello, and then 3 feet (7 syllables with a weak ending) in the second half of the line, spoken in sharp response by Desdemona. The way the text is formatted, with Desdemona's impassioned reply tabbed over to begin immediately at the end of Othello's line confirms that it is played as a shared line — the verse of one line shared by two or more characters. It takes her no time at all to respond because she is innocent. The shared line format is reinforcing what we know is true from the story.

Perhaps **a line of verse is stopped short, containing less than 10 syllables**. Here is an excerpt from the opening scene of *King Lear*, in which Lear makes it clear to his three daughters that each must "sing for her supper," expounding on how much they each love him as a condition to receive their inheritance. The older sisters, Goneril and Regan have played along, but the youngest (and his favorite), Cordelia, refuses to join in this vain pageant, after Lear asks her:

LEAR	What can you say to draw
	A third more opulent than your sisters? Speak.
CORDELIA	Nothing, my lord.
LEAR	Nothing?
CORDELIA	Nothing.
LEAR	Nothing will come of nothing: Speak again.

The space that should by occupied by remaining feet in the verse line is left blank. The other character picks up their line after a pause, with the length of the pause determined by the weight of the moment, guided by the absence of a certain number of syllables or feet. These are called **"short lines."** Something must happen during that pause: **the moment requires a response**, a decision must be made, or the situation needs to be assessed by a person, a group, or even a crowd. When we encounter short lines, we can navigate that next step (of deciding what has to happen before the next line is spoken), by putting brackets around the space of the **[empty feet]** and jotting down within them a few things that might need to happen, either for our character, or for the character who needs to speak next. In many instances, someone needs to gather their thoughts, think about how to respond, and decide what to say or do next, and the **missing feet** provide the space to do so.

Determining whether or not lines have fewer than ten syllables (less than 5 feet) is important so that we know if we should pick up a cue, perhaps responding impulsively with a prompt retort, or playing a specific choice to support the dramatic need of the moment, finding the length of that moment in the **empty feet.**

First, of course, with new text, we read the text aloud twice and then begin with the scansion, revealing four lines in a row that begin with a fixed trochee, repeating the same introductory word, but only the fourth line is a complete line of verse, leaving [empty feet] for thoughts and actions:

	/ ˇ ˇ /	
CORDELIA	Nothing, my lord. [	]
	/ ˇ	
LEAR	Nothing? [	]
	/ ˇ	
CORDELIA	Nothing. [	]
	/ ˇ ˇ / ˇ / ˇ / ˇ /	
LEAR	Nothing will come of nothing: Speak again.	

But are these empty feet or shared lines? In this version, they are formatted as short lines, and therefore contain empty feet, missing feet of verse, amounting to time when something must transpire. Hypothetically, if they were meant to be shared lines, with no empty feet, they would look like this:

CORDELIA	Nothing, my lord.
LEAR	Nothing?
CORDELIA	Nothing.
LEAR	Nothing will come of nothing: Speak again.

The emotion and tension can't be conveyed if they are played as shared lines, and the scansion doesn't support the meaning or the high stakes of the moment. What needs to happen in the scene takes time. The writer has built the time into the text by leaving out the remainder of the verse for each line.

As empty feet, we can sense the weight of this moment on young Cordelia. She's in a public setting, with her two suitors, the Duke of Burgundy and the King of France watching, as her father asks her to perform a trick for the crowd. This is not Cordelia's way, and she bravely (and methodically) disobeys her father's order to "Speak" – like a trained dog, rather than love him deeply in her own way. Lear needs time to process what is happening, as does everyone around them. Most importantly, everyone in the scene needs to play the empty feet, since that's why they exist. Imagine what glee Goneril and Regan are trying to conceal, how loyal-to-Lear Kent is figuring out how to stop this from going any further: all these actors are working an angle during these gaps in the verse.

Mark and then notate the empty feet in this way, putting the thoughts or action in a box in the space where the [*missing text*] would be [imagined in brackets *in italics here*]

>   1   2   3   4   5
> CORDELIA: Nothing, my lord. [C: There, I said it.] [L: Is she joking? I love you, so try again.]
>
>   1   2   3   4   5
> LEAR: Nothing? [C: I stand by my answer. I will not play this game.]
>
>   1   2   3   4   5
> CORDELIA: Nothing. [L: I'm furious! She's humiliated me. I'll disinherit her.]
>
>   1   2   3   4   5
> LEAR: Nothing will come of nothing: Speak again.

To which Cordelia replies, dutifully and thoughtfully, in complete and regular verse lines:

> Unhappy that I am, I cannot heave
> My heart into my mouth: I love your majesty
> According to my bond; no more nor less.

The time needed for this intense action to transpire requires the use of empty feet. The scene's tension builds during the pauses between lines, using the absent verse as a guide for the pace. **Any actor in the scene will want to mark and note what they are playing during empty feet onstage.** When something monumental or nuanced happens, everyone responds, whether they have a line of dialogue or not.

One of the challenges in working with shared and short lines is that in some published versions of the plays, shared lines may not be formatted across the page, so they appear to be short lines. After some practice with the rest of the basic tools, you will be able to determine which interpretation or scansion serves the story best, if it's unclear from the edition you're using.

The basic rules of scansion can help actors unlock the meaning of the text by understanding its structure and purpose. So many intricate exceptions and further variations of scansion exist. If you are as curious and filled with wonder by the intricacies of verse as I am, there are many other unique and rare examples in the "Geek-Out on Scansion" Appendix. Check out the other resources listed below, including George T. Wright's seminal work, *Shakespeare's Metrical Art,* a page-turner for those of us who find this topic fascinating.

SUMMARY

In this important opening chapter,

- we learned that **scansion** is the first step in the actor's homework process with heightened text, noticing and marking the iambic pentameter or other verse form:

> **Two** (the number of alternating light and strong [˘ /] syllables in an **iambic** foot)
> ×
> **Five** (the five iambic feet in a line of verse: that's the **pentameter** part.)
> = 10
> **Ten** is the number of syllables in a line of **Iambic Pentameter**.
> Two syllables, **one light and one strong in a |foot|** of [˘ /] × 5 iambic feet.
> A **foot** is a little set of two sounds, that **alternates light, then strong**, and there's five feet of them strung together in a row to form a line of iambic pentameter verse.
> Sometimes, there's **an extra syllable or syllables**, for which there is always a rationale.
> **Short lines** (containing empty feet without text) have action that needs to occur in place of lines being spoken. **Shared lines** happen without a gap, one line leads right to the next, sharing the scansion of the line.

- we learned that reading aloud supports this work in profound ways that assist in making discoveries.
- we gained awareness of the rules in regular verse lines, and how to identify the signs of variations and irregular verse lines, and why those variations matter.

- we learned specific tools and techniques to uncover the purpose and the power of the heightened language.
- we understand why something is written a particular way, and how rhythm and meter are intrinsic components of verse structure, which support actors grasping this important first step to acting heightened text. **Additional selections of text for scansion practice** are available in the Appendix.

RESOURCES FOR FURTHER EXPLORATION

One infinitely readable resource that can support your practice and study of scansion in iambic pentameter and other verse forms is George T. Wright's *Shakespeare's Metrical Art*. It offers a deep and thoughtful analysis of the iambic pentameter line. This remarkable volume contains geek-out chapter titles like *Syllabic Ambiguity, Lines with Omitted Syllables,* and *Trochees,* and an appendix that includes *Main Types of Deviant Lines in Shakespeare's Plays*. This is one of my "Desert Island books," along with my well-worn copy of the Pelican edition of the *Complete Works of Shakespeare,* held together with gaff tape since 1985.

Connecting text to acting was the life's work of John Barton, whose book (and 1982s RSC/PBS-TV series *Playing Shakespeare*) introduced generations to the power of heightened language featuring actors who began their careers grounded in verse plays, and have gone on to employ those skills in film, theatre and television spanning all genres. The episode with Ian McKellen working with Barton on Antonio's opening speech from *The Merchant of Venice* is one of the experiences that drew me to working with classical texts.

There are some **indispensable scansion-based materials** from master voice and speech teachers Patsy Rodenburg, *Speaking Shakespeare,* Cicely Berry's *The Actor and the Text,* and Kristin Linklater's *Freeing Shakespeare's Voice* that provide in-roads with exercises to open up the voice, the body, and the imagination using heightened text.

An example of **the wide range of variations in printed editions** of classical plays could be any reliable edition of *Hamlet,* including the Arden, Pelican, Folger, and an obscure volume called the *Variorum Edition,* which was first printed in the 1870s. Only a few lines from the actual play appear on each page, because the notes are so extensive and the number of variations among different editions is so enormous. It's like an archaeological dig of a play.

Websites that can offer teaching and learning resources on scansion (and so much more!) some offering downloadable online versions of text (which saves time retyping them) include:

- The Folger Shakespeare Library https://www.folger.edu/teach/
- Shakespeare's Globe https://www.shakespearesglobe.com/discover/#discover-shakespeare
- The Complete Works of William Shakespeare (MIT) https://shakespeare.mit.edu/
- The Stratford Festival of Canada https://www.stratfordfestival.ca/Learn

2

A FOUNDATION OF MEANING

INTRODUCTION

Building on the discoveries made during scansion, the next step is to **determine what the words, ideas, images, and emotions mean** by paraphrasing the lines, to make them seem like our own. Using the same examples of text from the previous chapter, and adding new ones, the stories start to come alive through both the scansion and paraphrase process. This second phase of text homework for the actor is **paraphrasing: putting the heightened language into our own words**, using a dictionary such as the Oxford English Dictionary or other open-source dictionaries to help us understand what's being said, or at least what was meant at the time the play was written. A key element of navigating heightened text is a thorough understanding of how **punctuation** factors into the homework, including how punctuation choices vary among editors working with public domain text. Punctuation impacts thought and breath: two critical needs for actors playing any kind of text. Specific examples and exercises build skill in connecting breath to the integrity of the thought, using punctuation as a guide, providing the basis for acting the work in later chapters. **A thorough exploration of images and metaphors used in the text** is essential, and embedded into this process is a commitment to anti-racism and inclusion, as we encounter archaic phrases and references that can be problematic to navigate given what we care about

DOI: 10.4324/9781032695310-3

and value in being collaborative artists in the theatre. Strategies for approaching how to make thoughtful changes in material that is in the public domain must maintain the integrity of the story and also serve the structure of the verse. A short scene from *Othello* provides an opportunity for foundational practice, which will serve as a scaffold for acting exercises in later chapters.

FINDING OUR WAY THROUGH PUNCTUATION

As we look closely at the structure of the verse through the lens of scansion, we notice something that helps organize and understand the language and ideas: **punctuation**. Some of these marks are signposts for separating, connecting, and ending ideas. Other forms of punctuation help us clarify words or phrases, or lean toward giving us direction on how to convey what we mean. As actors, two of our primary jobs are to be **heard** and **understood**. Processing how the punctuation impacts the thought impacts the latter (being understood), and almost by osmosis (without much effort), solves the former (being heard), by its connection to breath. Punctuation in heightened text (and in any text for that matter) helps the person speaking know when they need to breathe, so that **the integrity of the thought remains intact**. In ordinary speech, we incorporate punctuation through our inflection, when we pause, trail off, interrupt, ask questions, or say something with special emphasis. We need to apply the same principles to speaking text that's prepared with written punctuation, to make the thoughts seem as if they are our own.

Maybe you remember watching "Schoolhouse Rock" when you were younger, learning about history, grammar, and math with whimsical cartoons to help children understand important concepts. Debuting in 1973 on ABC Television, and still available on YouTube, one of my favorite episodes is *"Conjunction Junction, What's Your Function?"* which taught the difference between [and], [or], and [but]. Similarly, understanding the function of each form of punctuation in text helps us shape the idea, find the place for breath if it's needed, and organize the thoughts so that we can be understood by the audience. This allows us to maintain the **integrity of thought**: an idea that needs to be sustained by a single breath. We need to view punctuation as a friend in order to achieve this integrity of thought, as a helpful companion on the road to understanding. From the outset, as we read aloud, punctuation's role in scansion leads us onward to our destination of clear, imaginative, textually supported choices as actors.

Using the familiar lines of text from our scansion homework, reading aloud, let's break down the most common punctuation marks we will see employed in heightened text:

> The duke is very strangely gone from hence.

One might say there's no punctuation at all, but there it is at the end: a **period [.]** also referred to in heightened text (and telegraphs) as a **full stop.** The technical requirement for a period might be the end of a declarative statement or sentence. The use of a period means that this particular thought or point is over. We can take a breath and move on to a new thought.

Here are two related thoughts from *Richard III* that are joined by internal punctuation leading to a full stop at the end.

> I never did incense his Majesty
> Against the Duke of Clarence, but have been
> An earnest advocate to plead for him.

Making an appearance in the middle of these three verse lines is our friend, the **comma [,]**, signaling to us that the thought is not over, not yet complete. Think of a list of things you might need from the grocery store, and observe how the comma functions in this everyday speech line:

> Go to the store and buy some milk, eggs, cheese, fish, and bread.

A comma in the middle of a list tells us to keep going, separating things slightly, but not measuring a pause each time. Imagine how tedious it would be if we paused between each of those items? (Unless the meaning was that we couldn't remember each item, and needed time to think, but then the commas would be ellipses… right?)

In this *Richard III* case, it reminds us to keep going, but with a slight pause to make a point, expressing "rather" or "in fact" but using the comma for implying that expression. Because there is no punctuation at the end of the first line, when reading it aloud we should continue through the first line into the second one until we arrive at the comma, take a slight pause to change our focus, and then continue speaking without a pause for the remainder of the line until we get to the full stop. The comma serves as if to say the "rather," or "in fact," which conveys her meaning. The comma's function in this instance is not specifically to pause, but to think, and that thinking may require a breath, or a moment, or not. But the phrasing, the integrity of the thought, is divided into two distinct parts based on the use of the comma, until we reach the full stop [.] at the end.

Here's another example we know, that has lots of internal punctuation:

> To be, or not to be, that is the question:
> Whether 'tis nobler in the mind to suffer
> The slings and arrows of outrageous fortune,
> Or to take arms against a sea of troubles,
> And by opposing, end them. To die, to sleep –

See how the punctuation gets a little more complicated? In the first line, we notice our friends the commas, helping us separate the two options Hamlet has, but after the word "question," we have a **colon [:]** which sets up the more elaborate "or" statements that follow. A colon sets up a related clause or statement but requires energy on the part of the reader, so that we know something else is coming. The colon is like a springboard, a jumping-off point. Imagine a schoolteacher says to their third graders, "I'm going to be in the hallway for a few minutes talking to the principal, and while I'm gone, you should do the following things: put your name on the top of your paper, write down your answers to the prompts on the chalkboard, and remain quiet until I return." The colon serves to reinforce the dynamic of teacher-to-student by leading directly into the instructions. The punctuation serves the clarity of the idea, and the actor has to read the sign and perform the choice needed to sell the relationship.

In the second line, notice how an **apostrophe [']** appears to shorten the phrase "it is" into an elision of one syllable ['tis] but otherwise has very little impact on the phrases or ideas, in the same way as if it indicated a possessive, as in "the happy cause of Hamlet's wildness." The apostrophe sometimes is the signal to elide the word rather than elongate the syllables, often to help support the meter of the line, as in this line of Iago's from *Othello*:

I see this hath a little dash'd your spirits.

This **elision,** indicated by the apostrophe, is our signal to say "dasht," rather than say "dash-ed" pronouncing the word as a monosyllable, tightening up the scansion, as well as the abruptness of the word, which means killed, shortened, and ended. The elision accomplishes two things: it fixes the scansion and makes the meaning clearer.

The close relatives to the apostrophe are **quotation marks [" "]** indicating what someone else has said word-for-word, or setting off a phrase for a special reason, and actors must attend to the energy needed to isolate those for clarity. Sometimes, a set of apostrophes is used in lieu of quotation marks. Important grammatically, and for reading the words clearly, the apostrophes and quotation marks make quick appearances without deeper analysis required. Look for examples of these as you encounter more heightened text, and take the opportunity to make a strong choice. If a pause or breath is required, it's because we're playing back something someone said, just as we do in everyday conversation.

Looking now to the end of this *Hamlet* excerpt "To die, to sleep—" we have a longer **dash [--]**, also known as the longer **em dash** – used to indicate a break of some kind, either to cut off one's own train of thought, or to be interrupted by someone else. An em dash is sometimes used instead of a comma, a colon, or parentheses, for slightly different reasons. In this particular instance above, the dash indicates Hamlet has a quick reflex to what he has just said, he interjects another phrase but then returns to this theme of "to die, to sleep" a few lines later. A momentary distraction, and for the actor, most certainly a breath to change the thought. The brain signals the new thought and the motor cortex responds to that impulse with a breath. However, as in this example below from *Measure for Measure*, if the dash occurs at the end of one character's line and then another character begins speaking, they have interrupted the other person:

> LUCIO   Assay the power you have.
> ISABELLA   My power? Alas, I doubt—
> LUCIO   Our doubts are traitors.

In this excerpt, Isabella starts a new thought but is interrupted by Lucio. As actors, they each have a job to do on the dash: she has to know what the rest of her sentence is (even though she's not likely ever to say it), and he has to cut her off and interject his response. The actress would write her complete thought out as if it were the rest of her line: "Alas, I doubt I have any power at all." Even if the actor playing Lucio forgets to cut her off during a rehearsal or performance, the actor playing Isabella is living in the moment of having something to say. The em dash is an essential mark for actors, requiring both attention and action.

The shorter length dash is called an **en dash [-]** or **hyphen** and is used in compound words, such "empty-handed," "self-conscious," or an expression like "free-for-all."

Another common punctuation mark is the **semi-colon [;]** which resides in the spectrum between a comma and a period. A semi-colon usually separates two independent but related clauses that could read as complete sentences, and when a coordinating conjunction such as [for, and, but, or, yet, so] is not present, as we have seen in this line of Cordelia's from *King Lear:*

> I love your majesty
> According to my bond; no more nor less.

Punctuation varies widely from edition to edition. This line above is an example, where a semi-colon is often used, but sometimes it's a comma after "bond" instead. The word "nor" is often used instead of the first "no more." The use of "nor more" might make the line seem archaic in that placement, but less so if it was used on "nor less."

Here is another example from *Othello:*

> Now do I see 'tis true; look here, Iago,

The presence of the semi-colon instead of a comma indicates a change is occurring, perhaps a shift in tactic, and most certainly earns a pause as an opportunity for a breath to fuel the new thought.

Two other forms of punctuation represent full stops in addition to the period, the **question mark [?]**

> EMILIA
> Why should he call her whore? Who keeps her company?

and the **exclamation point [!]**

> OTHELLO   Swear thou art honest!
> DESDEMONA   Heaven doth truly know it.

In both instances, the actors speaking play the level of energy, emphasis, and inflection needed to convey the moment. Emilia's questions mean "Why would he do such a thing? Doesn't Othello know I'm always by her side?" She's flustered and angry, wondering how Othello could suspect such behavior of Desdemona. Othello's demand is a harsh command, "Go ahead, swear the opposite! I dare you!" She replies with a calmer though vehement tone, trusting in God that he knows she is honest. She does not match his level of anger, and the regular full stop of the period is the actor's clue that she is attempting to diffuse the tension.

On rare occasions, you might encounter something (especially in the later plays of Shakespeare), like these two passages from Act I, scene ii of *The Winter's Tale:*

> LEONTES   Is whispering nothing?
> Is leaning cheek to cheek? is meeting noses?
> That would be unseen be wicked? is this nothing?

The question mark does not always indicate a full stop, but **when followed deliberately by an uncapitalized word, is played as a comma question mark,** with the pace of a comma but the energy of a question mark. This speech is a rapid succession of questions, a list, a rampage of words seeing nothing be betrayal.

Later in the same scene, Polixenes urges Camillo to help him escape the wrath of jealous Leontes:

> I will respect thee as a father if
> Thou bear'st my life off. Hence! let us avoid.

In the same vein, the exclamation point, which typically indicates a full stop, is treated as a **comma exclamation point when deliberately followed by an uncapitalized new thought**, a quick continuation of the emphasis of the moment before.

Parentheses ( ) are found more in modern published editions of Shakespeare and other playwrights than in the Quarto or Folio texts, where commas serve to separate parenthetical phrases. Within parentheses, we find additional information, comments, or clarifying phrases, such as the line from *Two Gentlemen of Verona:*

> O Eglamour, thou art a gentleman
> (Think not I flatter, for I swear I do not)
> Valiant, wise, remorseful, well accomplish'd.　　*Silvia, IV:iii*

The actor must identify the main thought "O Eglamour, thou art a gentleman wise, remorseful, well-accomplished," and then insert the parenthetical phrase within it, adding the marks if they are simply expressed as commas. This serves to subjugate the comment that she isn't flattering him, she swears, by picking up the pace of the parenthetical phrase as well as lowering the pitch ever so slightly. Making the commas into parentheses is a key step here, in order to signal the eyes and brain to do what's necessary to make the phrase a sidebar, maintaining the integrity of the main thought. We do this in everyday speech, making thoughts parenthetical by the subtle changes in pace and pitch.

Brackets [ ] are often used around stage directions, for which authorship cannot always be proven, and for editorial notations, which direct us to footnotes or endnotes to understand what choices have been made. A fascinating array of decisions are made by editors and scholars, indicated by these brackets. For actors, it serves as a resource for further exploration and understanding, rather than related to how the specific text might be played.

In the Arden edition of Shakespeare's *Measure for Measure,* brackets appear on either side of two blank lines in the middle of Duke Vincentio's speech in Act III, Scene ii:

O, what may man within him hide,
Though angel on the outward side!
How may likeness made in crimes,
Making practice on the times
[
                                                          ]
To draw with idle spiders' strings
Most ponderous and substantial things!

The **brackets** direct us to the editor's notes at the bottom of the page, where it suggests "a couplet is missing" and then goes on to propose how the lines might be inferred for clarity. Other editions add a comma after "times," allowing the previous thought to be further explored by "to draw with idle spiders' strings…" We have no way to unravel this mystery, so a choice must be made to suit the moment, with the editor's note as a guide.

Less frequently, and often with an editor or typesetter's hand, we encounter the **ellipsis** […], which signals to us that our thought trails off, and the actor needs to slow down, finish their final word, but not know where the next thought will land. Another character might chime in, or the character themselves might return to speaking after a pause. The pause is motivated by what's happening to their thought, it's fading away, or the next thought isn't clear enough to speak. The energy and focus needs to be on what is happening instead of speaking, as with most pauses in acting. In early modern printing, these marks vary from being long dashes (---) or three periods (…) but the impact is the same, shown in this example from *King Lear:*

I will have such revenges on you both
 That all the world shall --- I will do such things ---
What they are yet I know not, but they shall be
The terrors of the earth!   *Act II, scene ii*

Lear is so enraged in this moment of betrayal by two of his daughters, that he's unable to think up a punishment to suit them, but he will, soon, and when he does it will be horrible. The ellipsis, or breaking off, trailing off, needs to sustain the energy of the moment, in this case, high stakes and fury. In other situations, the speaker might be lacking energy or focus. But no matter the case, the ellipsis is a signal to make a change and support the loss of thought with the pause and energy required.

With few exceptions, most forms of punctuation in text call for vocal intonations, an intake of breath, the suspension of an idea, a change in pitch, or a lifting of a final word in order **to convey the nuance of the moment they punctuate**. A semi-colon, for example, maintains the thought's buoyancy, perhaps raising the pitch slightly, as if it to indicate, "I'm not quite finished yet," and finishing sentences with a downward inflection when encountering an end stop of a period, question mark, or exclamation point. Navigating the river of the thoughts and ideas is aided by punctuation, allowing the breath, voice, and acting choices to enhance understanding.

PARAPHRASING: PUTTING THE TEXT IN YOUR OWN WORDS

The second step in the homework of heightened text in verse (after scansion) is **paraphrasing, translating the line into your own words**, another way to say the same thing, the way you might say it today, your personal version of what is being said. (I just paraphrased three ways to convey the main idea.) We paraphrase to make sense of the language, to ensure we understand its meaning, so that we can adequately convey it to the audience. Paraphrasing is something we do every day, not just with heightened text, especially in situations when you recognize you're not being understood. **Clarifying the meaning of what we say** is a critical phase in acting heightened text, including understanding any images, metaphors, or references with which we are not familiar. We may encounter words that seem problematic today – times have changed and along with it, our sensibilities, and what we value. We must find reasonable solutions to help keep the audience in the story, not turning to their smartphones to look up words, or to compose an indignant reaction to a choice we've made, whether it was to remain true to the printed text or change it to suit the need in a production.

At the outset of paraphrasing, the first step is – no surprise here – we read aloud:

> The duke is very strangely gone from hence.

What does this line mean? Do we understand all the words? If we throw around ideas, we might come up with the following brainstorming session:

Duke implies a male figurehead, likely inheriting a title over a dominion. That's a fancy way to say "the man in charge here."

Very means to a great extent, a lot.

Strangely has a little more complexity, since it could mean "odd," but it's very strange, and it doesn't seem like he left moving sideways, or backwards, so perhaps it's more "unusual" that he left at all. And it's "very strangely" so maybe he rarely leaves.

Gone is a simple definition: not here. No longer in this place, which in *Measure for Measure* is Vienna.

From hence repeats that idea for emphasis, "from here," but when I look it up online for a definition, because I wasn't really sure, the word "Archaic" appears, as well as the definition "from here" (Source: Oxford Languages), and it was the third definition down the list. I had to look up "archaic" as well, to discover it means "old-fashioned, no longer in everyday use." That helped me know I'd found the best one for this line.

Consequently, my paraphrase for this line could sound clinical:

> The royal man in charge has, under rare and strange circumstances, left Vienna.

Or it could sound like we might say it today:

> The main dude, totally out of character, blew out of town.

Perhaps, we can merge the two approaches:

> The governor, uncharacteristically, and for no known reason, has fled from here.

That's my paraphrase. I know what the line means, and I've covered everything in it. My paraphrase is like a savings account, I have it in case I need it, to support me, but it isn't what I actually rely on as my primary text.

> ### TRY IT! PARAPHRASE IN YOUR OWN WORDS
>
> Read each of these two familiar passages aloud and then construct a paraphrase for each. Use an online dictionary as a definitive source, especially for archaic and obsolete words we might find only in classical texts. Write out your paraphrase in the space opposite the verse line itself.
>
> **I never did incense his Majesty**
> **Against the Duke of Clarence, but have been**
> **An earnest advocate to plead for him.**   *Richard III*
> **And**
> **To be, or not to be, that is the question:**
> **Whether 'tis nobler in the mind to suffer**
> **The slings and arrows of outrageous fortune,**
> **Or to take arms against a sea of troubles,**
> **And by opposing, end them. To die, to sleep –**   *Hamlet*

In both examples above, it would be essential to know the full story of the play, as there are situations and circumstances that help make the information clear (more on that in Chapter 4). Here is how I might paraphrase these sections of text, placed *in italics* to the right of the lines. Compare these to what you wrote in above:

I never did incense his Majesty	*No! I didn't get the King fired up*
Against the Duke of Clarence, but have been	*about his brother, but rather*
An earnest advocate to plead for him.	*have been arguing on the Duke's behalf.*
And	
To be, or not to be, that is the question:	*To live, or to die, that's my dilemma:*
Whether 'tis nobler in the mind to suffer	*Is it better to just let my thoughts be at war*

> The slings and arrows of outrageous fortune,   *with everything that's happening to me,*
> Or to take arms against a sea of troubles,   *Or should I fight back against my fears,*
> And by opposing, end them. To die, to sleep –   *and by doing so, put them to rest. Because dying is a kind of rest.*

Many helpful websites and publications offer paraphrasing or summaries of plays in verse, as it is an essential step in building understanding and comprehension. As actors, if we can understand what Hamlet is saying in our own words, it supports the weight of the poetic language when we return to that text. Using those sites can be efficient, but **the ownership of meaning comes from deciphering the text yourself**, and putting it into your words is so much more worthwhile than the shortcut of what someone else has written. If you do use a paraphrase from another source, be sure to cite it clearly, especially if you submit it as homework in a class.

The **paraphrase** is not the same thing as **subtext,** which is an unspoken idea, theme, or meaning adding a layer of complexity to what is spoken aloud, how a character really feels but could not possibly be spoken aloud or played in a way that it could be seen by the other character. An example of subtext could be that a character is lying, or making a false claim in order to gain footing, to fool someone, or to gain favor, as in this exchange from *Othello:*

> **EMILIA**   What handkerchief?
> Why, that the Moor first gave to Desdemona,
> That which so often you did bid me steal.
> **IAGO**   Hast stol'n it from her?
> **EMILIA**   No, faith, she let it drop by negligence,
> And, to th'advantage, I, being here, took't up.
> Look, here it is.
> **IAGO**   A good wench! Give it me.

Here it is with the **paraphrase marked "P" and in bold** and the **subtext marked** *"s" (not in bold and in parentheses)* below and beside each line, shaded. The paraphrase is what must be conveyed using the words, and the subtext is what else can be conveyed, albeit subtly and cautiously, through an acting choice in order to achieve their goal or objective, but not be obvious to the other character:

> **EMILIA**
> **What handkerchief?**
>   *P: What hanky? (s: Are you serious?)*
> **Why, that the Moor first gave to Desdemona,**
>   *P: The one Othello gave her as a gift. (s: Do I really have to remind you?)*
> **That which so often you did bid me steal.**
>   *P: The hanky you asked me many times to try to swipe.*
>   *(s: You've been bugging me about this non-stop. Why do I bother?)*
>
> **IAGO**
> **Hast stol'n it from her?**
>   *P: Did you manage to steal it? (s: Nice work! I'll play along.)*
>
> **EMILIA**
> **No, faith, she let it drop by negligence,**
>   *P: Of course not! She just happened to drop it.*
>   *(s: You idiot. I wasn't ever going to steal it.)*
> **And, to th'advantage, I, being here, took't up.**
>   *P: But I fortunately happened to be right here, and picked it up.*
>   *(s: And because I'm smart and pay attention, I might be willing to please you.)*
> **Look, here it is.**   *P: I've got it right here in my pocket, see?*
>   *(s: How badly do you want it? Will you be nice to me now?)*
>
> **IAGO**
> **A good wench! Give it me.**   *P: You're a doll! I'll take it.*
>   *(s: I have to treat her a little better to make this plan work.)*

These passages show the vital connection between close reading of the text and actors making textually supported choices in their work. The scansion provides us with the pacing and the structure of emphasis, and the paraphrase gives us the meaning we must convey clearly and effectively. There may not be subtext for every single line, but it's possible to add complexity to the choices if it's appropriate.

Calling back our short line example from the scansion work, look at **the interplay of empty feet, subtext, and paraphrase** in the exchange between Cordelia and Lear:

> **CORDELIA**   Nothing, my lord.
> **LEAR**   Nothing?
> **CORDELIA**   Nothing.
> **LEAR**   Nothing will come of nothing: Speak again.

When there are empty feet, we need to fill them with action, with what is visibly happening, but also with unspoken thoughts, or subtext. The actors have to do both things at the same time, not saying anything, but not giving away what they're really thinking.

As before let's add the **paraphrase** in **bold** and the subtext underneath *in italics* to avoid confusion.

> **CORDELIA:** Nothing, my lord.
> Cordelia's paraphrase: **I'm not saying anything.**
> (Her subtext: *This is a ridiculous game!*)
> **LEAR:** Nothing?
> Lear's paraphrase: **Are you sure? That's it?**
> (His subtext: *Do you realize what you're doing?*)
> **CORDELIA:** Nothing.
> Cordelia's paraphrase: **Absolutely.**
> (Her subtext: *There's no going back after this.*)
> **LEAR:** Nothing will come of nothing: Speak again.
> Lear's paraphrase: **No land will be the result of not speaking. One more chance!**
> (His subtext: *I can't be kind to you in front of all these people. I'm begging you!*)

The level of nuance in this scene is extraordinary, and it's only the first scene of the play! No one, especially Lear, expected Cordelia to behave this way. Lear's ability to use the same word twice in one sentence, with two totally different meanings shows how sharp he remains, though he seeks to retire from being King. "Nothing" means "no land" and also "not speaking" and it's clear to everyone how much it hurts him to say it. The **paraphrase** in this section is a reflection of what they are saying, their actual text, not to be confused with what they are thinking while no one is speaking, or what they are trying to show to the public during this painful and awkward exchange. If the actors playing the roles of Lear and Cordelia think that paraphrasing the word "nothing" isn't necessary, because they know what that word means, they're missing the point. Drill down into what is happening, and let the paraphrase step include what they are playing externally, and what they have to cover up as well.

DICTIONARY WORK: BEING CURIOUS ABOUT WORDS

One of the challenges of paraphrasing is when we don't know what a word means. Even more challenging is thinking we know what a word means, when we really don't. **Being curious about meaning** is part of what makes the paraphrase a rich and rewarding step in our homework.

Let's look at more of the Emilia and Iago handkerchief scene from *Othello* as the reference point for what I call **"dictionary work:" looking things up and folding what we discover into the paraphrase**. After reading it aloud and scanning it (putting our scansion marks above each line), and noticing what emerges from the scansion alone, we move into the paraphrase step: and identifying words that need some dictionary work is a part of that. This process can happen before you start paraphrasing at all, or after you've given it a try and want to look up the words you don't know. I've scanned it, and then identified the words I think I need to look up and placed them in the right margin *in italics* for quick reference, realizing that sometimes there's a root word I am more likely to find in the dictionary

EMILIA

˘ ˘   /Ap˘ ˘   /Ap ˘ / ˘   empty ½ foot
I am glad I have found this napkin: [picks it up]   *napkin*

/   ˘ ˘   / ˘ /   ˘   /   ˘   /
This was her first remembrance from the Moor: *remembrance*
   Moor

˘ / ˘ / ˘ / ˘ / ˘ /
My wayward husband hath a hundred times   *wayward*

/ ˘ ˘   / ˘ EC ˘ / ˘ / ˘ / ˘ w
Woo'd me to steal it; but she so loves the token,   *woo'd (woo)*
   token

/˘ / ˘   / ˘ ˘   /˘ / ˘   w
(For he conjured her she should ever keep it),   *conjure(d)*

˘ / ˘ /   ˘ /˘ /   ˘ / ˘   w
That she reserves it evermore about her   *evermore*

˘ / ˘   / ˘ EC ˘ / ˘   / ˘   /
To kiss and talk to. I'll have the work ta'en out,   *work (taken) out*

˘ /   ˘/˘   / ˘ ˘   / ˘ /
And give't Iago: what he will do with it

/ ˘   /   ˘   /   empty feet
Heaven knows, not I; [*I wish I did...*]   *Heaven knows*
   (expression)

˘ / ˘   / ˘ /   ˘ / ˘ /
I nothing but to please his fantasy.   *Enter Iago*   *please fantasy*

IAGO

˘ /   ˘   / ˘ /   ˘ /
How now! what do you here alone?   *How now*
   (archaic
   expression?)

EMILIA

˘ /   ˘ /   ˘ / ˘ /   ˘   /
Do not you chide; I have a thing for you.   *chide   thing*

IAGO

˘ /   ˘ / u / u / u   /
A thing for me? it is a common thing--   *thing (in a*
   different sense)
   common

> **EMILIA**
> ⁄
> Ha!
> ˘ ⁄ ˘ ⁄ ˘ ⁄   empty feet
> **IAGO** To have a foolish wife. *[Oh yeah?]*   *foolish*

For the sake of example, here's what I found for two of these words. (You can look up the rest, and any more of your own, making notes of what you find, and fold those meanings into your paraphrase of the rest of the scene.)

- **chide**: "to scold, rebuke; to dispute angrily" (Oxford English Dictionary)
- *I have a **"thing"** for you*: "an inanimate object distinguished from a living being" (Google, Merriam Webster's Dictionary)
- *a "thing" for me*: "a strong liking or attraction" (WordUp)

My paraphrase, now composed based on my reading aloud, understanding of the situation, and doing a little dictionary work is as follows for these two lines:

> **EMILIA**
> Do not you chide; I have a thing for you.
>   *Stop scolding me like a child. I have a little something you want.*
> **IAGO**
> A thing for me?
>   *Oh yeah, you think I want what you have to offer?*

Now you can paraphrase the entire scene using the dictionary work you did, and utilize this step with every piece of heightened text you encounter moving forward.

PARAPHRASING REFERENCES, IMAGES, METAPHORS, ARCHAIC PHRASES, AND WHAT TO DO ABOUT PROBLEMATIC WORDS (IF IT'S NOT OKAY TO SAY THEM!)

Heightened text often contains archaic phrases and references, using imagery and allusions that strengthen the verbal rhetoric conveying the ideas. We use analogies and examples in our everyday conversations, often saying "it's like when you ..." and then going on to explain something that might help our idea come across effectively. Mythological figures and folk tales were widely used in analogies in early modern plays, and like recurring clues in crossword puzzles, these are references we should know. But how do we find out about them to support our paraphrase? Let's use "Like Niobe, all tears" – a phrase from within this impassioned speech of Hamlet's, drafting our *paraphrase*:

> "Let me not think on't— Frailty, thy name is woman! —
> *I can't even think about it! Women are weak!*
> A little month, or ere those shoes were old
> *It's only been a month, her shoes not broken in*
> With which she follow'd my poor father's body,
> *From the funeral of my father, following it*
> Like Niobe, all tears:--why she, even she--
> *Like _____, crying non-stop, my mom--*
> O, God! a beast, that wants discourse of reason,
> *Jeez! an animal, that has no mind to know,*
> Would have mourn'd longer—"
> *Would have stayed in grief longer than 30 days.*

A quick internet search and some investigation into a few Greek mythology resources turn up lots of versions of the story of Queen Niobe, a prototype of the bereaved mother. Niobe had boasted to one of the gods of her ability to bear so many children; then as punishment for her pride, saw her seven children murdered by the gods, was turned to stone, but was unable to stop weeping. Hamlet offers this comparison in reference to the nerve of his mother Gertrude, to marry her brother-in-law Claudius so soon after her husband's death, perhaps even speculating that she may have been involved.

Our paraphrase for that line could now read:

"Like the bereaved Queen turned to stone for her hubris, crying non-stop…"

References might also be personifications, like Fortune, Hydra, metaphors like "the green-eyed monster," (meaning jealousy), or terms relevant to the time in which the play was written, like "nineteen zodiacs." A little sleuthing is needed, from reliable sources, (such as those listed in the resources at the end of this chapter), that can help us understand the reference or image, and subsequently, convey that meaning to the audience with clarity. If we understand it, that goes a long way toward convincing others, rather than merely saying the words with no meaning or context attached. Sometimes, images can accompany the information, "like Patience on a monument" from *Othello* is an example, with the initialized capital letter as a clue that something deeper is at play, as we discover images of a young woman sitting with her hands in her lap, watching the drama happening below, "smiling at grief," unable or unwilling to act or get involved, without judgment or action. In every instance of a reference or metaphor, the character speaking is choosing it as another way to express what seems inexpressible. The text becomes doubly heightened in these moments, as characters reach to higher realms of rhetoric and imagery to make themselves understood.

Sometimes, phrases or words in texts written long ago mean something very different today, and we need to be mindful of how they sound and their impact on the audience. It might be words that are no longer in common usage, that take an audience member out of the story, thinking "Huh? What did they say?" In *Twelfth Night*, for example, Viola says, "How will this fadge?" when speculating how things will turn out. There's no need to change that word just because no one uses it today, since it's clear from the context that she's unsure of the whole situation she's gotten herself into. The meaning of the archaic word is most likely clear through her actions (taking off her hat and shaking her head) and her choice (to think this through a little bit), so "what's going to happen next?" is the paraphrase, which helps the actor commit to that meaning, even though the word sounds a little nonsensical. No change in the text is needed.

In other cases, problematic words activate us (and audiences) based on their contemporary meaning. No matter where you land on the issue of altering or cutting text in the public domain, you will find passages that are archaic or problematic and need to decide if a change is needed. In a production, this kind of attention paid to these issues might be undertaken by a dramaturg or the director. As actors, we have a responsibility to ask the question and make requests for changes in a setting that is appropriate. When a change is implemented in iambic pentameter, it should retain the scansion of the word you're removing, for example, "miserly rascal," meaning a person who is stingy and mean, should be substituted for the adjective used in the 1500s that has an unequivocal and profoundly racist meaning today (that I choose not to dignify with putting it here in print). Lines can be cut or changed with rationale that supports the values you bring to the work, and actors have the right to approach a dramaturg or a director with concerns about what's not okay to say from their perspective, and provide suggestions of words that might provide what's needed without causing harm.

Here are a few examples of line changes that might be considered that retain the meaning and the scansion yet eliminate an archaic or charged word and honor the scansion:

> From *Much Ado About Nothing*, Act V, scene i:
> LEONATO: Art thou the **rogue** that with thy breath hast kill'd Mine innocent child?
> From *The Comedy of Errors*, Act II, scene i:
> ADRIANA: Neither my husband nor his **man** return'd?

Harvey Young, in his 2013 book *Theatre and Race,* offers us "an invitation to reflect upon and evaluate the legacy and enduring relevance of race," and provides "an economical model that allows for a better appreciation of the shifting perspectives on race and theatre over time." Descriptive terms have changed over the years, and categories of any kind are essentially divisive. We can no longer simply make excuses or provide rationales that dismiss concerns with statements like "That was a different time," or "If we set it in a different period, it will be okay." Nicole Brewer and her *Anti-Racist Theatre Ethos* provides tools to make changes in individual and organizational ways that matter. Even the "Golden Age" is renamed the "Olden Age" now, acknowledging that we need to reimagine material with the permission of late authors' estates to consider changes to support, as Brewer states, "that our collective liberation is tied to one another and the way forward is together." We have evolved as a society and a global culture, and the language we use matters.

TRY IT! PRACTICE PARAPHRASING VERSE TEXT (AND REINFORCING SCANSION)

Here is the entire scene from *Othello* when Iago obtains the handkerchief Desdemona has left behind, unwittingly offered up by his wife Emilia, then speaking directly to the audience about his plans to trap Cassio and Othello in a web of deceit. Begin by reading it aloud, then repeating it aloud while mapping out the scansion. Make your scansion marks [˘ /] above each unstressed or stressed syllable. Then move onto the paraphrase step, using dictionary work along the way to unlock the meanings of words or references, or to look up familiar words that might be used in unique ways.

OTHELLO Act Three, Scene iii (lines 294 – 333)
EMILIA
I am glad I have found this napkin;
This was her first remembrance from the Moor.
My wayward husband hath a hundred times
Wooed me to steal it; but she so loves the token –   5
For he conjur'd her she should ever keep it -
That she reserves it evermore about her
To kiss and talk to. I'll have the work ta'en out

And give't Iago: what he will do with it
Heaven knows, not I,   10
I nothing know, but for his fantasy.   *Enter IAGO.*
IAGO
How now! What do you here alone?
EMILIA
Do not you chide, I have a thing for you -
IAGO
A thing for me? it is a common thing -
EMILIA
Ha?
IAGO   To have a foolish wife.
EMILIA
O, is that all? What will you give me now   15
For that same handkerchief?
IAGO   What handkerchief?
EMILIA
What handkerchief?
Why, that the Moor first gave to Desdemona,
That which so often you did bid me steal.
IAGO
Hast stol'n it from her?
EMILIA
No, faith, she let it drop by negligence,
And, to th'advantage, I, being here, took't up.   20
Look, here it is.
IAGO   A good wench! Give it me.
EMILIA
What will you do with't that you have been so earnest
To have me filch it?
IAGO   Why, what is that to you?
EMILIA
If it be not for some purpose of import
Give't me again. Poor lady, she'll run mad   25
When she shall lack it.
IAGO
Be not acknown on't, I have use for it.
Go, leave me.   *Exit Emilia.*

> I will in Cassio's lodging lose this napkin   30
> And let him find it. Trifles light as air
> Are to the jealous confirmations strong
> As proofs of holy writ. This may do something.
> The Moor already changes with my poison:
> Dangerous conceits are in their natures poisons,   35
> Which at the first are scarce found to distaste,
> But with a little art upon the blood
> Burn like the mines of sulphur.

A completely paraphrased version of this scene is found in the Appendix.

SUMMARY

In this chapter:

- we delved into punctuation, like signs on the map of our heightened text, to help us navigate how the ideas are structured;
- we found opportunities for breath without sacrificing the integrity of the thought;
- we learned how to paraphrase the text, putting it into our own words;
- we enlisted a dictionary to use in discovering the meaning of unfamiliar or archaic words and became more curious about words we think we know;
- we gained awareness of how words can be charged with different meanings, and strategies for making changes to reduce and prevent harm, without erasing or minimizing the story.

RESOURCES FOR FURTHER EXPLORATION

Harvey Young's book *Theatre and Race* is a slim but mighty volume that emerged from conversations in his graduate seminar at Northwestern University. At only 80 pages in length, it can be read in an afternoon, but its ideas can take a lifetime to process.

Asimov's *Guide to Shakespeare Volumes 1 and 2* has been reprinted in one edition and is an indispensable compendium of the historical and mythological references in each play of Shakespeare's. When I am working on any of the plays, one of my first reads is "the Asimov chapter" on it.

WEBSITES

- Nicole M. Brewer, Anti-Racist Theatre https://www.nicolembrewer.com/anti-racist-theatre
  An indispensable up-to-the-moment guide to how to incorporate Anti-Racist values in theatre.
- Folger Shakespeare Library https://www.folger.edu/explore/
  This site has a wealth of information about each Shakespeare play, including scene by scene analysis.
- Schoolhouse Rock, Conjunction Junction, YouTube: https://www.youtube.com/watch?v=LjdCFat9rjI
  Lyrics by Bob Dorough, with Jack Sheldon on lead vocal and Terry Morrell backing vocal, this short, animated musical entertains while educating about the importance of "hooking up words and phrases and clauses" with "and, but, or." The leading character is a train conductor who has those words printed on the side of the train cars.

3

CONVEYING THE IDEAS
Emphasis on Words, Thoughts, Ideas, and Images

INTRODUCTION

This chapter demystifies the third step in acting heightened text: **conveying the meaning** of what we discovered in the paraphrase to the other actors and to the audience using **operative words**. **We mark the key words that help ideas come across effectively**. Identifying and underlining the operative words in each line, discerning the difference between primary and secondary operative words, and using parenthetical phrases, images, and metaphors make the main ideas clear. Attaching the appropriate vocal emphasis using a nuanced combination of pitch, rhythm, and volume is essential to achieving this goal. Using examples of text from previous chapters, building on the first and second steps in the homework process (scansion and paraphrase) reinforces how the steps support each other and allow us to pursue the acting choices we discuss in future chapters. Longer sections of text and dialogue allow for practice, revealing a myriad of variations and interpretations that can be employed through operative words.

IDENTIFYING OPERATIVE WORDS IN OUR DAILY INTERACTIONS

Once we determine what it is we're trying to say through our paraphrase and dictionary work, we must figure out how to get these

DOI: 10.4324/9781032695310-4

ideas across clearly to our scene partners and the audience. Since this process is no different than what we do in everyday life, we'll begin with ordinary exchanges and identify the operative words, then test whether our choices are effective by reading them aloud. When we move forward to using heightened text, we'll clarify metaphors, images, and parenthetical phrases, navigating how to weigh certain words over others to convey the ideas effectively.

Let's start with some scientific understanding about how thoughts get put into words. How does one person understand another person when they speak, receiving and processing the idea in order to respond? The brain is the nerve center of this activity, but playing an important role, more specifically, is a small part of the left frontal lobe called "Broca's area," which spontaneously processes and codes thoughts, chooses words, and then sends signals that form speech. Imagine a little chip in your head that spits out the right thing to say at the right moment. The challenge, of course, is not having the words sound like a computer when we say them!

To avoid sounding like a machine, humans in all languages make some words sound more important than others. Those words are called **operatives**. The operative words we choose **emphasize and control the function of the idea** – they make the thought happen clearly and effectively because of a specific choice. As human beings with emotions, we use pitch, rhythm, and volume to help differentiate important words from less important words, which aids in the communication and comprehension of the ideas.

Our tool for identifying operative words is to underline them. In our marked-up scripts, as the third step in our homework, a primary operative word gets a solid underline, and a secondary operative word gets a dotted or dashed underline, either from a keyboard (using the Font menu) or an old-fashioned pencil on paper. I prefer to use a pencil, since it's likely I'm going to change my mind, or make a mistake – it's all part of the growth mindset! We distinguish using the word **emphasis** from the word **stress** when talking about operatives, since stress is now associated with the marks [˘ /] used in **scansion**. Operatives are the words we emphasize over other words, taking into account how they might be scanned in the verse line. A challenge can be figuring out which monosyllabic words are operatives, so let's tackle that first. There's no right or wrong in choosing operative words, it's whether they work or not in conveying the meaning.

EMPHASIS ON WORDS, THOUGHTS, IDEAS, AND IMAGES **67**

When we say the lines aloud, we emphasize these words to varying degrees as primary and secondary operatives, to allow for some flexibility and variety in our expression. A <u>primary</u> operative word receives the <u>most</u> emphasis, the <u>secondary</u> operative a little <u>less</u>, and then regular stressed and unstressed words no more than what they need to serve their purpose. In words with more than one syllable, the whole word gets the emphasis, though the scansion within it doesn't change. With monosyllabic words, we have to determine how much emphasis it needs, above and beyond if it's already one of the stressed syllables in the line. If a monosyllabic word seems like it's actually working well as an operative, and you've marked it as unstressed, you'll need to change it to be a stressed syllable. (It's not possible to emphasize a word you decided wasn't even stressed.) In iambic pentameter, in regular lines with no variations, unstressed and stressed syllables fall into "positions" – where they normally land. For example, the first syllable in a regular line is unstressed, the second syllable is stressed, and so on. We might say of those syllables that they are in a "stressed position" or "an unstressed position" as a way to help us think about operative levels of emphasis, especially on monosyllabic words:

˘ / ˘ / ˘ / ˘ ˘ / ˘   w
To <u>be</u>, or <u>not</u> to be; <u>that</u> is the <u>question.</u>
1 2   3 4 5 6   7   8 9 10   11

In this example, the 2nd, 4th, and 6th words are monosyllabic and fall in **stressed positions**: that's just where they land naturally in the regular iambic part of this line.

The operative words are the first [<u>be</u>] and [<u>not</u>], but we leave the second mention of [be] alone, relying on its weight as a stressed syllable to be enough to carry the meaning of Hamlet's thought. This conveys the **antithesis** of "being" and "not" being. If both "be" instances are emphasized, it confuses the meaning.

In the later part of the line, which has two variations (a trochee "that is" and a weak ending "the question"), we operate on both of the remaining strong stresses in the line, even though "question" is two syllables and the second syllable is weak. The <u>scansion</u> remains <u>intact</u>, and the entire <u>word</u> receives emphasis as an **operative**. Since "is" is a tiny word with little significance beyond being the verb, and "that" references the dilemma set up by the preceding phrase, these operative choices are reinforced by the work we did earlier on scansion.

Here's another example in which the line has an operative word right off the bat, but it starts with a trochee, the stressed syllable coming first:

> / ˘   ˘   / ˘ / ˘   / ˘ /
> <u>Nothing</u> will come of <u>nothing</u>; <u>Speak</u> <u>again</u>.

As we learned in our paraphrase, the two instances of the word "nothing" mean two totally different things. One of the best ways to support this in conveying it to Cordelia, as well as the audience, is to make the first one a <u>primary</u> operative, and the second one <u>secondary</u>. (However, the reverse choice also works!) The same logic applies to the remainder of the line – Lear ordered her to "Speak" a few lines back, and now he asks her to do it "<u>again</u>," an appropriate reason to use secondary emphasis on "<u>Speak</u>" and <u>primary</u> emphasis on "<u>again</u>."

It takes a little practice to get used to how to talk about what you're doing, but the way you're saying the line is usually effective. When you get stuck on which words are operatives, the best method to test your choice is to say it that way **aloud**. If it <u>works</u>, <u>mark</u> it and move <u>on</u>. If you get caught up in the weeds of whether an operative is <u>primary</u> or <u>secondary</u>, just <u>underline</u> it, <u>emphasize</u> it when you <u>say</u> it and move <u>on</u>. In most cases, the <u>secondary</u> element of it comes out effectively when you focus on conveying the <u>idea</u>, rather than <u>how</u> you're trying to say the <u>line</u>. Just <u>do</u> it.

FINDING THE ANTITHESIS: RELATED WORDS THAT FORM IDEAS

Finding the **antithesis** in a line of text helps us gravitate to the idea, which then leads us to choose operative words to support it. **Antithesis** can mean contrasting words, opposites, related or different words. <u>**Antithetical words must be lifted**</u> above and beyond their level of stress or emphasis, as this is a primary literary device, not only in heightened text, but in everyday conversation.

Examples of **antithesis at play** include:

From *Richard III:* Now is the **<u>winter</u>** of our discontent
Made glorious **<u>summer</u>** by this son of York.

The antithesis is seasons, very different ones, perhaps. "Winter" is pitched up, and then "summer" is a response.

From *King John:* **Husband**, I cannot pray that thou mayst win;
Uncle, I needs must pray that thou mayst lose;
Father, I may not wish the fortune thine;
Grandam, I will not wish thy fortunes thrive:
Whoever wins, on that side shall I **lose:**
Assured loss before the match be play'd.

The antitheses here are Blanche's **familial relations**, and **win/lose** – on opposing sides of a war. Blanche's level of detail in conveying her predicament: a new husband, on an opposing side, and family members who all have a stake in winning the war, is conveyed by her careful and passionate delineation of the situation for all of them, as a means to get them to all to stop.

If the first multi syllabic word of the line seems like an **operative**, like in the above *King John* example, the **whole word** is underlined and emphasized, regardless of whether it's a regular iambic beginning or a trochee. Let's look at these lines we've already scanned to see how it's done:

˘ / ˘ / ˘ / ˘ / ˘ /
I never did incense his majesty
˘ / ˘ / ˘ / ˘ / ˘ /
Against the Duke of Clarence, but have been
˘ / ˘ / ˘ / ˘ / ˘ /
An earnest advocate to **plead** for him.

Above, we see the second line has an operative right off the bat, "Against," and it's a two-syllable word. The emphasis applies to the word – the scansion doesn't change.

The **antithesis** is reflected in bold, and underlined, even though the word "for" might seem like the antecedent to "against," she is "pleading," which implies the same idea – on Clarence's behalf.

> **TRY IT! OPERATIVE WORDS IN EVERYDAY INTERACTIONS**
>
> Think of a short list of things you might need from the grocery store and say it aloud a couple of times, as if you were talking to someone else:
>
> **Go to the store and buy some milk and eggs.**
>
> Even though we aren't dealing with a line of verse, this one happens to be ten syllables, and every one of these words is monosyllabic. Our first task is to figure out what's important among them.
>
> What words come to the surface as operative words? <u>Underline</u> them and say those words with a little more emphasis in order to make the idea clear. (You don't have to hit them like a newscaster, just a bit more volume or a slightly higher pitch will do the job.)

Here's how I hear it when I speak it aloud:

<u>Go</u> to the <u>store</u> and buy some <u>milk</u> and <u>eggs</u>.

It's clear what to do, where to go, and what to get. I would understand this if you said it aloud to me with these operative words emphasized.

If we want to break it down further and explore other options or "what-if's" (like we do in scansion), let's try the "nuclear option" and make <u>every</u> <u>single</u> <u>word</u> a primary operative:

<u>Go</u> <u>to</u> <u>the</u> <u>store</u> <u>and</u> <u>buy</u> <u>some</u> <u>milk</u> <u>and</u> <u>eggs</u>.

Whoa! That's way too much, and a ridiculous example of operative overkill. Let's look instead at all the options in between.

What if one assumes the main verbs (go, buy) should both be the primary operatives? It would sound like this:

<u>Go</u> to the <u>store</u> and <u>buy</u> some <u>milk</u> and <u>eggs</u>.

If you said that to me aloud with those operatives, emphasizing that I <u>go</u> and <u>buy</u> the milk and eggs, I would assume that <u>this</u> time, you want me to <u>buy</u> them, not <u>steal</u> them (like I did <u>last</u> time!).

What if you wanted to be clear about <u>where</u> to go and what to <u>get</u>? The sentence might look like this:

Go to the <u>store</u> and buy some <u>milk</u> and <u>eggs</u>.

Obviously, from the way you conveyed it, I must've gone to the "7-11" last time and bought potato chips and soda. The emphasis is on going to <u>this</u> particular place and buy <u>these</u> particular items.

One last what-if could be if I wanted to be clear about the quantity of milk and eggs I wanted from the store (with my Broca's area adding a couple of other words to do so), but there's no confusion about where to go and that I intend to buy them:

Go to the <u>store</u> and buy a <u>gallon</u> of milk and a <u>dozen</u> eggs.

What matters most in this example is how much milk and how many eggs. The operatives are structured to help make that clear.

In the end, the most logical use of operatives in this sentence might be as follows:

<u>Go</u> to the <u>store</u> and <u>buy</u> some <u>milk</u> and <u>eggs</u>.

TRY IT! FINDING PRIMARY AND SECONDARY OPERATIVES IN VERSE

Using the familiar lines of text from our scansion and paraphrase, reading aloud, let's hear what words stand out as crucial (operative) in conveying the meaning:

The duke is very strangely gone from hence.

It's helpful to review the work with a line or a speech that you've already done your homework on, so the steps happen in this order: scansion, paraphrase, operatives. Maybe you may find it's easier and more natural to read aloud and jump right to the marking the operatives, which might help you sort out the paraphrase, and then you can use scansion to check your work. What matters most is that you complete all three steps, but how you get there is up to you.

The scansion for this line is regular, so there's no need to mark it. If there was a variation, you would mark it, and honor that difference as you proceed into reviewing our paraphrase before finding the operatives.

I came up with these ideas to paraphrase what the line above means:

- The royal man in charge has, under rare and strange circumstances, left Vienna.
- The main dude, totally out of character, blew out of town.
- The governor, uncharacteristically, and for no known reason, has fled from here.

Here's what we might come up with for operatives, reading aloud, if we emphasized **every** component of the idea:

>The <u>duke</u> is <u>very</u> <u>strangely</u> <u>gone</u> from <u>hence</u>.

When too many words are marked as operatives, it's too much, and the nuances of meaning get lost in the volume and force of landing so heavily on every word, especially every word that starts with strong stress. Unless you're talking to someone on the other side of a wall, there isn't the need for this level of emphasis.

As we strive to find the balance, we can efficiently use our scansion and paraphrase to help guide us:

- Choosing <u>duke</u> as a primary operative is critical since it's the subject of the sentence and the main point of what Lucio wants to convey: "The person who's usually in charge is gone."
- If we underline <u>very</u>, making it an operative means we have emphasized the modifying word without conveying what's "very." Let's leave the word as it is, just allowing the stress of the word to do its job.
- Then we can rely on <u>strangely</u> to carry the heavy luggage of the idea that it's unusual and rare for the duke to be away. The actor's job is to convey that "strangely" means both things.
- The unstressed monosyllabic words should not be made into operatives: "the" "is" and "from" do not carry the weight of the ideas. If we did make them operatives, we'd have to go back and

change our scansion, since you can't give words more emphasis if they don't even merit strong stress. That dog doesn't hunt.
- The phrase "gone from hence" is a challenge, since "gone" means "left where we are." Since "from hence" means "left here," which in this case is Vienna, we have to make a choice to lift one or the other, or choose one as <u>primary</u> and make another a <u>secondary</u> operative. There's no right or wrong choice here, except not to make either of them an operative in any way.

Here are some options to try aloud that vary the weight in order for Lucio to convey the context to Isabella, setting up the circumstances for why her brother is in jail:

The <u>duke</u> is very <u>strangely gone</u> from <u>hence</u>.
The <u>duke</u> is very <u>strangely gone</u> from hence.
The <u>duke</u> is very <u>strangely</u> gone from <u>hence</u>.

You may not notice a big difference between <u>primary</u> and <u>secondary</u> operatives, and making rules isn't often helpful, since each line varies in its complexity. Play with the weight a few ways until it seems to serve the idea effectively, and move on.

Let's try another example of familiar text that we've scanned and paraphrased, reading aloud a few times to help find the operatives that naturally rise to the surface

In the Hamlet speech we've been working with, we have metaphors of weapons and a body of water to establish:

To be, or not to be, that is the question:
Whether 'tis nobler in the mind to suffer
The slings and arrows of outrageous fortune,
Or to take arms against a sea of troubles,
And by opposing, end them. To die, to sleep—

The metaphors must be set up by the strategic use of operatives. We often use metaphors to aid in understanding, or to express how what we mean is like something else. These are frequent literary devices, as common in our everyday conversations as in heightened text to great poetic effect.

For simplicity, here is the passage using only primary operatives, with the lines numbered:

> To <u>be</u>, or <u>not</u> to be, <u>that</u> is the <u>question</u>:   1
> Whether 'tis <u>nobler</u> in the <u>mind</u> to <u>suffer</u>   2
> The <u>slings</u> and <u>arrows</u> of outrageous <u>fortune</u>,   3
> Or to take <u>arms</u> against a <u>sea</u> of troubles,   4
> And by <u>opposing</u>, <u>end</u> them. To <u>die</u>, to <u>sleep</u> –   5

I had to make some tough choices to ensure I wasn't hammering away on operatives on almost every strong stress. The most challenging for me was the 3rd and 4th lines, since there are so many things to convey, that fortune can be outrageous (I felt the word "outrageous" covers that ground on its own without being operative), and that if I take arms, it assumes that I am taking them against something, so I choice not to operate on "against" as well.

Using <u>secondary</u> operatives is like having more than just a <u>flat-edge</u> screwdriver in the drawer, you get more choices of finding the <u>right</u> <u>tool</u> for the <u>right</u> <u>job</u>.

Here, then, is the same speech using a mix of <u>primary</u> and <u>secondary</u> operatives:

> To <u>be</u>, or <u>not</u> to be, <u>that</u> is the <u>question</u>:
> Whether 'tis <u>nobler</u> in the <u>mind</u> to <u>suffer</u>
> The <u>slings</u> and <u>arrows</u> of <u>outrageous</u> <u>fortune</u>,
> Or to take <u>arms</u> against a <u>sea</u> of <u>troubles</u>,
> And by <u>opposing</u>, <u>end</u> them. To <u>die</u>, to <u>sleep</u>—

Playing with operative words might feel like trying different line readings, which leads some actors to believe they are setting things too early in the rehearsal process. Remember that finding operative words is part of the homework, the work you want to complete to be prepared for a rehearsal, audition, or callback. It's the basic, investigative work that sets you up to make textually supported acting choices. When an actor or director has done thorough homework, rehearsal becomes an opportunity to explore and respond. Operative words are changeable, they are your choices at this point in your work. Just like in life, when the need arises, you can make a new choice.

Operative words help us navigate every conversation or exchange, and we clarify what we need by emphasizing certain words to help our ideas come across clearly. This happens in a split second in the brain. Think of someone in your kitchen about to reach for a pan that you just took out of the oven: you take a quick urgent breath and shout: "Watch out – that handle is hot!"

If we mark the operatives we used, it might look like this: "Watch <u>out</u> – that <u>handle</u> is <u>hot</u>!"

The weight we give these words comes out naturally, to suit the situation. It doesn't sound clinical or forced, we just blurt it out, and what's important comes to the surface. There's no magic number of how many operatives you use, just as many or as few as it takes to be clear. If we aren't clear, the other person says, "What?" and we often repeat the sentence or phrase with a little more attention to conveying the meaning. We talk so fast sometimes there's only one or two operative words in a line, because we understand each other in terms of context. We have to read aloud, or else we won't hear the weight of the operative as it relates to the rest of the idea. You can't identify and practice operative words in your head.

Scene partners hear operatives the same way your friends do in ordinary conversation, understanding what's going on and responding in the moment, like this:

> **A:** Do you want to go to <u>dinner</u> tonight?
> **B:** <u>Sure</u>! What <u>time</u>, though?
> **A:** We could go at <u>6</u> or <u>8</u>.
> **B:** <u>8</u> would be better for <u>me</u>, I'm working <u>late</u>.
> **A:** Then <u>8</u> it <u>is</u>! Do you want to <u>meet</u> there or should I <u>pick</u> you <u>up</u>?
> **B:** <u>Oh</u>, I'll meet you <u>there</u>. <u>Thanks</u>!

Let's look at the familiar Emilia and Iago exchange to see how a scene partner feeds off their partner's operatives in heightened text:

> EMILIA What will you <u>give</u> me <u>now</u>
> For <u>that</u> same <u>handkerchief</u>?
> IAGO What <u>handkerchief</u>?
> EMILIA   <u>What</u> <u>handkerchief</u>?
> Why, that the <u>Moor</u> first <u>gave</u> to <u>Desdemona</u>,
> That which so <u>often</u> you did bid me <u>steal</u>.
> IAGO   Hast <u>stol'n</u> it from her?
> EMILIA   <u>No</u>, faith, she let it <u>drop</u> by <u>negligence</u>,
> And, to th'<u>advantage</u>, <u>I</u>, <u>being</u> here, took't <u>up</u>.
> <u>Look</u>, here it <u>is</u>.
> IAGO   A <u>good</u> wench! <u>Give</u> it me.

With practice, actors gain skill in conveying a natural exchange employing different weights of emphasis for primary and secondary operatives.

WADING THROUGH TOO MUCH INFORMATION: PARENTHETICAL PHRASES AND LISTS

Operative words are essential in helping set off parenthetical phrases from the main thought. Parenthetical phrases offer support to the main idea, often additional information, or a clarification. These phrases can be set off by parentheses, (like this), or might be separated by commas, another reason to consider how a comma might be used in a particular line. In everyday conversations, we set off parentheticals by lowering our pitch for the duration of the phrase and picking up the pace of the parenthetical slightly. This has the impact of subjugating the information (making it a little less important) and returning to the established pitch and pace of the main thought when the parenthetical phrase is complete.

Since many classical texts were typeset using blocks of letters to form words, the sets contained only periods, with the comma and parentheses introduced around 1521. The addition of these two internal forms of punctuation assisted in making legal documents clearer and brought more nuanced readings of novels, plays, and songs. Imagine our communication without any internal punctuation! An example of an archaic printed text is in a link at the end of this chapter.

We'll begin with everyday use of parenthetical phrases (providing more information that may not be critical, but aids in our understanding), reading the sentence aloud to raise awareness of how we naturally differentiate parentheticals from main thoughts:

> My brother, John, (he graduated from the University of Michigan), is coming over for dinner tomorrow night.

What is the main thought? "My brother is coming over for dinner tomorrow night."

All the rest of the information is parenthetical, not as important as the main thought (whether it's set off by parentheses or not): that he graduated from the University of Michigan.

That's why "John" is set off with commas, because it's parenthetical to the main thought.

Why is his name parenthetical? Because I have more than one brother, and only John went to Michigan.

Why would I say, "he graduated from the University of Michigan"? Because my other dinner guest went to Ohio State, and I thought it would be fun to mention it (especially if it's a Saturday and they're playing football this afternoon).

If you don't know me well, I might say it this way:

> My brother is coming over for dinner tomorrow night, he graduated from the University of Michigan.

I changed the main thought to just say that my brother who went to Michigan is coming over for dinner. It's a bit of an afterthought, but now it's more important, and a separate clause all on its own. If you don't know or care that I have more than one brother, his name doesn't matter right now, but I do want to mention the Michigan thing.

The sentence we started with would be marked like this:

> My brother (John), (he graduated from the University of Michigan), is coming over for dinner tomorrow night.

All this parsing about is to make the point about how to identify a parenthetical phrase. The reason we need to identify it is to be sure to lower our pitch and pick up the pace while we say it. The best way to mark the text is to add parentheses (if they aren't already there as part of the text), and then practice "making it parenthetical." When choosing operative words, make sure there are only secondary operatives within parentheticals, otherwise they become more important than the main thought.

> **TRY IT! FINDING PARENTHETICALS AND PRIORITIZING THE MAIN THOUGHT**
>
> Here's a brief example from Othello's soliloquy over Desdemona's sleeping body, moments before he murders her for believing she has been unfaithful. Read it aloud, put your scansion marks in if there are irregular lines, and then place parenthetical marks ( ) where you think they belong, then read the speech again and mark your operative words, indicating <u>primary</u> and <u>secondary</u> when it suits:
>
> **Put out the light, and then put out the light:**
> **If I quench thee, thou flaming minister,**
> **I can again thy former light restore,**
> **Should I repent me; but once put out thy light,**
> **Thou cunning'st pattern of excelling nature,**
> **I know not where is that Promethean heat**
> **That can thy light relume.**   *Othello V: ii*

Let's break this one down below once you've had a go at it.

The paraphrase step is critical in identifying parentheticals here since Othello is referencing both the light in his room (the candle) and the light of his life (Desdemona). Knowing which one he's talking about is essential. Since he repeats the same four words "put out the light" and then begins with the light he can restore, we are clear that it's the candle first. Othello looks at the candle as he considers these consequences. He has told us already that he can't bear seeing her in the light, so putting it out is essential to carrying out his plan. Now he thinks for a moment about how one action can be revoked, and the other one can't. Here is how one might mark it to highlight the main thought by adding the *paraphrase*, identifying the operative words, and then marking the parentheticals (**read only the lines themselves aloud**, not the *paraphrase*):

> Put <u>out</u> the <u>light</u>, and <u>then</u> put out the <u>light</u>:
> *Blow out this candle, and then extinguish the light of my life:*
> If I quench <u>thee</u>, (thou <u>flaming minister</u>),
> *If I douse you, (my burning guide),*
> I can again thy <u>former</u> light <u>restore</u>,
> *It's easy to re-light you again,*
> Should I <u>repent</u> me;
> *If I change my mind.*

The scansion step becomes integral in the second half of the speech, so below I mark up the variation to help convey that switch from the candle to Desdemona, with the help of two trochees and the strategic use of primary and secondary operatives:

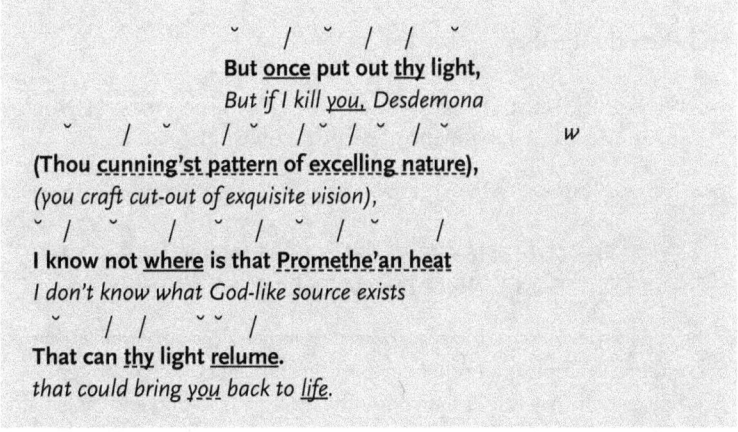

A 5000-ft. observation is important here: this is an author working at the top of their game, sending clear signals to the actor with the words, which requires that the actor know how to read the signals and convert them to choices and actions that tell the story. (In the next section on Imagery, we will return to this speech, showing how Othello tries to talk himself out of doing this horrible deed using logic and metaphor to keep his impulse to kill her under control.)

When working on any text in which the thought seems clunky, long, or complex, maybe containing a list, we break it down to find the parentheticals, or bring rhetorical shape to a list. The exercise we use to practice the subjugation of the parenthetical or part of a list is to take it out – not say it – saying only the main thought aloud, then put the parenthetical phrase(s) or parts of the list back in, one at a time. This helps keep the main thought as the focus, and lessen the weight on the parentheticals but maintain their connection.

Think about the sentence we used to identify parentheticals, and leave them out this time:

My brother is coming over for dinner tomorrow night.

Then, we add in the first parenthetical, John:

My brother, John, is coming over for dinner tomorrow night.

And then the final parenthetical:

My brother, John, (he graduated from the University of Michigan) is coming over for dinner tomorrow night.

TRY IT! IDENTIFYING MAIN THOUGHTS AND PRACTICING KEEPING THEM CLEAR

Here is an example of a speech of Desdemona's from *Othello* that contains multiple parenthetical phrases and lists, even though it employs commas rather than parentheses. Read it aloud and look for the signs, mark the parentheticals, then try the exercise I described above to leave out speaking the phrases or parts of a list to keep the main thoughts clear:

> **DESDEMONA**
> O good Iago,
> What shall I do to win my lord again?
> Good friend, go to him; for by this light of heaven,
> I know not how I lost him. Here I kneel:
> If e'er my will did trespass 'gainst his love,
> Either in discourse of thought or actual deed,
> Or that mine eyes, mine ears, or any sense,
> Delighted them in any other form;
> Or that I do not yet, and ever did,
> And ever will--though he do shake me off
> To beggarly divorcement--love him dearly,
> Comfort forswear me!   *Othello, IV:ii*

Let's review what you discovered. The main thought in the section that begins "Here I kneel" includes a huge list of potential reasons why she would accept his rejection of her with "Comfort forswear me!" While each of the examples is important, the weight of her logic is carried by the sheer number of deeds she suggests might make her guilty, had she been capable of doing them.

By numbering the ways she might have upset him, then singling out each one by **saying that number aloud**, adding the parentheses, and then closing the thought with "Comfort forswear me!" we see how the list contained within the speech serves to build the argument, with operative words helping make the case for why these accusations are ridiculous:

>   Here I kneel:
> 1. If e'er my <u>will</u> did <u>trespass</u> 'gainst his <u>love</u>,
>   Either in <u>discourse</u> of <u>thought</u> or <u>actual deed</u>,
> 2. Or that mine <u>eyes</u>, mine <u>ears</u>, or <u>any</u> sense,
>   <u>Delighted</u> them in <u>any</u> other <u>form</u>;
> 3. Or that I do not <u>yet</u>, and ever <u>did</u>,
>   And ever <u>will</u>—(<u>though</u> he do <u>shake</u> me off
>   To <u>beggarly divorcement</u>)--<u>love</u> him <u>dearly</u>,
>   <u>Comfort</u> <u>forswear</u> me!

As an exercise, the actor playing Desdemona practices creating the build by reading it this way once, and then going back and retaining that sense that the first thing she says at the time may be the only thing she says, but then she decides to provide another example, and then another, leaving out the parenthetical, finally landing on "Comfort forswear me!"

> **Here I kneel:**
> **If e'er my will did trespass 'gainst his love,**
> **Either in discourse of thought or actual deed,**
> **Comfort forswear me!**
>
> **Or that mine eyes, mine ears, or any sense,**
> **Delighted them in any other form;**
> **Comfort forswear me!**
>
> **Or that I do not yet, and ever did,**
> **And ever will—love him dearly,**
> **Comfort forswear me!**

After creating this sense of how the pieces of the list connect, the actor goes back to the complete speech, including the parenthetical, building the energy with a connection to the end of the main thought, to convey her frustration and innocence.

MAKING IMAGES AND IDEAS CLEAR AND EXPRESSIVE

Heightened text is often filled with poetic language using mythical references, metaphors, allusions, analogies, and similes (ways we express how something is like something else) to convey the ideas. The actor's job is to make these images clear, since it is the character who is using the metaphor to express what they feel or what they mean. When we paraphrase them, we retain the metaphor, but also connect with why the character is using the metaphor – they need another way to express it to make their point.

In this case, in Act V, scene ii, Othello is trying to convince himself of the consequences and finality of killing Desdemona, so these two versions of paraphrase retain the metaphor to the right in *italics*:

When I have plucked the rose,	*If I pulled a beautiful flower off the vine,*
I cannot give it vital growth again.	*There's no way to bring it back to life.*
It needs must wither. I'll smell it on the tree.	*The flower dies. I'll enjoy it once more.*
O balmy breath, that dost almost persuade	*I feel her warmth, which almost makes*
Justice to break her sword!	*The very personification of Justice give up!*

Attention must be paid to how the character needs to be convinced that this is the right thing to do, which is why Othello uses the metaphor and reference to Justice in the first place:

When I have plucked the rose,	*If she were a flower I plucked,*
I cannot give it vital growth again.	*I wouldn't be able to bring her back to life.*
It needs must wither. I'll smell it on the tree.	*She'd be dead. I'll kiss her before I kill her.*
O balmy breath, that dost almost persuade	*Her warm lips are almost convincing me*
Justice to break her sword!	*To throw aside my righteous vengeance!*

The personified image of Lady Justice from Roman mythology (though her origins are in Egypt) is often a statue outside courthouses, portrayed wearing a blindfold, in a flowing robe, carrying scales in one hand and a sword in the other. By the 16th century when Shakespeare wrote *Othello,* the virtue of Justice served as an inspiration to uphold the law, in the same way the Statue of Liberty in New York implies freedom. **The character of Othello is using the reference to Justice** as a reminder of the power of authority, and that justice can be final.

Useful resources exist that can help actors find visual representations of mythical references, as well as websites and image libraries of museums. **The characters knew what they were referring to**, so we have an obligation to understand and connect to these images as we prepare our text.

> ### TRY IT! PRACTICING POETIC TEXT AND REINFORCING OPERATIVE WORDS
>
> Using the scene between Emilia and Iago, apply the skills from this chapter by reading aloud and marking the operative words and parentheticals as you go. It's helpful to use a pencil in case you change your mind, or if you're working with a partner, to mark the operatives on their lines. Working the whole scene (rather than just your own lines) will be important as we move forward in this book. If you encounter references or images, be sure to do the research to investigate their visual representation, and understand the context for the character employing that device.
>
> **OTHELLO Act Three, Scene iii (lines 294–333)**
> **EMILIA**
> I am glad I have found this napkin;
> This was her first remembrance from the Moor.
> My wayward husband hath a hundred times
> Wooed me to steal it; but she so loves the token –
> For he conjur'd her she should ever keep it -   5
> That she reserves it evermore about her
> To kiss and talk to. I'll have the work ta'en out
> And give't Iago: what he will do with it
> Heaven knows, not I,
> I nothing know, but for his fantasy.   *Enter IAGO*   10
> **IAGO**
> How now! What do you here alone?

EMPHASIS ON WORDS, THOUGHTS, IDEAS, AND IMAGES   85

EMILIA
Do not you chide, I have a thing for you -
IAGO
A thing for me? it is a common thing -
EMILIA Ha?
IAGO
To have a foolish wife.
EMILIA
O, is that all? What will you give me now   15
For that same handkerchief?
IAGO   What handkerchief?
EMILIA
What handkerchief?
Why, that the Moor first gave to Desdemona,
That which so often you did bid me steal.
IAGO
Hast stol'n it from her?
EMILIA
No, faith, she let it drop by negligence,   20
And, to th'advantage, I, being here, took't up.
Look, here it is.
IAGO   A good wench! Give it me.
EMILIA
What will you do with't, that you have been so earnest
To have me filch it?
IAGO   Why, what is that to you?
EMILIA
If it be not for some purpose of import   25
Give't me again. Poor lady, she'll run mad
When she shall lack it.
IAGO
Be not acknown on't, I have use for it.
Go, leave me.   *Exit Emilia.*
I will in Cassio's lodging lose this napkin   30
And let him find it. Trifles light as air
Are to the jealous confirmations strong
As proofs of holy writ. This may do something.

> The Moor already changes with my poison
> Dangerous conceits are in their natures poisons,   35
> Which at the first are scarce found to distaste,
> But with a little art upon the blood
> Burn like the mines of sulphur.
> A complete marked-up version with operatives is found in the Support Material accompanying this book at www.routledge.com/9781032695297.

SUMMARY

In this chapter:

- we demystified the third step in acting heightened text homework: identifying and using operative words;
- we learned to emphasize some words in each line by underlining them as primary or secondary operative words and adding vocal energy to how we say them;
- we found the antithesis as a means to lift the main idea or new information;
- we identified parenthetical phrases, (and marked them to serve as reminders if commas were used) which provide additional or clarifying information that serves the main thought;
- we practiced attaching the appropriate vocal emphasis to operatives and parentheticals by using a nuanced combination of pace, pitch, rhythm, and volume essential to achieving clarity of thought;
- we gained confidence in all three steps of the homework, understanding how the steps support each other;
- we read aloud as a primary tool to find the operatives, marking parentheticals and lists, revealing a myriad of variations and interpretations that can be employed through operative words, enriched by a wealth of images and references.

RESOURCES FOR FURTHER EXPLORATION

Here are some references to concepts and historical information from this chapter:
- How Thoughts Are Converted to Words: Mass General Journal: Aug 23 2018
https://advances.massgeneral.org/neuro/journal
- Information on Broca's Area of the brain:
https://www.verywellmind.com/how-the-broca-s-area-of-the-brain-functions
- The Printed Word: A Little Printing Press History:
https://www.history.com/articles/printing-press
- The History of Punctuation:
BBC.com article "*The Mysterious Origins of Punctuation*," by Keith Houston, 2 September 2015
- An Example of Text with no punctuation:
https://en.wikipedia.org/wiki/Scriptio_continua#/media/File:Vergilius_Augusteus,_Georgica_141.jpg
- The History of Lady Justice:
https://en.wikipedia.org/wiki/Lady_Justice

CONNECTING TO THE PARTNER AND THE SITUATION

INTRODUCTION

Now, we advance the text homework from earlier chapters and place it into the context of realistic acting of the story, leading us to a fully inhabited and truthful portrayal of the given circumstances of the play, the conflict and stakes at the heart of the scene, and the nuances of the relationships with other characters. The foundation of acting is responding actively to a partner (whether real or imaginary) during moments when actions, topics, or tactics change. Marking these changes as beats or shifts and then engaging physically and vocally with those changes allow for a responsive and dynamic performance of heightened text that seems as natural as everyday conversation. Using a short excerpt from *Othello* as a guide, we will navigate playing the moment, having achieved a thorough understanding of the heightened language. Further refining the ability to work moment-to-moment means an actor needs to play conflict, and its adjacent concepts obstacles and stakes, a skill which is illustrated with examples from classic and contemporary texts. Short scenes will allow us to practice these skills with partners or classmates, and we will develop strategies for working on monologues on our own.

DOI: 10.4324/9781032695310-5

GIVEN CIRCUMSTANCES: JUST THE FACTS

Given circumstances are the things we know from the text, the facts we are given by the author. In order to fully support acting choices for each moment, we think of given circumstances as the building blocks of the production. This common term of script analysis, **given circumstances** (which I call **"GC's"** for short), may have been conceived and coined by the Russian actor-director Konstantin Stanislavski, around 1912, which he explored in his acting theory and practice thereafter. The GC's include all the material in a play or script that clarifies the environment, characters, relationships, and situations in which the story takes place – essentially creating the special world of the play. We will work through examples for these building blocks (and what we do when we don't find a concrete answer or fact in the play), to improve our ability to make choices that are grounded in the GC's.

Information is gathered from dialogue (something that gets said) or actions (something that happens) in the text itself and answers questions like Who? What? When? Where? and Why? to help us understand the unique world of the play. Sometimes, these facts are found in part of the stage directions, usually written in *italics*. Stage directions might be words the original production used to describe movements or objects specific to their choices, or an editorial note, not even written by the playwright.

Let's examine each of these questions and provide brief examples of GC's mined from the text. In almost every instance, asking one of these five questions reveals answers to the others, a helpful and efficient way to gather information from close reading of the text through the lens of looking for GC's.

Who are these characters? Do we know their ages, their relationship to each other? What kind of facts are given (or at least believed by other characters to be facts) that can help support our acting choices? What can we learn about the characters Ruth and Walter Lee from Lorraine Hansberry's *A Raisin in the Sun* from two brief lines of dialogue and the accompanying stage direction below?

> RUTH: What kind of eggs you want?
> WALTER LEE: Not scrambled.
> *Ruth starts to scramble eggs.*

These **GC's** about Who? come from the above text:

- Ruth waits on her husband Walter Lee a bit when she makes his breakfast.
- Walter Lee is tired of scrambled eggs.
- The *stage direction* reflects that Ruth does what's easiest for her and rejects his criticism.

These GC's give the actors the information they need to make strong choices moment-to-moment, to convey the story and their relationship. Ruth makes an effort to please her husband in asking how he wants his eggs, Walter Lee complains about having scrambled eggs every day, and Ruth scrambles his eggs anyway because it's easy and quick. They both play the choice that this is a routine, and that some tension is in the air about things always being the same.

What is the current situation for these characters, (often called "stasis" in formal script analysis), at the beginning of the play? What facts are established about the location, time, and events of significance? In the opening scene of *Hamlet,* the character Horatio has been roused out of bed by a few of the palace guards to witness what they have seen two nights in a row:

HORATIO: What, has this thing appeared again tonight?
These **five** GC's about **What?** come from this **one line of text**:

- The guards have seen a ghost, and want Horatio to see it.
- Horatio seems skeptical, calling the ghost "a thing" – he doesn't believe in ghosts.
- Whatever has appeared, it's happened before, since Horatio says "again."
- We know it's nighttime, from the mention of "tonight." (That's a When? answer, too.)
- Horatio's opinion would be respected more than theirs. (That's a Who? answer, too.)

When does the story take place? We need to uncover every clue about time period for the play, especially if it's crucial to setting for the story. Is it happening in the past, present, or future; perhaps in a particular historical period, or is the play's time period open to a different interpretation? Often, the setting is written on the title page, or within the text of the play, where information about season, span of time, or time of day can be found.

Shakespeare's *Julius Caesar* is a dramatization of historical events that happened in 44 B.C., but productions often set it in another period or the present day, since it resonates today as a story of political upheaval. *Hamlet* has no designated historical time period, meaning it is up to the production's director and designers to determine what time period works best for the world they wish to create, such as 1600 (about the time the play was written), or 1941 or 2001.

In *A Raisin in the Sun* by Lorraine Hansberry, however, the time period is distinct and important: the play is set in the 1950s prior to the Civil Rights Act of 1964, depicting the struggle of the Younger family to own a home and live a better life in the face of discrimination and racism in America. This epic story may be timeless in theme, but it cannot be set in the 1600s or even the 1940s. It has a fixed given circumstance that relies on the specific time period.

No matter the time period, establishing the season, span of time in which the play takes place, or the time of day in each scene is critical, and these details are usually contained (or can be surmised) from within the dialogue or actions. What can we learn about the time of day for each scene? In both of our previous examples, we see the importance of time of day and how it impacts the actors' choices, whether it's early morning or late at night.

Where does the action of the play take place? There might be multiple locations, ranging from the general to the specific, or the whole play might occur in one room.

Hamlet is set in the kingdom of Denmark, but scenes take place inside various rooms or outside the castle, at Polonius' house, an open plain, or in a church graveyard.

In *A Raisin in the Sun,* the setting is the South Side of Chicago in an apartment building shared by many families. This detail is critical to the plot. The Younger family wants to own their own home and leave this apartment building, but the scenes all happen in one room.

Why is the story important? What is motivating each character, and what do they want from one moment to the next? Actors need to uncover the reason, the desire, the need for something to happen.

In Shakespeare's *Romeo and Juliet,* the Count Paris wants to marry Juliet, who is "not yet fourteen" years old. Juliet's father, Lord Capulet, prefers to have his daughter marry at age sixteen, but why?

> | PARIS: | Younger than she are happy mothers made. |
> |---|---|
> | LORD CAPULET: | And too soon marr'd are those so early made. |
> | | The earth hath swallow'd all my hopes but she." |
> | | *Act I, scene ii* |

These GC's about **Why?** rose to the surface:

- Paris is eager to be wed and have children, urging that girls often marry young and become mothers.
- Lord Capulet warns Paris of the dangers: women often died in childbirth.
- Juliet's father adds that she is his last living child, alluding to previous children who are dead and buried, "swallowed" by the earth. He has no other "hope" but Juliet.

PREVIOUS ACTION AND THE MOMENT BEFORE: WHAT JUST HAPPENED?

Another kind of GC is called **Previous Action**: What happened before the play begins that impacts the story?

In both *Hamlet* and *A Raisin in the Sun,* the characters are reeling in the aftermath of a father's death. The events of these two plays are sparked by something that already happened, often called an inciting action in formal script analysis. Hamlet's father died (we find out very soon that he was murdered); and Walter Lee's father recently passed away (we find out later that a large insurance check is on the way). The deaths occurred prior to the start of the play, but are still the spark that starts the fire of the story.

Previous Action, like other GC's, is also found in the dialogue, stage directions, or actions. A helpful exercise in rehearsal is to improvise short imagined scenes to support the weight of those events on the action of the play. Here are some ideas for improvisations using the examples above:

- Hamlet receiving news of his father's death while he's at school;
- His mother Gertrude telling her son she plans to marry Claudius, the king's younger brother (Hamlet's uncle) only a month after the funeral.

- Mama sharing the revelation that the life insurance policy of their father will pay out $10,000 with Walter Lee, Beneatha, and Ruth;
- Walter Lee cooking up the scheme about the liquor store with Bobo, overheard by Ruth.

Finding the Previous Action helps inform the actors of their characters' history, as if there was another whole play full of events beforehand, necessary to the story we are about to tell.

THE MOMENT BEFORE: WHAT JUST HAPPENED?

The final critical component of given circumstances is called the **Moment Before**. What happens or is said right before the start of the play, or in your scene or monologue? What has to take place in order for that line to be spoken? Think about the opening line of *Hamlet:*

BARNARDO: Who's there?

That's only two little words, but a lot of information is packed in them. An actor has to ask themself why they would say such a thing, "Who's there?" Clearly, a sound of some kind has to happen in order for Barnardo to say this line. The script doesn't offer what the sound is, but it does express the need, as a Given Circumstance, for there to be a noise that Barnardo hears in order to start the play. Moreover, it has to be the kind of sound that leads him to believe someone else is there.

Reading on, we learn that Francisco is on their post, at the end of their shift on the watch. Maybe Francisco has fallen asleep and their weapon hits the ground and makes a noise. Another great acting teacher, Sanford Meisner, believed that something has to happen to make the next thing happen. The line can't happen just because it's the next thing on the page. The Moment Before could be that Francisco (or something else on stage) makes a noise that startles Barnardo.

Barnardo jumps to the conclusion that someone else is there by saying "who" as his first response, but it also leads us to the GC that the expectation is that no one else should be here. He is alone, and he did not expect to encounter anyone. The Moment Before is critical.

A second example of **Moment Before** is the opening line of *A Raisin in the Sun:*

RUTH: Come on now, boy! It's seven thirty!

Ruth has been trying to rouse young Travis out of sleep on the sofa in order to get him into the shared bathroom in the hallway. If he doesn't stay on schedule, Walter will be up and not be able to get to work on time if Travis is still in the bathroom, or if someone else gets in there before either of them. Ruth's urgency itself is a GC, as well as the time of day, but the Moment Before is that Ruth has already tried unsuccessfully to get him out of bed.

A **Moment Before** helps you prepare for the launch of your work. It's your own personal Why? Why do I say this? What has led up to this particular moment? If you are working on a monologue, or a scene in a class, rather than doing a production of a full play, you will need to find it, and write it down at the top of your script, so you are always reminded of what happened in the Moment Before.

> ### TRY IT! UNCOVERING GIVEN CIRCUMSTANCES
>
> Uncover more GC's in the opening passage from *Hamlet* below, starting with what we already discovered about the first line.
>
> - Read the text aloud alone or with a partner.
> - Read it a second time through, still aloud.
> - Line by line, note any GC's on the left-hand side of your text with a pencil.
> - Circle GC's that stand out, write the facts you discovered next to the letters "GC," and do this all the way through the text. It can be messy, but it's your mess!
>
> From *Hamlet*, Act I, Scene I Excerpt for Given Circumstances:
> *Enter Barnardo and Francisco, two sentinels.*
>
> | | | |
> |---|---|---|
> | BARNARDO | Who's there? | |
> | FRANCISCO | Nay, answer me. Stand and unfold yourself. | |
> | BARNARDO | Long live the King! | |
> | FRANCISCO | Barnardo? | |
> | BARNARDO | He. | 5 |
> | FRANCISCO | You come most carefully upon your hour. | |

| BARNARDO | 'Tis now struck twelve. Get thee to bed, Francisco. |
| FRANCISCO | For this relief much thanks." |

Compare your findings to the marked-up copy of a GC's list for this exercise found in the Support Material at www.routledge.com/9781032695297.

FINDING THE CHANGES: BEATS AND SHIFTS

Beats and Shifts are acting constructs we use to delineate changes in the action of a scene. A **beat change** is a big change, and a **shift** is a subtler change. When we move from one beat to another, there's a beat change, or when there's a subtler one within a beat, it's a shift.

Why do we care about and indicate beats and shifts? Stanislavski wanted actors to inhabit roles rather than simply perform them. He believed the foundation of authentic acting was **truthful behavior in imaginary circumstances**. He wanted audiences to believe the characters onstage were real people, that what's happening on stage is really happening, even though we bought a ticket and we know that it's just a show.

This kind of **moment-to-moment acting is achieved by paying attention to the changes** and making choices that mirror real-life behavior. We have to find the beat changes and shifts, understand why they're happening, and then make a specific choice based on that change. Stanislavski called the units of scenes "bits" – like little bits of action in a scene that happen before something else happens that makes things change. This bit, that bit, the next bit, and so on, until we get to the end of the play and the very last bit. Finding the transitions that separate them, and making choices about them, is the key to authenticity in acting.

In theatre lore, the "beat" came into use after Stanislavski hosted some English-speaking actors to share his ideas about acting, the Russian-to-English translator pronounced the word as "beet" [bit] – with a long "ee" sound, which was interpreted and spoken as "beat." We also might call it a beat change – though some playwrights use the word "beat" in stage directions to account for a pause, or to "take a beat." For our purposes, we're going to stick with the original idea, that a beat is one thing, a small unit of action, until there is a change (a beat change) and then the next beat begins. Within that small unit of action, we might discover subtle changes, or "shifts," which indicate a tactic change, even though we're still living fully within the same beat. There's a difference between a beat and a shift, though they both reflect a change. What's most important is that we **identify the change** (whether big and obvious or small and subtle) as an opportunity to make a new choice.

A beat change or a shift can occur because of something that's said in the dialogue, or because of an action, just like with GC's. If I am unsure if something is a beat or a shift as I'm working, I'll mark "something changed!" with a / or // mark and figure it out later which one it is. Getting bogged down in deciding if something's a beat or a shift can take the fun out of finding them.

To understand beats and shifts a little better, let's use an invented example from everyday life:

If Avery and Jordan are having a friendly conversation about the tulips and the weather on the front porch, and suddenly Avery's phone rings inside the house, they have to make a choice about what to do next: Avery could acknowledge the interruption but not get up to answer it, saying something like "It's not important – let it go to voice mail," and keep the conversation going. Or Avery could jump up and say, "I'm sorry but I have to get that, it's the doctor's office calling about my dad!" Or Avery could notice the ringing but try to ignore it, which makes Jordan say something like "If you need to take the call, go for it. I have to get back home anyway."

Avery and Jordan were having a nice conversation about tulips and weather out on the porch.

The phone rings.// (That's a **beat.// Two slash marks.)**
What changed?

That's a big change. Is the phone call about the tulips or the weather? Not likely.

Now the new "beat" is about how Avery is going to respond to the phone ringing. Avery has to deal with what's happening.

Avery: //I'm going to let it go to voice mail. //You were saying?

Avery's trying to get back to the previous beat! Another Beat Change! Where were we?

Jordan: /No, no, please – take the call – I have to get home anyway.
 /We'll catch up soon.

*Jordan stays in the beat of what to do about the interruption, but **shifts** to making it their choice to end the conversation about the weather.*

A **shift** is a more subtle change in tactic that is within a beat. (That's a **shift. / One slash mark**.)

If what one character says flows directly into what the next character says, there's no change.

It's a response, plain and simple, whether it's an answer to a question or a continuation of the same beat with no significant tactical change.

Here are two examples in which there's **neither a beat nor a shift,** since the next line is a direct response with no change in topic or tactic:

Avery: This warm weather has been unbelievable.
Jordan: I know – my tulips are starting to come up, and it's only February! *Note that you could put a / as they shift to the mention of tulips at the dash.*

Or:

Jordan: Do you have a few minutes to chat?
Avery: Sure, I have the whole day off.

Now let's look at two alternatives, using the same two opening lines as above, but adding a change in topic //(Beat) or tactic /(shift) in the response:

Avery: This warm weather has been unbelievable.
Jordan: /(*shift*) Has it? I've been trapped inside with a cold all week.

Or:

Jordan: Do you have a few minutes to chat?
Avery: //(*Beat*) Uh-oh. What did I do this time?

In analyzing heightened text for performance, it's important to find the changes and mark them, just like above: the big ones (Beats) with a // (double slash mark) and the subtle ones (shifts) with a / (single slash mark) to help shape the action and the story.

Actors play the change by making a specific choice supported by that discovery. The next phase of this work is to read the scene aloud again, line by line, and add **saying "beat" or "shift" aloud** when we think there's a change. This helps the actor embody the change, hear themselves say there's a change, and figure out what choice can support that change. After a few readings like this, we drop saying the words "beat" or "shift" aloud but we **continue to play the changes**, since we now have embedded what is happening into our choices.

So, the little scene out on the porch might look like this in a marked-up script, and we say aloud the word "beat" or shift" when it's your change happening:

> AVERY: //*Beat* This warm weather has been unbelievable.
> JORDAN: I know – my tulips are starting to come up, and it's only February!
> *(A PHONE RINGS INSIDE THE HOUSE.)*
> AVERY: // *Beat* Oh, I need to get that. /*shift* It might be the doctor calling about my dad.
> JORDAN: /*shift* Absolutely! //*Beat* I can come back later this afternoon.
> AVERY: //*Beat* Please don't leave, it'll just take a minute.
> //*Beat* I really want to talk to you.
> JORDAN: Okay. I'll wait. // *Beat* I didn't realize your dad hasn't been well. *RINGING*
> //*Beat* Quick! You better get answer it before it goes to voice mail!

TRY IT! FINDING BEATS AND SHIFTS IN HEIGHTENED TEXT

Let's put this tool into practice with some heightened text. As you read this *Othello* excerpt aloud, work on your own or with a partner to find the beats and shifts (action, topic, tactic changes in action or dialogue). You've already done the text homework!

Using a pencil, mark the beats with **two slash marks (//) where the beat change is**, or mark **one slash mark if it's a shift (/)**. When in doubt as to which it is, think of any change as "something" and just put one slash mark, move on, and figure out later if it's a beat or a shift.

Let what we learned about punctuation guide you:

- Full stops (period, exclamation point, question mark) indicate the end of something, so what comes next is some kind of change. It could be a beat or a shift.

- Semi-colons may indicate beats or shift changes, commas rarely so. If the thought is in motion, it won't likely have a shift just because there's a comma. Figure out what the comma is doing there, and act accordingly.

Once you're through marking the changes, take things up a notch by **saying aloud the word "Beat" or "shift" depending on what choice you made**, and let the way you say that word support the change. Act the word a bit.

Remember: A **beat** is a unit of action within a scene. The scene is about something specific until it changes and becomes about something else. You are marking the beat changes, as well as any shifts within those beats (units of action). Beat changes can be a result of something that's said or something that happens. A **shift** is a change in tactic or thought within a beat – more subtle, perhaps, but still aiming at the same intention.

To get things started, the first few beats and shifts are marked *(any notes by the actor about their choices are in italics)*:

OTHELLO, Act Three, Scene iii (lines 294–333)

EMILIA **//** Beat *(I see the handkerchief that Desdemona must have dropped and pick it up.)*
// Beat I am glad I have found this napkin;
/ *shift* This was her first remembrance from the Moor.
// Beat My wayward husband hath a hundred times
Wooed me to steal it; /*shift* but she so loves the token –
/*shift* For he conjur'd her she should ever keep it   5
That she reserves it evermore about her
To kiss and talk to. // *Beat* I'll have the work ta'en out
And give't Iago: /*shift* what he will do with it
Heaven knows, not I,
/ *shift* I nothing know, but for his fantasy.   10
Enter IAGO. //*Beat (I hide it away before he can see it. I want him to appreciate me.)*
IAGO *(I am on my way somewhere, and what's my wife doing here without Desdemona?)*
//*Beat* How now! /*shift* What do you here alone?

Now take it from here on your own

EMILIA
Do not you chide, I have a thing for you -

IAGO
A thing for me? it is a common thing -

EMILIA
Ha?

IAGO   To have a foolish wife.

EMILIA
O, is that all? What will you give me now
For that same handkerchief?

IAGO   What handkerchief?

EMILIA
What handkerchief?
Why, that the Moor first gave to Desdemona,
That which so often you did bid me steal.

IAGO
Hast stol'n it from her?

EMILIA
No, faith, she let it drop by negligence,
And, to th'advantage, I, being here, took't up.
Look, here it is.

IAGO   A good wench! Give it me.

EMILIA
What will you do with 't, that you have been so earnest
To have me filch it?

IAGO   Why, what is that to you?

EMILIA
If it be not for some purpose of import
Give't me again. Poor lady, she'll run mad
When she shall lack it.

> **IAGO**
> Be not acknown on't, I have use for it.
> Go, leave me.   *Exit Emilia.*
> I will in Cassio's lodging lose this napkin   30
> And let him find it. Trifles light as air
> Are to the jealous confirmations strong
> As proofs of holy writ. This may do something.
> The Moor already changes with my poison
> Dangerous conceits are in their natures poisons,   35
> Which at the first are scarce found to distaste,
> But with a little art upon the blood
> Burn like the mines of sulphur.   *Othello*, Act III, scene iii

Let's take a few moments to process what just happened in the scene, and how you fared with marking and saying aloud beats and shifts.

As we know from the paraphrase we completed in an earlier chapter, Emilia stumbles upon the lost handkerchief, acknowledges how upset Desdemona will be to discover it is missing, but also wants to please her husband, who, for some strange reason, has asked her to get it for him. Her solution is to take it to someone who could make a copy of it, and give the copy to Iago, returning the prized possession to Desdemona.

Reading the first few beats and shifts aloud helps the actor playing Emilia realize the struggle she's having: does she try to make her husband happy, or does she do the right thing and simply get this precious memento back to Desdemona, or better yet, after having a copy made for Iago?

The time it takes for these thoughts to cross her mind is the time it takes to say "Beat" or "shift." Eventually, the actor won't say those words aloud but will "play" the beats and shifts, having observed what happens and created time for it to take place. The language comes alive at the same time each change is discovered.

A version of the scene marked-up with beats and shifts is included in the Appendix.

IDENTIFYING CONFLICT: WHAT'S AT STAKE?

Conflict is what makes drama interesting. Actors need to identify what's at stake within the text, and what types of conflict are at play as their characters interact with other characters and the things they cannot control. Opposing forces create conflict in a story and move it forward. These can be internal, a character struggling against self as in *Hamlet,* or external, a character struggling against other characters or against society norms as in *A Raisin in the Sun*. Other external conflicting forces can be found in nature (King Lear in the storm), or the supernatural (Titania casting a spell on Bottom in *A Midsummer Night's Dream)*, or with technology (as in the film, *The Terminator)*.

How these types of thematic conflict impact our character choices in the moment is what matters most. This is an important element in actors working in heightened text because the scope and size of the human condition is its primary theme. Both the language and the stakes are higher.

As actors handling heightened text, unearthing the conflict, finding out what's at stake, helping lift up the moment, and supporting the scene, lifts up the themes of the whole piece. We have a responsibility as actors to make choices that are deeply rooted in the text, and identifying the conflict is a key tool in fully inhabiting the language and the situation. Powerful examples of how identifying conflict can lead to bold choices and the propulsion of the story result from the actor's thoughtful and detailed analysis of internal and external forces.

Here are some ways we might see conflict manifested in some stories with circumstances that may or may not be familiar to you, using these major categories of Internal and External Conflict from formal script analysis:

- **Self** (Internal): Hamlet struggles with his inability to act, due to his grief and anger.
- **Others** (External): Ruth doesn't want Walter to use all the insurance money.
- **Society/Norms** (External and Internal): In *Hamilton,* Angelica has to marry a wealthy man.

- **Supernatural** (External and Internal): The guards, Horatio and Hamlet have to confront a ghost.
- **Technology** (External): In *Dear Evan Hansen,* social media complicates the lives of young people struggling with isolation.
- **Nature** (External): In *The Wizard of Oz,* Dorothy seems to be transported to another world by a tornado.

If you're familiar with Lin-Manuel Miranda's musical *Hamilton,* it's a contemporary example of heightened text in song lyrics. The conflicts include characters being at odds with themselves, others, and the expectations of society. When the character Angelica Schuyler sings the song *Satisfied,* we identify what her character is struggling with and what kinds of conflict are at play, and see how an actor can make specific choices that convey how the character navigates conflict moment by moment. Here are the lyrics from the section we'll explore for conflict:

LAURENS:	Now everyone give it up for the maid of honor, Angelica Schuyler!
ANGELICA:	A toast to the groom!
GUESTS:	To the groom!
ANGELICA:	To the bride!
GUESTS:	To the bride!
ANGELICA:	From your sister, Who is always by your side! To your union And the hope that they provide May you always... Be satisfied.

The song *Satisfied* is told through the eyes of Angelica while giving a toast at the wedding of Alexander to her younger sister Eliza, all the while struggling with her own feelings for him. Angelica loves her sister deeply, and is infatuated with Alexander since their first meeting, but also has a sense duty to her wealthy and prominent family. Internal and external forces are both at play. The actor identifies the conflict – what is the struggle? – and makes specific choices.

The lyrics are in **bold,** the type of conflict(s) as a bullet point, *and the choice she might make in italics:*

> LAURENS: **Now everyone give it up for the maid of honor, Angelica Schuyler!**
>
> - Self & Society: *Uh-oh. I have to make a speech!*
> - Self, Society, Others: *Lean into it, smile, and pretend to be happy.*
>
> ANGELICA: **A toast to the groom!**
>
> - Self, Others, & Society: *Make it seem normal, do what's expected of me.*
>
> GUESTS: **To the groom!**
> ANGELICA: **To the bride!**
>
> - Self & Others: *I will honoring my sister, celebrating our relationship, and the current moment.*
>
> GUESTS: **To the bride!**
> ANGELICA: **From your sister,**
>
> > **Who is always by your side!**
> > **To your union**
> > **And the hope that they provide**
>
> - Self, Others, & Society: *I will add a secret, coded message in public, though only Alexander will truly understand its real meaning.*
>
> > **May you always...**
> > **Be satisfied."**
>
> - Self: *And now I flashback to the moment we met...*

The song begins with a joyful public moment covering up her private, aching heart. Three kinds of conflict (vs. herself, her sister and Alexander, and society's expectations of her) are in play, as Angelica is thrust into the spot light to comply with a societal tradition of making speeches at a wedding, while suppressing her feelings for her sister's husband, and seeing the love in Eliza's eyes for Alexander.

With the last five words of her toast, "May you always… Be satisfied," including the author's strategic use of an ellipsis, we witness Angelica struggling to figure out what to say to serve the purpose of a public speech, and yet reconcile her love for Alexander and her devotion to her sister. She cannot, and will not, ruin the wedding of her sister by proclaiming her love of Alexander. She has a duty to her family as the eldest daughter to marry into a wealthy family. She would never betray her sister, but she also pays attention to her own heart.

How does she navigate this quagmire of conflict?

Angelica is thinking (for the short length of the ellipsis provided and supported in the music) of a way to send a secret message to her would-be lover, Alexander, calling back a phrase that shocked her when they first met.

The toast ends with demonstrating how Angelica found a way to share words publicly – "Be satisfied" – to serve the occasion, though only she and Alexander know is really about each other, as a way to live through this heart-breaking moment with the only man she has ever really been attracted to, who is now marrying her sister.

Her resolution at the end of the song, sparked on by the memory of what she has just spoken aloud, permits Angelica to move on, make her sister happy, and keep Alexander a part of her life.

GOING IT ALONE: HOW TO ACTIVATE A MONOLOGUE OR SOLILOQUY

Having a partner in class or in a scene can make everything seem manageable. You can share the work by bouncing ideas off one another, finding GC's, and marking your beats and shifts together.

But what about when you have a monologue all by yourself for a class assignment, an audition, or a production of a play? How do you go it alone? How do you keep your work active when there's no one there to respond to? Just like in life, you are enough. There are ways to practice skills and technique on your own – just like that rebounding wall at a tennis court, or the goal net out on the soccer field to practice penalty kicks. In the world of acting heightened text, the language is our partner, and the good news is: it never lets us down. The text has our back, every time.

What is a monologue anyway? It's when one person does all the talking – that's the "mono" part. Look back at our example from *Hamilton,* and how Angelica is in a reverie of feelings, having to sort through the current moment, her past, and her future, all on her own, but in front of a hundred wedding guests. Her thoughts, spoken aloud, but only to herself, are considered a soliloquy.

But sometimes, the monologue is actually part of a scene, and there's another character right there, supporting you, giving you what you need. They don't actually say anything, but that doesn't mean there's not trying to talk, or at least listening with intent and planning their next move. In those cases, we approach the monologue with the same process we always rely upon: reading aloud, scansion, paraphrase, operatives, dictionary work, and then exploring the given circumstances, beats and shifts, tactics, intentions and actions. It's always the same dish, like chili, but each person's recipe has different ingredients, different cooking temperatures, and different spices, and unique, detailed, and interesting results. The homework process is the recipe for success with heightened text every time.

WALKING A MONOLOGUE

Once you've completed your text work on your monologue, circled and played with punctuation, marked up your beats and shifts, you're ready to **take your monologue for a walk**. The technique of walking your monologue is a way to reinforce the beats by changing directions as you come to them. This means walking in one direction while reading your lines aloud, coming to a full stop when there's ending punctuation, turning around, saying "Beat" aloud, and then going back in the other direction. With your beats marked, it makes the decisions very clear, something has changed, and moving in a new direction and saying it aloud helps ground the change physically and vocally.

If you have a shift within a beat, the character is changing tactics, you turn on a slight diagonal, to continue walking in the same direction, driving through the idea, but at a different angle. It might feel like you're in the marching band, making a pattern on the football field, when a phrase or certain moment causes you to change direction, but in this exercise, it's the meaning and the intention that drive the journey, rather than a change in the music.

The secret bonus of walking the monologue is that it helps you learn your lines while reinforcing beats and shifts. Memorizing by staring at the page and repeating lines over and over can be a thing of the past if you do your homework, mark your beats and shifts, and take your monologue out for a walk.

> ## TRY IT! WALKING THE MONOLOGUE
>
> Here's an example using some of Cordelia's lines from *King Lear*, Act I, scene i. The beats and shifts are marked, and, at least for the first few lines, instructions for how to get started walking your monologue. Remember to say "Beat" and "shift" aloud, coming to a full stop on beat changes, and to pause slightly and turn diagonally on the shifts.
>
> Do this walking exercise in a large room or studio, or outside in a park, or simply around the block if there's a sidewalk. (People may look at you strangely, but this is for a good cause.) You may not get very far in any direction, but you do need a bit of open space to physicalize the length of the thought before there is a change.

> ## CORDELIA:
>
> *//Beat (start walking straight ahead)*
> *//*What shall Cordelia speak? *shift (turn diagonal: keep walking)*
> */*Love, and be silent.
> *Beat (turn around walk in the opposite direction)*
> *//*Unhappy that I am, I cannot heave
> My heart into my mouth: *shift/diagonal / *I love your majesty
> According to my bond; nor more nor less.
> *Beat (turn around and walk)//*Good my lord,
> You have begot me, bred me, loved me: *shift to diagonal /*I
> Return those duties back as are right fit,
> Obey you, love you, and most honor you.
> *Beat //*Why have my sisters husbands, if they say
> They love you all? *shift /*Haply, when I shall wed,
> That lord whose hand must take my plight shall carry
> Half my love with him, half my care and duty:
> *shift /*Sure, I shall never marry like my sisters,
> To love my father all.

Here's a crude but helpful diagram mapping out how I walked this monologue. It's not necessary to make such a record of what you did, it's more important to just do it. I carry the script in my hand and say "beat" or "shift" aloud a few times, while I'm turning around and changing directions. Sometimes I go outside on a sidewalk and simply walk around the block, changing directions

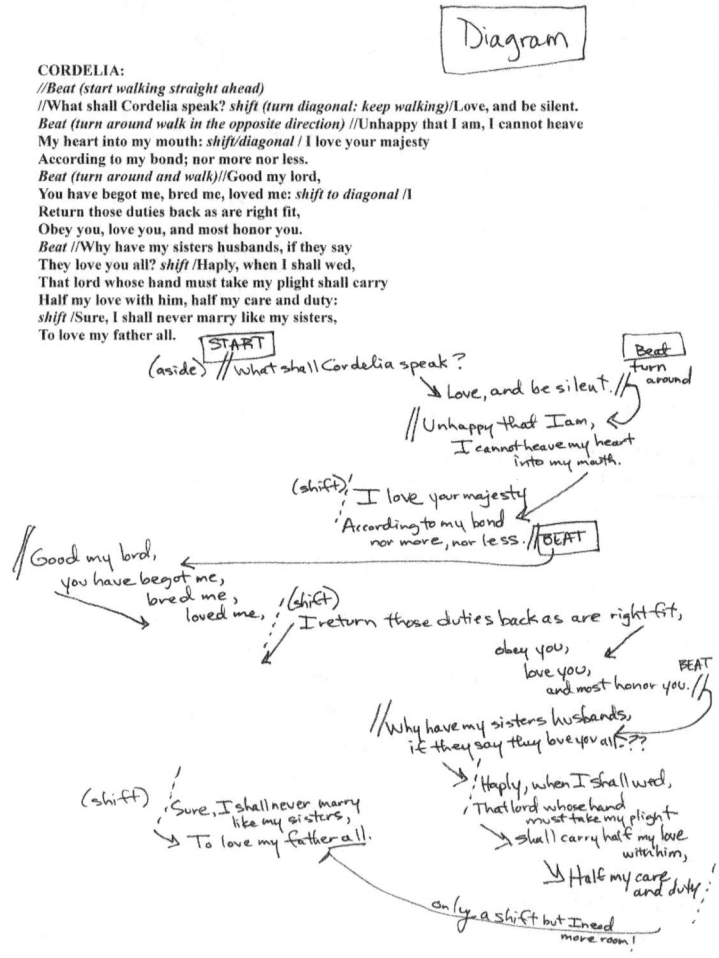

Figure 4.1 Diagram of Cordelia Walking.

on any changes, whether they're beats or shifts. The changes get grounded in the body, the lines get memorized, and you get a little exercise to boot!

HOW TO APPROACH WORKING ON A SOLILOQUY

Sometimes, a character is speaking their thoughts aloud to themselves, or talking directly to the audience, letting them in on a secret, laughing at their success, or seeking advice or input. This can be either "**soliloquy**" or "**direct address,**" and it isn't necessarily indicated in the script when it's either one. The actor investigates the reason the character is speaking, and how they might benefit from utilizing direct address. Do they need something from the audience, or are they speaking their thoughts aloud?

Hamlet, for example, speaks his innermost thoughts aloud, struggling with what's happening in his world since his father died, his uncle married his mother, his girlfriend Ophelia seems to be breaking up with him, and some friends from school suddenly show up and seem very interested in his every move. Other characters even see him talking to himself, and they assume he is going mad, or worse, pretending to be mad. Hearing his thoughts made manifest helps the audience understand his real predicament, and how confused, conflicted, and angry he is at what's happening. Sometimes, an actor (and the director) may have utilized direct address, and certain lines are spoken to the audience, such as "What a piece of work is man," as if to say to us, "Isn't man an incredible thing?" Or he may be processing that thought to himself. The choice is yours, but a choice must be made. It makes sense either way, and the speech can be a mix of the two modes of address.

Soliloquy isn't just used in Shakespeare, but also in contemporary plays, or movies. It's something that we often do in our own lives, but we just might not label it as such. We also don't always say our thoughts aloud, but we do think fully formed thoughts in order to work something out. Have you ever been hungry late at night and headed down to the kitchen for a bite? Imagine your thinking this train of thought, or even saying it out loud (if no one's home):

"I am so hungry. What is there to eat? There's toast. I could make toast and peanut butter with honey. With milk! Is there any milk? *Goes to the fridge and opens it.* No milk. Oh, but what's in that take-out container? Oh, it's my sister's mac and cheese from the potluck on Sunday. But today's Thursday, so is that still any good? If I microwave it, everything will be ok, right? *Pulls out the container and shuts the fridge.*"

Speaking your thoughts aloud, working out a problem: this is what's happening to Hamlet, Viola, Imogen, Puck, and Caliban in Shakespeare, Elegba in *In the Red and Brown Water*, Prior in *Angels in America*, Faulkland in *The Rivals*, and thousands of other characters in plays.

> **TRY IT! GOING IT ALONE: WORKING ON A SOLILOQUY**
>
> One exercise that can support exploring a monologue that's a character speaking alone is similar to the walking exercise but divides the working space you have into three areas:
>
> 1. an area of space to represent another person or the idea of them,
> 2. another area to make comments, and
> 3. another focused area or the other side of the argument or problem.
>
> Always locate the comment space in the center of your available room to ground yourself.
>
> Make one or more of these areas direct address or talking to oneself.
>
> Move as quickly as possible to the three different parts of the room every time the focus of the text changes.
>
> **If you don't have a lot of space**, choose three strong focus points:
>
> 1. at a 2 o'clock angle to your right, representing the other person or the idea of them,
> 2. on the wall in front of you straight ahead, representing the comments, and
> 3. at a 10 o'clock diagonal to your left to give yourself a different place to look as the focus or argument changes.
>
> Here is an excerpt of Viola's lines from *Twelfth Night*, Act II, scene ii, as she's disguised as Cesario, with the focus points listed:

- **Center** (for comments spoken aloud, either to the audience or to herself in exasperation),
- **Right** (where Malvolio just left, and where Olivia lives), and
- **Left** (where Orsino resides, with whom she is in love) along with suggestions from direct address or soliloquy.

Try quickly hopping from one space to the next and saying the whole line as if it were in a box, then dash over to the next area, until the end. She's got to figure out what's going on and what to do next. That's why the speech is in the play.

VIOLA
Center (Direct address, looking at audience)
I left no ring with her: what means this lady?
Right – pertaining to Olivia
Fortune forbid my outside have not charm'd her!
She made good view of me; indeed, so much,
That sure methought her eyes had lost her tongue,
For she did speak in starts distractedly.
Center (Direct address, looking at audience)
She loves me, sure; *Right* the cunning of her passion
Invites me in this churlish messenger.
Left – towards Orsino, who sent no ring
None of my lord's ring! why, he sent her none.
Center (Direct address, looking at audience)
I am the man: if it be so, as 'tis,
Poor lady, she were better love a dream.*Center (Soliloquy, talking to herself, "what have I done?")*Disguise, I see, thou art a wickedness,
Wherein the pregnant enemy does much.
Center (Direct address, looking at audience)
How easy is it for the proper-false
In women's waxen hearts to set their forms!
Alas, our frailty is the cause, not we!
For such as we are made of, such we be.
How will this fadge? *Left – towards Orsino* my master loves her dearly;
And I, poor monster, fond as much on him;
Right – towards Olivia And she, mistaken, seems to dote on me.
Center (Direct address, looking at audience)

> What will become of this? *Left* As I am man,
> My state is desperate for my master's love;
> *Right* As I am woman,--now alas the day!--
> What thriftless sighs shall poor Olivia breathe!
> *Center* O time! thou must untangle this, not I;
> It is too hard a knot for me to untie!   *Exit Viola*

A monologue can also contain a combination of part of a scene (with another character present), some direct address, and some moments in soliloquy. Rarely does a script tell you which to do – though sometimes the clue might be in italics *(Aside)* or *(to herself)* or *(They look to the audience for help.)*

In the Support Material link at www.routledge.com/9781032695297, an extensive list of other monologues for practice is provided, including some soliloquies to figure out the focus points for yourself!

SUMMARY

In this chapter:

- we connected the text homework to the foundation of authentic acting of living truthfully in imaginary circumstances.
- we uncovered the given circumstances, previous action, and moment before, and found the changes in the scene by identifying and saying aloud the beats and shifts.
- we gained awareness of the kinds of conflict most common in drama, and highlighted the conflicts that create nuances in relationships and situations using song lyrics and soliloquies.
- we learned that acting heightened text requires finding moments when actions, topics, or tactics change, and playing those beat changes or shifts fully with the partner.
- we found ways in monologues, without the benefit of a partner on stage, to play out these actions and ideas through physical exercises, providing ways to navigate where the focus should be, in thoughts spoken aloud, or as direct address to the audience.

RESOURCES FOR FURTHER EXPLORATION

Script analysis: one of the most helpful writings on script analysis is Elinor Fuch's essay, *EF's Visit to a Small Planet: Some Questions to Ask a Play,* available online at https://web.mit.edu/jscheib/Public/foundations_06/ef_smallplanet.pdf

Dramaturgy: The Basics by Anne M. Hamilton and Walter Byongsok Chon, Routledge, 2022.

This is a comprehensive introduction to how script analysis is applied in production. Both authors are former students of Dr. Elinor Fuchs and take her work to a new level of practical and aesthetic heights.

Acting: direct from the source, a dynamic new text of Stanislavski's first two books in one easy-to-read volume: *Konstantin Stanislavski: An Actor's Work,* Routledge Classics, 2016.

Voice and Speech in Heightened Text: Written by one of the great voice, speech, and text teachers, *The Actor and the Text* by Cicely Berry (Applause, 2000) has exercises to help access the power of the language through the human voice using heightened text as a guide.

The Appendix contains a partial list of monologues for practice.

HELPFUL WEBSITES

Shakespeare's Complete Works Online play by play, able to be downloaded in Word https://shakespeare.mit.edu/

HOOKING
Active Listening and Responding to Impulses

with Hooking Illustrations by Leanna Yatcilla

INTRODUCTION

This chapter introduces a technique I developed while working with student actors on inhabiting heightened text that I call "hooking." I saw a need to provide a transitional level of process between the homework phase and getting on your feet with a scene in rehearsal. Once the scansion, paraphrase, operatives, and beats and shifts have been introduced and practiced, students (and many actors) didn't know what to do next, they didn't seem to connect the dots and cross over into making their discoveries manifest. Hooking grounds the text work within the context of acting by building awareness and responsiveness to what is happening in the moment, using the hook of what one character says as the launching pad for the next line. Activating the listening skills involves impulse exercises, both non-verbal and verbal working with a partner. This attentive work leads to discoveries and surprises, which then transform into specific acting choices rooted in truthful behavior and a high level of responsiveness to what's happening moment-to-moment. The goals of this chapter are best achieved with access to a classroom, rehearsal studio or open room, a couple of chairs, the scene text, a partner, and a pencil. Building on the skills learned in previous chapters, actors undertake a three-step process of identifying and using hooks (the words or actions that make saying the next line necessary), whether in a scene or a monologue. The hooks are spoken aloud

DOI: 10.4324/9781032695310-6

for two of the three steps, and then dropped out in the third phase, making the scene's lines emerge with a profound level of connection. Using familiar text from *Othello*, these steps will be laid out clearly, with accompanying illustrations, and marked-up text as well as additional scenes for practice in the Support Material at www.routledge.com/9781032695297.

HOOKING: WORKING WITH A SCENE PARTNER, ACTIVE LISTENING, AND RESPONDING TO IMPULSES

Up until this point in this book, we've been able to work on our own, exploring the text through the stages of homework in preparation for rehearsal: doing our scansion, paraphrasing our lines, identifying operatives, doing some dictionary work, and marking the beats and shifts. We know how the verse is structured, what ideas we need to convey, and the beat changes that lead us to make textually supported choices. Now, we cross the threshold into bringing the text to life, and we do so by creating dynamic exchanges between the characters that reveal the drama moment-to-moment. The technique we will use next, what I call "hooking," uncovers, then manifests the reason we say each line by speaking it aloud. Hooking's basis is in active listening, a method of communication that emerged in the 1950s from leaders in the fields of psychology, parenting, and conflict resolution. Essentially, active listening means utilizing more effective communication skills, which improves one's ability to be responsive. Sharing discoveries openly during hooking completes the process, but active listening, the brainchild of Carl Rogers and Thomas Gordon, is at its core. In the clinical application, active listening improves relationships, which is also the goal of hooking: to improve the relationship to and with the scene partner, to focus on what we hear, our "hook," say it out loud, and then determine how to respond using the next line.

What is a hook anyway? In fishing, it's the thing that catches the fish (in addition to the bait); in popular music, it's an opening string of notes or a phrase that hooks you, whether it's written by Marvin Gaye, Lady Gaga, Beyoncé, or Beethoven. In acting, a hook connects to things and draws you in and helps you refine every acting choice you make, reinforcing why you do something and what you say next, based on what just happened. If acting were a game of ping-pong, hooking is the ball. You go where the ball is, not where you want it to be. You deal with what's actually happening.

Hooking clarifies the connective tissue from one line to the next. An actor shouldn't say their next line unless something happens that makes them say it. This is the basis of Sanford Meisner's work that developed into "The Meisner Technique," a method of repetition that helps actors rely upon each other for what they need in order to proceed. Hooking manifests the Meisner idea further by speaking aloud the unspoken connection, saying the "what I need" or "what I get" from the partner (or action) aloud, and then saying the next line. The improvisational aspect I've added of using impulse and chair exercises builds on fundamental skills developed by Viola Spolin, who believed that everyone (not just actors) has a natural ability to be responsive in the moment. In acting heightened text, we fold together these two theories and add active listening skills. The result is that hooking brings physical energy to the text (and the scene) that is dynamic, focused, and partner-centered.

Before we dive into the details of the hooking technique, let's spend some time practicing the underlying skills of active listening and responding to impulses.

ACTIVE LISTENING

Active listening sounds simple: pay close attention to what's being said. The Decision Lab's website defines it as "an attentive approach to a speaker's verbal and non-verbal forms of communication that can make interactions more meaningful and effective." The operative words for our purposes are "verbal and non-verbal" as we think about connecting them with heightened text. Instead of being focused on your next line (which is most actors are thinking about), active listeners give their "free and undivided attention to the speaker," concentrating on what's being conveyed. Relationship communication and counselors recommend repeating what's been said as a technique for making sure you are hearing and understanding a partner or loved one during difficult conversations. Acting listening goes beyond the words, by taking in as much information as possible, not just from words, but also from behavior that accompanies the words.

In everyday conversation, even though you may not realize it, you have an **impulse** (maybe you're hungry), and it leads to a **stimulus** (you say to your close friend, "Hey, do you want to go get something to eat?"), and then you pay attention to their **response** (they say, "I do!" vigorously). Your hunger is the impulse, the question is a stimulus, but the response includes two distinctive things: an **answer** (the information that they do want to get something to eat) and a **reaction** (the behavior that they're excited). In this benign example, the **answer** is "I do" (which is basically a "yes"), but the **reaction** (accompanied by the exclamation point) is surprisingly enthusiastic! An active listener is attentive to both of those components, and deals with the **whole response**, and says jokingly, "Okay, calm down, I'm not proposing marriage, just dinner."

Here's a more dramatic example of active listening, involving an **impulse, stimulus,** and **response.** An active listener is standing next to a stranger at a busy intersection, when the traffic light changes to green and the "WALK" sign kicks on (that's the **impulse**). Just as the stranger starts to walk ahead, a bus comes speeding along and the active listener flings their right arm out to hold the stranger back so they won't get killed (that's the **stimulus**). After a terrifying moment, the stranger takes a breath, gently grasps that outstretched arm with both hands, turns and says, "Thank you" (taken as a whole: what happened + the words, that's the **response**). The answer/information of "Thank you" communicates "I'm grateful," but the reaction/behavior of their deep breath and the physical connection conveys, "that's the scariest thing that's ever happened to me in my entire life. I almost died." The active listener takes all that in, processes what they might say next, given how shaken up the stranger appears, and says, "I'm going over to that bench for a minute to have a seat. Want to join me?" Can you imagine if someone replied with an automatic "You're welcome" to their "Thank you"? Or admonished them with "You really ought to look where you're going!" Thomas Gordon's *12 Roadblocks to Communication* reads like a manual of **In**active Listening, and it underscores the importance of paying attention to the whole response, which serves, for us, as the backbone of hooking.

Since these exchanges happen naturally and quickly in life, they need to seem that way in a performance. In acting heightened text, active listening is essential to staying in the moment, making a specific choice, playing a beat change or a shift, or anything else called for in the script. The impulse and the stimulus come from anything that happens: an anticipated arrival, a sudden noise, a line of dialogue: "Who's there?" and then an awkward silence. The next thing that happens is connected by that thread that started with the impulse – what remains is what causes the next moment to happen, "Nay, answer me!" and boom! we're in the opening scene of *Hamlet*.

TEXTUAL ACTION: WHEN THE STAGING IS BAKED-IN TO THE TEXT

As a director who trained as an actor, I appreciate it when the text seems to stage a moment for me. I don't have to create a blocking move, the text is telling me there's a move. A big part of active listening for me (and subsequently, hooking) is paying attention to my own lines and mining them for **Textual Action.** In the same way that given circumstances give us information about the time, place, and situation, the dialogue can also tell us what's happening physically on stage through **textual action**. During the paraphrase part of homework, you may discover something is happening, even though there are no stage directions, indications of props or actions. Here are some examples from everyday life, of the text and what *actions the text implies:*

Text: **I'm going.**
Action: *I am on the move. If I'm seated, I get up. If I'm up, I move away.*
Text: **Let's go!**
Action: *I want both of us to leave. There's some kind of gesture of inviting you to come along, and I am happy to lead the way.*
Text: **Leave that alone, please.**
Action: *You must have touched something, or made a move towards touching something. There's something there that shouldn't be messed with: a game of Risk? a cake cooling?*

Now, let's reverse the exercise and play an action (without speaking), and then make up a line of text that expresses that **textual action**, revealing something that's unspoken. If you have a partner to work with, this is a great warm-up before you start rehearsing a scene.

Non-Verbal Action: *Standing with one hand on hip, the other outstretched and pointing down.*

Possible Text:	**Put that down!** (clearly you have something in your hand)
Non-Verbal Action:	*Walking towards your partner with arms open wide.*
Possible Text:	**It's so good to see you again!** (reveals a former relationship of some kind)
Non-Verbal Action:	*Standing or sitting, then turning and facing another direction and crossing both arms, shaking your head.*
Possible Text:	**I can't believe you just did that.** (something just happened)

In this excerpt from *Julius Caesar*, it's the morning when Caesar is heading off to the Capitol in spite of his wife Calpurnia's haunting dream that he will be murdered. Read the lines aloud a couple of times, and answer the prompts below:

CALPURNIA:
> **What mean you, Caesar? Think you to walk forth?**
> **You shall not stir out of this house today.**
> *Act II, scene ii*

What is happening during these lines, even if you don't know the play?
What is Caesar doing when she comes into the room?
What changes do you notice?
What is the textual action? What's happening because of what the lines say?

Doing our scansion and paraphrase homework can serve us well. Take a few moments and read the lines aloud again and make some observations about the verse, and come up with a paraphrase.

There's a lot to unpack from this speech in response to these prompts:
What is happening during these lines, even if you don't know the play?

- Calpurnia is surprised right off the bat. "Whoa! What's going on?"
- She asks him that question and he doesn't answer.

- She makes an assumption that he's leaving, asks him, and he doesn't answer, again.
- She gives him a direct order.

What is Caesar doing when she comes into the room?

- Caesar must be putting on his shoes or jacket, or getting ready to leave, otherwise she wouldn't say he'd be "walking forth."

What else do you notice?

- She asks two questions and then makes a statement.
- She takes charge.
- She speaks almost entirely in monosyllabic words, except for *"Caesar"* and *"today."*
- First line ends in a pyrrhic/spondee pair [you to | walk forth], like "you're not **going out**"

What is the textual action? What's happening because of what the lines say?

- Caesar is readying himself to leave on her entrance.
- Caesar heads toward the door at some point.
- Calpurnia either gets in his way or tries to stop him from leaving.

CALPURNIA: What <u>mean</u> you, Caesar? <u>Think</u> you to <u>walk</u> <u>forth</u>?
You shall not <u>stir</u> out of this <u>house</u> today.

Here's what happens next:

CAESAR: **Caesar shall forth.**

The textual action is a direct result of active listening. Caesar's response is defiant: "Nobody tells Caesar what to do!" based on what Calpurnia said (verbal stimulus) and did (non-verbal stimulus). Actors need to pay close attention to both things, what's spoken (or written) and what's happening. Stage directions are rare, but these stage directions are baked-in to the text, not written separately in italics. Imagine in this scene, if Caesar is just sitting by the window reading a book. Calpurnia could still say her first line, "What mean you, Caesar?" because it could mean, "What are you doing?" if he's fully dressed and has his coat on, maybe she could say her next line, "Think you to walk forth?" But something has to happen (besides his not answering her), that prompts her to assume he's going to stir out of the house, or she wouldn't say "You shall not stir out of this house today." Caesar's next line is clearly active – "Caesar shall forth." He's going, he's not minding her warning, and he's certainly not going to let her dream that he's going to be murdered make him stay at home. He even pulls rank (or tries to be objective) and refers to himself in the third person!

The best way to find textual action is to say the line a few times aloud (of course). Try to feel what's happening by repeating the line, and then allow the action to occur. Just like in active listening, actors pay attention to what's implied in their line, what actions or moves seem to be indicated in their text. Not every line has textual action, but with practice, it will stand out as you're reading aloud while doing your homework and serve you well in rehearsal.

NON-VERBAL EXERCISES TO ACTIVATE IMPULSIVE RESPONSES

One way to increase awareness of impulses and practice responding to them in the moment is through a simple game of standing and sitting. You'll need a sturdy chair and a partner. Face each other several feet apart to begin, and able to comfortably stand facing each without feeling too close together, and be able to sit back down in the chair behind you without much effort: up and down, standing and sitting, a couple of times on your own to practice. It's best to land in the center part of the seat, rather than leaning back or resting against the back of the chair, as in these drawings (Figure 5.1).

By landing in the center of the chair, you are both able to activate and respond to impulses with immediacy. Focus forward, facing your partner. Eyes are open, hands on the tops of your thighs, in case you need them for support and energy in rising or sitting. You're ready for something to happen.

Figure 5.1 Partners Sitting and Standing Face-to-Face.

The rules of the game are simple: you respond to impulses, and you do so by standing, sitting, staying standing, or staying seated, as in the drawings above. This changes every time you feel an impulse. You can respond by moving or choosing to stay standing or seated (but not the whole time, of course). The point of the exercise is to practice responding and to allow the other person to impact your actions.

Begin by moving in unison with your partner, without deciding or talking about who's going to move and when. Allow it to happen spontaneously, impulsively. Someone, one of you, eventually, will stand. (It's not about quick or slow, just about the initial impulse, so just get up!) The partner senses the impulse and stands along with you, and then someone has the impulse to sit and you both sit. This is a non-verbal exercise. There's no need to talk, you know exactly what to do: stand, and sit. After you've done this a few times, fold in the option to stay standing or stay seated when your partner moves, and then change it up, but always by responding to an impulse (not just sitting down and standing up at random). It might look like a seesaw if you're working in opposition, or like a Simon Sez game if you're always sitting or standing in unison. Shake it up. Allow this to happen for a few minutes, and then find a way to end it. Then talk about what happened with your partner. Play the game again by taking a few breaths and beginning whenever you are ready (Figure 5.2).

In this exercise, you learn to work off of someone else. You learn that you don't have to generate everything and that you must engage fully in response. The partners, whether sitting or standing, create impulses to which the other responds by choosing to stand, sit, stay standing, or stay seated until the next impulse comes along. (If all you do is generate by standing and sitting one move right

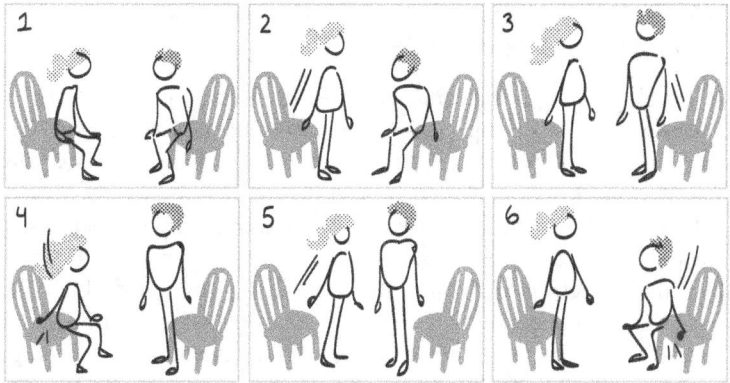

Figure 5.2 Various Configurations with Partners Facing Each Other.

after another, you will not be responding to anything.) There is risk involved (very low risk), but it's important to begin to feel the uncertainty of not knowing what will happen next and being okay with that. Something will happen and it will make the next thing happen: if you allow it to happen.

Play this game together, responding to each other's movements for a few minutes without using words, getting the feeling of choosing to stay standing or stay seated sometimes, but always responding (making a choice) based on what happens. If you crack up or lose focus, that's okay, it happens, we're human. Use the exercise to get your focus back, standing or sitting in response to the other person and move past the diversion. Find a way to end it, (often by both sitting), and check in for a few moments with each other, processing what happened with a few short observations. Your responses were based on impulses, "hooked" to them, as we call it, to what your partner did and vice versa: "You stood, then I stood as soon as I felt the impulse that you were standing, then we both sat at what seemed like exactly the same moment;" "You stood and I stayed seated, you sat down and I stood up. That felt like we abandoned each other;" "We sat there for a few moments and then we both stood up, again, working so closely fused to the impulses (and our partner's energy) that we didn't even know who started it!" It doesn't matter who started it, what matters is that both responded, and both did so as soon as they felt the impulse.

MATCHING ENERGY AND ADDING VERBAL RESPONSES TO IMPULSES

To develop the next building block in hooking, we add the verbal component of matching energy. For this exercise, step forward from your chair (we'll use them again later), and stand facing your partner (Figure 5.3).

Take turns initiating a brief exchange, using simple greetings, as pictured, with one person leading and the other responding with the same greeting matching their energy, using only "Hi," and "Hello," as your dialogue, as in #2 below. If I say an enthusiastic "Hi!" you respond immediately with your version of that energy. If I am low-key and playful and say "hellooo," you play back in the same vein. Do that a few times back and forth, tossing different greetings back and forth but making strong choices and supportive spontaneous responses based on what you've been given. Switch

Figure 5.3 Two Actors Stand, Facing Each Other, Offering Stimulus and Response.

who goes first so each of you gets practice being the stimulus and the response. The bits of dialogue are like a rubber ball being tossed back and forth between you, sending the energy to the partner and back, changing the dynamics a little, but always by working off of what's was given.

Moving on to new dialogue, as in #3 above, use the dialogue "You're late," and "I know" as the stimulus and response, changing who starts every few go's. Be sure to return the same or slightly more energy back, and in the same vein as what you receive from your partner. This isn't an exercise about trying to create difference or be funny, it's to notice, share, and match the energy. By throwing out a simple phrase like "You're late" to our partner as the stimulus, we see that their **response** includes **behavior** that accompanies their **answer,** "I know." If you say, "You're late," like you're the boss, and I have a perfectly good reason for my lateness, I might respond, "I know," but with a positive tone, rather than defensive. Try saying "You're late" as stern, understanding, frantic, upset, or sad. If you're responding, be sure to make it connected to that stimulus choice, rather than making up your mind about how you want to play it as a response. Switch it up so that each person gets to go first. If they are stern, you might respond with confidence, or sass. If they're sad, that's a very different offer, so be attentive – imagine it's two siblings outside a parent's hospital room. Remember the active listener example at the intersection: engaging with what's happening, not just with what they hear. There is no right or wrong, just practice listening and responding.

There's no diagram anymore to show what happens next. In this next improvisation, one person provides a stimulus or prompt, and the other provides a response, taking turns coming up with your own word or phrase, and says it to them, like a word association game. We stick with one word or a short phrase to keep it simple, and trade back and forth who's providing the stimulus (saying the new word), and who's responding to it. I start with "umbrella" and you reply "rain." You might say back to me "cheese" and I say "Yum!" The next pair of words doesn't have to be connected to the previous set in any way, so start fresh every time.

This is a great way to practice staying in the moment, taking low-level risks, and responding truthfully to what's happening between you and your partner. You don't have to scan or paraphrase any lines. It matters not one bit that your choices be interesting or funny, you are simply arriving at a response based on the stimulus you receive. Learning to be comfortable not knowing what is going to happen next, living in a moment of uncertainty, creates a fertile environment for building confidence in dramatic situations, whether in a play, film, or real life.

Let's break down the difference between the answer and the behavior using the two examples above. The stimulus was "umbrella" and you said "rain." The **answer** is the word that you provided: a logical situation in which you might need an umbrella: in the rain. The **behavior**, however, was immediate and decisive – you know exactly what an umbrella is for, and you felt like you did the exercise right, you seemed proud of your answer. That's your **response**, a reveal of behavior, fused to your logical answer. If I were to speak further on this same topic, I would incorporate both your answer and behavior in my next line, saying "Ding! You got it right!" I saw that you were nervous about this exercise, relieved to have an easy word to work off of, and came up with a logical answer, wanting to do well. The behavior was much more interesting than the answer, and merged into a response, gave me plenty to work with.

In the next exchange, you provide the stimulus, saying, "cheese," and my face lit up and I said, "Yum!" That's barely an answer, but it's what I said! It was almost 99% behavior and, therefore, blended together with "yum," a rich response. If you were to speak again, you could go a few different directions, saying, "Calm down, I meant what kind of cheese do you want on your burger?" or "I know!" sharing your love of gooey melted cheese with me.

TRY IT! MATCHING ENERGY AND PAYING ATTENTION TO THE RESPONSE

Face your partner and provide a stimulus word. Pay attention to their whole response (answer + behavior). Take turns providing the stimulus, like a word association game.

Here are a few one-word prompts for stimulus if you're drawing a blank: planet, hockey, weather, strawberry, tall, habit, muffin, spaghetti, driveway, California, hope, tree, birthday, and sprinkler.

After you've played back and forth with your partner a few times, take a break and process aloud what happened using a few of the pairs as examples. Some exchanges may seem automatic and not need too much analysis; so, focus on the ones that elicited interesting behavior in addition to the answer. Even a long pause in-between is part of the response and merits attention.

For more complex practice, move on to asking open-ended questions of each other: Where do you dream about traveling? What's your favorite movie of all-time? What's something no one knows about you (that you feel comfortable sharing)? What is a lesson you've learned from a recent experience? Any question that doesn't have a yes-or-no answer is a great jumping-off point for active listening. Refrain from answering back with an "I statement," though.

Keep the focus on their **whole response** (their answer + their behavior) and stop after a few exchanges. Pay attention to what they do, how they respond, not just what they say. Think about in daily conversations how many times we ask someone how they're doing, and they respond with "OK," when we (and Taylor Swift) know that we're "not fine at all." That's the basis of hooking, recognizing that the literal answer isn't everything.

HOOKING PHASE ONE: FINDING THE HOOKS IN THE SCENE (WITH OR WITHOUT A PARTNER)

Now, we're ready to **find the hooks** in a scene: the thing that one character says or does that catches the other character, draws them in, and compels them to say the next line or do something in response. We will circle hooks as we find them.

If you're playing Barnardo, you speak first in *Hamlet*, but what happens to be able to say the first line?

    BARNARDO   "Who's there?"

What has to happen? What's the hook? Something has to scare Barnardo – a noise of some kind.

You can **write or type in your hook**: "a noise" or make a circle or box and write it in, that also serves as your "moment before."

Hook: "A noise!" / "What's that?" / "Yikes!"
BARNARDO   **Who's there?**

The **textual action** of "Who's there?" also means Barnardo needs to be focused somewhere else first, probably looking off in one direction hoping for Marcellus to show up with Horatio. You might be looking over **here**, when your partner playing Francisco, who's fallen asleep on the watch over **there,** suddenly wakes up and his helmet falls to the ground and makes a noise, startling you. You respond to the impulse, take in a fast breath, turn the opposite direction and say "Who's there?" You don't have to act startled: you were startled.

In this phase, **finding and saying our hooks,** two things can be what draws us in and compels us to say our line: something that's said, or something that happens (an expression or an action). In this example, it's something that happens, and it's a noise Barnardo hears, and he says his hook aloud (choose any one of the suggestions below) and then immediately after it, the line:

> **SAY** *"A noise!" / "What's that?" / "Yikes!"*
> **BARNARDO** *then say*   **Who's there?**

If it's an action or part of the dialogue, we **say the hook out loud**. We're responding to what's happening, or what the other person is doing or saying, and we say it out loud. You are not trying to rehearse the scene at this point, you're just **finding and saying your hooks**. At first, it's clunky, and it's going to seem like you're making a big deal out of everything. That's exactly the idea: to find every relevant moment, and make sure you know why it's happening, and what leads to the next thing happening. Hooking requires paying attention so clearly to each moment that it becomes obvious why you say (or do) the next thing. Hooking teaches us that the reason to say your next line can't be just because it's next. There has to be a reason to say it. If your next line has a beat change, then you have to make a hook out of that and say it aloud, and play that change. Your "beat-change-hook" (I just made that up!) might be, *"well, this isn't* *going well, I'll try something else,"* or *"why are you ignoring me?"* — this isn't the same as your subtext (what you're really thinking inside and wish you could say aloud). Your hook is what's actually happening, and you are naming it, aloud and proud, so that you and your partner are aware of what is going on between you, spoken or unspoken. In this first phase of hooking, phase one, it's all spoken, as well as in phase two. In phase three, we'll go back to just saying our lines, but by then, we'll know why we're saying them. After a few rounds of hooking, we'll also probably know our lines! You see, memorization is over when you start to hook: an added bonus of reading aloud and focusing on the work instead of just on learning the lines.

The **Hook is spoken aloud as if it's a comment to yourself** *(did she really just say that?)* so that **your line is spoken with full energy,** "Ok, fine, here's what I think." You say your hook aloud first, the bit you need for your next line, and then your actual line:

> *(Francisco's helmet falls to the ground next to where he's fallen asleep – CLANK!)*
>
> **BARNARDO:** *(What's that noise?)*   **Who's there?**
> **FRANCISCO:** *(Who's there? /shift Flip that!)* **Nay, answer me! Stand and unfold yourself!**
> **BARNARDO:** *(Unfold myself? OK! Don't shoot!)*   **Long live the King!**
> **FRANCISCO:** *(Long live the King? //Beat I recognize that voice –)* **Barnardo?**
> **BARNARDO:** *(Barnardo! Whew! He knows me.)*   **He.**

It can seem a little confusing and chaotic, but bear in mind: we're hooking, not acting. The hooking exercise allows us to make sure we know why we're saying our line; so, there's some back and forth that might feel like all you're doing is repeating your partner's line. See if you can go deeper than that, investigating how to make a hook out of what they say (or how you are responding to what they say), and then say your actual line. You may need to repeat a line a couple of times to find the hook, and use what line comes next as a guide: "If I say this next, then what am I responding to?"

TRY IT! HOOKING PHASE ONE: FINDING AND SAYING THE HOOKS ALOUD

Using the scene between Iago and Emilia, sit in chairs facing each other, with your scene scripts and a pencil (or your tablet) in your hand. Find your hooks in your partner's lines (or actions) as you repeat the lines of the scene back and forth to each other. What do they say (or do) that you need in order to say your next line? The hook could be using their exact words, their words re-phrased from your point of view, or an action – something that happens, like the noise from Francisco's helmet dropping. You might have to invent a spoken hook that conveys a beat change or shift. Do this for the entire scene, which will take about two or three times longer than it takes to read your scene.

OTHELLO, Act Three, Scene iii (lines 294–333)

EMILIA
// I am glad I have found this napkin;
/ This was her first remembrance from the Moor.
// My wayward husband hath a hundred times
Wooed me to steal it; / but she so loves the token –
/ For he conjur'd her she should ever keep it   5
That she reserves it evermore about her
To kiss and talk to. // I'll have the work ta'en out
And give't Iago: / what he will do with it
Heaven knows, not I,
/ I nothing know, but for his fantasy.   *Enter IAGO.* //   10

IAGO
// How now! / What do you here alone?

EMILIA
//Do not you chide, / I have a thing for you -

IAGO   / A thing for me? / it is a common thing -

EMILIA
/ Ha?

IAGO /   To have a foolish wife.

EMILIA
// O, is that all? / What will you give me now 15
For that same handkerchief?

IAGO / What handkerchief?

EMILIA
// What handkerchief?
/ Why, that the Moor first gave to Desdemona,
/ That which so often you did bid me steal.

IAGO
// Hast stol'n it from her?

EMILIA
/ No, faith, she let it drop by negligence, 20
/ And, to th'advantage, I, being here, took't up.
// Look, here it is.

IAGO
// A good wench! / Give it me.

EMILIA
// What will you do with't, that you have been so earnest
To have me filch it?

IAGO / Why, what is that to you?

EMILIA
/ If it be not for some purpose of import 25
Give't me again. // Poor lady, she'll run mad
When she shall lack it.

IAGO
// Be not acknown on't, / I have use for it.
// Go, leave me.   *Exit Emilia.*
// I will in Cassio's lodging lose this napkin 30
And let him find it. // Trifles light as air
Are to the jealous confirmations strong
As proofs of holy writ. // This may do something.
// The Moor already changes with my poison

> // Dangerous conceits are in their natures poisons,   35
> / Which at the first are scarce found to distaste,
> / But with a little art upon the blood
> Burn like the mines of sulphur.

HOOKING PHASE TWO: STANDING AND SAYING HOOKS

Now that we've found our hooks, we're going to **use** them. In phase two, we activate the hooking process by merging saying hooks aloud with the standing and sitting physical exercise in chairs. As an introduction, let's use the familiar everyday conversation from our first operative word exercise, since having the operatives in place shines a light on some of the hooks. Read this dialogue aloud including the emphasis on operatives as a review before we add in the hooks

> A: Do you want to go to <u>dinner</u> tonight?
> B: <u>Sure</u>! What <u>time</u>, though?
> A: We could go at <u>6</u> or <u>8</u>.
> B: <u>8</u> would be better for <u>me</u>, I'm working <u>late</u>.
> A: Then <u>8</u> it <u>is</u>! Do you want to <u>meet</u> <u>there</u> or should I <u>pick</u> you <u>up</u>?
> B: <u>Oh</u>, I'll meet you <u>there</u>. <u>Thanks</u>!

The main idea is that A wants to go to dinner with B, but there are a few details to be worked out. Now let's add **the hooks before each spoken line** *in italics* and **say the hook and then the line aloud**:

> A: *Hey, there you are!*
> A: Do you want to go to <u>dinner</u> tonight?
> B: *Do I want to go to dinner? (shift) Hmmm...*

> **B:** <u>Sure</u>! What <u>time</u>, though?
> **A:** *What time? Huh, well...two options*
> **A:** We could go at <u>6</u> or <u>8</u>.
> **B:** *6 or 8, huh?*
> **B:** <u>8</u> would be better for <u>me</u>, I'm working <u>late</u>.
> **A:** *Oh, you're working late? (shift) Let me help you out.*
> **A:** Then <u>8</u> it <u>is</u>! Do you want to <u>meet</u> there or should I <u>pick</u> you <u>up</u>?
> **B:** *Oh, meet you there or have you pick me up? (shift) That's thoughtful.*
> **B:** <u>Oh</u>, I'll meet you <u>there</u>. <u>Thanks</u>!

The drawings show how the hooks reflect what A and B are thinking, as they stand up, and then lead to their line, spoken aloud once they're standing. They sit back down after their line, to be ready for the next hook (Figure 5.4). Follow the numbered cells below, reading down the left column and then the right column to view the hooking and dialogue in the correct order:

Figure 5.4 Hooking the Scene, Rising and Saying Hooks, Standing Saying the Line, and Sitting Back Down to Listen.

> ### TRY IT! HOOKING PHASE TWO: STANDING AND SAYING HOOKS
>
> Now that the hooks have been found and practiced, we add **rising to a standing position while saying the hooks aloud**, and then **from the standing position we say our actual lines**. This part of the exercise utilizes the physical impulse exercises we played with earlier with your partner. As soon as you hear your hook, you rise while saying it aloud. By the time you're standing, you say your line. You sit back down at the end of saying each of your lines.
>
> - *Rise while saying your hook.*
> - Stand and say your line.
> - *Sit back down to be ready for your next hook.*
>
> Work slowly through the entire dinner dialogue scene above: rising, standing, and then sitting. It's a bit of a workout for the quads – all that standing and sitting, but the benefit of phase two is reinforcing what happens next and why. Look at your partner when they are speaking, so you focus on them, not just on your script and what you're going to say next. Hooking helps you rely on your partner, rather than the page, and increases the need for them, in a good way! You get almost everything you need from them to move forward in the scene.
>
> Once you've feel confident that you can navigate the rising, standing, and sitting with this short contemporary scene, move on to the Emilia and Iago scene with the hooks you found.

HOOKING PHASE THREE: PLAYING HOOKS (NOT SAYING THEM)

For phase three of Hooking, we keep the standing and sitting during our hooks and lines, but we no longer say the hooks aloud. We're playing them, just not saying them, similar to how we worked with beats and shifts. I have a nickname for phase three, which is "Nothin' but net!"– borrowing a term from basketball when the ball goes into the basket without any other contact – no backboard, no rim, just a straight clean shot. Now we let go of saying the hooks aloud and only say the lines, retaining the action/response of standing and sitting as we progress through the scene, giving the hook the physical energy of rising, focusing on standing and saying the lines, then sitting back down until you play (not say) your next hook, and so on.

You use the energy of what you hear (your hook) to propel you **into** your line as you stand to say it. Do this through the entire scene, which shouldn't take very long at all. Hooking now feels like you and your partner are on opposite ends of see-saw on a playground, because you're essentially standing up every time you speak and then sitting back down. But what you're really doing is connecting what you say and do to what was just said or done during the time it takes you to stand up. In some cases, you're also incorporating a change, either a beat (a big change) or a shift (a more nuanced change in tactic).

TRY IT! HOOKING PHASE THREE: NOTHIN' BUT NET! (PLAYING, NOT SAYING HOOKS)

Using our familiar scene with Emilia and Iago that you started earlier in this chapter, begin working phase three of hooking starting with Iago's entrance, and ending with Emilia's exit, setting aside each character's soliloquy until later in this chapter.

All the homework you've done thus far impacts the success of hooking in phase three, because you bring complete awareness of the words, the actions, and the responses to the table. Eventually, you get comfortable working without the script, even if you just work one small section at a time. Imagine the level of engagement you can bring to rehearsal after a session or two of hooking!

There are scenes in the Support Material www.routledge.com/ 9781032695297 that can be used for practicing the complete sequence of homework and the three phases of hooking, so that you can gain experience, skill, and confidence in every part of our process so far. Use your version of hooks that you found while working this chapter, or use the version of written hooks I prepared below as you embark on this phase (Figure 5.5):

Written Hooks for Emilia & Iago Scene (without soliloquies)

Enter IAGO // hook:Emilia hides the handkerchief before he can see it.

IAGO hook: What is going on? She's supposed to be with Desdemona!

// How now! / What do you here alone?

EMILIA hook: How now? // What am I doing here alone?

// Do not you chide, // I have a thing for you –

IAGO hook: You have a thing for me?

/ A thing for me? / it is a common thing -

EMILIA hook: a common thing? What? I have no idea what you're talking about.

// Ha?

IAGO hook: Ha?? // (let me finish...)// To have a foolish wife.

EMILIA hook: a foolish wife… common thing…

// O, is that all? // smart aleck /What will you give me now

For that same handkerchief?

IAGO hook: handkerchief? / What handkerchief?

EMILIA hook: What handkerchief?// What handkerchief?

Hook: What Handkerchief? / Why, that the Moor first gave to Desdemona, Hook: What Handkerchief.../ That which so often you did bid me steal.

IAGO hook: (Ding! Light bulb comes on) That handkerchief? / Hast stol'n it from her?

EMILIA hook: Stolen it? / No, faith, she let it drop by negligence,

hook: my wayward husband, you hath a hundred times wooed me to steal it…

And, to th'advantage, I, being here, took't up.

// Look, here it is. / Emilia shows him the handkerchief

IAGO hook: Wow – here it is. She got it! (play nice)A good wench! Give it me.

Iago reaches for it.

EMILIA. / Emilia takes charge and keeps it away from his grasp.

hook: Give it to you? Why?

// What will you do with 't, that you have been so earnest

To have me filch it?

IAGO hook: What will I do with it?

// Why, what is that to you? Iago grabs the handkerchief.

EMILIA hook: What is that to me?

// If it be not for some purpose of import

Give't me again. / Tries in vain to get it back. Hook: Give it me! // (Poor lady), she'll run mad

When she shall lack it.

IAGO hook: "She'll run mad?" uh-oh, "purpose of import…" (I need her to let it go…)

// Be not acknown on't, / I have use for it. hook for Emilia: What use?

Hook for Iago: (She isn't letting it go, and I can't have her suspecting me.) Give her a kiss.

// Go, leave me. // Exit EMILIA hook: oh, he understands, it must be for a surprise.

Figure 5.5 Hooks for the Emilia/IAGO Scene.

As you can see, I chose to show Iago being strategic with his last hook, taking in her whole response – he can't have Emilia telling Desdemona that she found the handkerchief and gave it to her husband, so he plays a little affectionate game to alleviate Emilia's concerns. She so desperately wants to please Iago that she's given up her idea of getting it copied by someone and giving that copy to Iago. Instead, she renders the actual precious memento directly to his scheming hands. We don't have the same play if she leaves in a huff, even if she isn't satisfied with his mysterious answer. The hooks (what they need) live in very close quarters with the paraphrase (what they mean) and subtext (what they really mean but can't say aloud), especially in this scene so critical to the plot.

HOOKING A MONOLOGUE OR SOLILOQUY

Hooks can be played with any text, not just in scenes. Hooks exist in monologues, speeches, and in the lyrics of musicals and operas. In the opening moments of this scene, Emilia's action (seeing the dropped handkerchief that Desdemona cherishes) creates the impulse and serves as the hook for her first line. A previous action – Iago asked her to steal it a number of times in the past – comes soon afterwards (Figure 5.6):

EMILIA // hook "Oh!" *She sees the handkerchief that Desdemona just dropped and picks it up.*
// I am glad I have found this napkin;   hook: "this napkin!"
/ This was her first remembrance from the Moor.
hook: "This napkin... I remember another thing, too--"
// My wayward husband hath a hundred times
Wooed me to steal it; / *hook: steal it? Her first remembrance?* / but she so loves the token --
/(For he conjur'd her she should ever keep it),   *hook: her first remembrance from the Moor*
That she reserves it evermore about her
To kiss and talk to. // *hook: my husband wooed me to steal it* I'll have the work ta'en out
And give't Iago: / *hook: my wayward husband (I do want to make him appreciate me)*
/ what he will do with it
Heaven knows, not I, *hook: my wayward husband*
/ I nothing know, but for his fantasy.   *Exit EMILIA*

Here is Iago's soliloquy after he manages to convince her to give him the handkerchief, hooked:

IAGO *hook: I have use for it (alright! Celebratory moment!!!)...*
// I will in Cassio's lodging lose this napkin
And let him find it. // *hook: lose this napkin – (tosses it)* Trifles light as air
Are to the jealous confirmations strong
As proofs of holy writ. // *hook: This napkin is a confirmation, proof, holy writ.*
This may do something.
// *hook: do something* The Moor already changes with my poison: *hook: poison +*
(all the ideas I've put into his head about Cassio...)
/ Dangerous conceits are in their natures poisons,
Which at the first are scarce found to distaste, *hook: conceits... this napkin, Cassio,*
But with a little art upon the blood *hook: distaste at first?...*
Burn like the mines of sulphur. *Exit IAGO.*

Figure 5.6 Emilia and Iago Soliloquies with Typewritten Hooks.

Looking at these two hooked versions, bookended together, we see the unraveling state of their marriage. In these soliloquies, the characters themselves are drawn to their next idea from what they've just said, or from something they've thought about in the past. Deeply invested in their commitments (whether honest or sinister), Emilia and Iago move forward based on their own logic and rationale. For Emilia, she imagines that giving Iago the thing he's been begging for will somehow improve their marriage. Iago believes having Desdemona's handkerchief will provide the evidence to Othello that she has been disloyal. Hooking helps the actor get from one moment to the next by staying in it, re-living a key word or phrase, and using it to propel them into their next line.

In a monologue or soliloquy, finding and saying the hooks is still the first step. The second step is sitting in a chair and saying the hook as they stand, then saying the line itself from the standing position, and then sitting again, allowing the next hook to provide the impulse for the next moment. Active listening, responding to impulses, and hooking are still possible without a partner and, in fact, are essential skills in staying in the moment-to-moment life of the speech. When you are in a scene and your partner has a long speech, you're there the entire time. You have to stay active, hooking with your own responses, or with what you might say if you had a line. This keeps you engaged, but it also forces the person speaking to work a little harder, deal with what you're doing – just like we do in real life.

MARKING YOUR HOOKS: CIRCLES AND ARROWS

For the purposes of introducing the hooking technique in this book, I put the hooks *in italics*. But in my actual script, which I make handwritten notes in, I couldn't possibly have room to do that (plus it would crowd the space I used for my paraphrase), and I can't make my handwriting look like italics! Instead, since my hooks are primarily what's just been said (or what was said earlier that I am referring to again), **I circle my hooks in my partner's line and draw an arrow to the line it inspires**. Sometimes, I use a highlighter in a different color than I'm already using for my lines. Actors might highlight hooks with a light green color, as if they've found what gives them a "green-light" to move forward, or yellow to highlight anything on the page that impacts them, signaling "pay attention." You do you!

Putting the focus on the partner's lines helps us listen for our hooks, and if you're working on your own (which you usually are when preparing for a role prior to the start of rehearsals), you may have to say every line of the whole scene aloud multiple times to unearth the hooks. You can complete the first phase of hooking – finding your hooks – on your own, working diligently in a close reading aloud of the entire scene. Circling hooks means you might end up circling the whole line, or a few words or phrases, sometimes even the question mark. Look for what supports what you say next, and when you find it, circle it.

Discoveries you make from hooking might impact how you approach marking up your script once you're cast in a new production. What's the first thing an actor usually does when they get their script (besides read it!)? Highlight their lines. Unfortunately, this can reinforce an assumption that their own character's lines are the most important thing when, in fact, what the other characters say to them should be their primary focus. Highlighting can serve a greater purpose than simply drawing our attention to what we do. Circles and arrows are a way to mark hooks should you prefer to highlight your lines, or use different colors. After all, it's your text. I prefer to highlight my character's **name** on any page of the script, to draw my attention to my presence on stage whether in dialogue or stage directions, but I leave off highlighting everything I say. It's not helpful. I don't want to be reading the play and just looking for my own lines, thinking to myself: "Not my line, not my line, not my line, Oh! MY Line!" and then highlighting it. Or, in cruder terms, "B★llsh★t, b★llsh★t, b★ullsh★t, MY LINE!" What I really want to focus on is why I say it. Just as active listening makes us more generous people in everyday conversation, hooking makes us less selfish, more attentive actors when we're playing a scene.

The Support Material at www.routledge.com/9781032695297 has a circled hooks version of the Emilia and Iago scene, full of observations, arrows, circles, and underlines that can be messy; but remember, the only person is has to make sense to is you!

> ### TRY IT! HOOKING HEIGHTENED TEXT: ALL THREE PHASES
>
> Here's a short scene from *Richard III* to read aloud with a partner to practice the three phases of hooking with what might be an unfamiliar text. If you choose, you can start from the very beginning with your

homework – given circumstances and paraphrasing would be crucial here if you don't know the play – but otherwise see what you can glean from it even as a cold reading. Starting with unfamiliar text will reinforce how important it is to do the homework as well as finding beats and shifts, action, hooks, etc. If you are on your own, you will still be able to accomplish up to phase one of hooking, but phases two and three are more like team sports.

Ideally, two actors would begin by sitting in chairs facing each other, speaking lines aloud and finding the hooks all through the scene, then going back again rising with each hook, saying their line while standing, and sitting back down until responding to the next thing, and then eventually "nothin' but net:" rising and saying only their lines while still "playing the hooks" by keeping the dynamics alive even though you're no longer saying the hooks aloud. (Sometimes the hooks just come out, you get so used to saying them aloud!) What's important is that we are making the text physical, and even more importantly, we are deeply connecting to our partner and their lines as the impulse for what we say and do next.

Richard III, Act III, Scene ii *Enter Catesby*
CATESBY Many good morrows to my noble lord.
HASTINGS Good morrow, Catesby; you are early stirring.
  What news, what news in this our tott'ring state?
CATESBY It is a reeling world indeed, my lord,
  And I believe will never stand upright 5
  Till Richard wear the garland of the realm.
HASTINGS How, wear the garland? Dost thou mean the crown?
CATESBY Ay, my good lord.
HASTINGS I'll have this crown of mine cut from my shoulders
  Before I'll see the crown so foul misplac'd. 10
  But canst thou guess that he doth aim at it?
CATESBY Ay, on my life, and hopes to find you forward
  Upon his party for the gain thereof;
  And thereupon he sends you this good news
  That this same very day your enemies, 15
  The kindred of the Queen, must die at Pomfret.
HASTINGS Indeed, I am no mourner for that news,
  Because they have been still my adversaries:

>   But that I'll give my voice on Richard's side
>   To bar my master's heirs in true descent,   20
>   God knows I will not do it, to the death.
> **CATESBY** God keep your lordship in that gracious mind.
> **HASTINGS** But I shall laugh at this a twelve-month hence,
>   That they which brought me in my master's hate,
>   I live to look upon their tragedy.   25
>   Well, Catesby, ere a fortnight make me older
>   I'll send some packing that yet think not on't.
> **CATESBY** 'Tis a vile thing to die, my gracious lord,
>   When men are unprepar'd and look not for't.
> **HASTINGS** O, monstrous, monstrous! And so falls it out   30
>   With Rivers, Vaughan, and Grey: and so 'twill do
>   With some men else that think themselves as safe
>   As thou and I, who as thou know'st are dear
>   To princely Richard and to Buckingham.
> **CATESBY** The Princes both make high account of you-   35
>   *[Aside]* For they account his head upon the Bridge.
> **HASTINGS** I know they do, and I have well deserv'd it.

A fully-hooked version of this scene in found in the Support Material at www.routledge.com/9781032695297.

SUMMARY

In this chapter:

- we learned a foundational technique for inhabiting heightened text called "Hooking," to uncover, then utilize the reason we say each line;
- we practiced active listening and responding to impulses, either from dialogue (what's been said before) or action (something that's happened);
- we worked through the three phases of hooking line-by-line, and became more generous and partner-focused actors by finding connections from the homework that activate explorations and discoveries in the rehearsal room.

RESOURCES FOR FURTHER EXPLORATION

Sanford Meisner's, *On Acting* is a book from the master acting teacher who taught that acting is rooted in the reality of doing, and in the behavior of the fellow performers based in the given circumstances of the play. I studied at the Neighborhood Playhouse, which Meisner founded, and I used his repetition technique as one of the bases for the hooking exercise, tailoring it to work effectively with heightened text.

My acting teacher in graduate school, H. Wesley Balk, believed that improvisation and responsiveness provided inspiration for exploring physical and vocal choices in musical theatre, drama, and opera. His book, *The Complete Singer Actor,* broke ground in helping opera and musical theatre performers inhabit the material with greater authenticity.

Viola Spolin's seminal work, *Improvisation for the Theatre* embraces the idea that every person has a natural ability to be responsive in the moment. Theatre games and improvisational exercises for rehearsal are critical in building skills and confidence in the performer. Verbal and non-verbal exercises in this book have influenced my teaching since my time studying at The Players Workshop and later The Second City Training Center.

Websites

Active Listening: https://thedecisionlab.com/reference-guide/psychology/active-listening

Roadblocks to Communication https://www.gordonmodel.com/work-roadblocks.php

6

PLAYING INTENTIONS, ACTIONS, AND TACTICS

INTRODUCTION

In this chapter, which could be considered part of the actor's homework or part of the what engagement happens in rehearsal, we incorporate the principles and techniques of acting that remain effective today and apply them to heightened text that may be centuries-old. Looking for clues in the script that contain textual action, and using verbs that convey our intentions and tactics keep actors focusing on what they are playing: actively seeking change in their partner and situation. Actions prompt the imagination and stimulate the vocabulary, so the verbs selected need to be specific and clear. These action verbs get added to scripts in the left-hand margin, so we see them before we say the line, utilizing test phrases that activate the text. Combined with the hooking techniques of active listening and responding to impulses from Chapter 5, you will practice using tactics and then changing them based on the results you do or do not achieve. Using references to contemporary plays, we learn how every text has its own style, or creates its own world.

DOI: 10.4324/9781032695310-7

ART IMITATES LIFE VS. LIFE IMITATES ART: HOW WE INCORPORATE INTENTIONS, TACTICS, AND ACTIONS EVERY DAY, AND HOW TO APPLY THOSE SKILLS TO ACTING IN HEIGHTENED TEXT

Though Plato, the Ancient Greek philosopher, coined "Art imitates life," Oscar Wilde, the 19th-century playwright and satirist, offered the counterpoint with "Life imitates art." The inspiration for drama is deeply rooted in real-life experience, with ordinary characters dealing with extraordinary circumstances. In this same vein, we have been comparing how ordinary conversations include the same process as acting, and observing how scenes in plays, television, or film must seem "as if" they are being spoken by real people, not merely characters.

The foundational acting skills we will be working on in this chapter may be terms with which you're familiar: intentions (or objectives), actions, and tactics. In aligning these skills with heightened text, we will be using a lot of verbs. Ironically, a verb is a noun. It's a thing that happens, an action that takes place, something that is done. Whether it's a small everyday action, like putting on a coat, or a big action, like trying to flag down help by the side of the road, it is rooted in the given circumstances.

Let's take a few moments to clarify each of these terms in the context of how we'll be using them in our work (this may be a review or brief introduction for you):

- An **Intention** (or objective) is what you want, *your overall goal*. For example, you need money. Sometimes, you might have a big picture intention, or super-objective: perhaps, it's because you need to leave town in a hurry. You're not going to leave town in this particular scene, necessarily, but you need to borrow money in order to leave town. Your intention in this scene is to get someone to loan you money.
- An **Action** is what you do (try to get someone to loan you money), think of it as *your plan*.
- A **Tactic** (your specific approach) is how you do it, your *tangible strategy* or steps you will employ to make your plan work, and

achieve your goal. These last two terms (Action and Tactic) have quite a bit of overlap in use, since more often than not, in life and in plays, we go after what we want in a certain way, using a more detailed strategy. For example, you might plead, threaten, or call in a favor to get someone to loan you money. While it's possible to think of the actor playing the tactic (because we're learning it as a technique), in actuality, the character is the one being tactical, so this process of attaching a tactic allows us to inhabit the character's psyche and figure out how they're going to try to get what they want in any particular moment.

In life, we have intentions, play actions, and employ tactics on a daily basis: it's how we navigate life's situations. Sometimes, in anticipation of a difficult conversation, a jury duty summons, or a job interview, we think about our intentions and tactics in advance – how do we try to get the outcome we want? We may not be writing them down, but in the moment, we play a tactic, we try something, and pay attention to how it lands. The same holds true for acting, since we are replicating real life in the imaginary circumstances of the play.

In *Actions: The Actor's Thesaurus*, an enormously helpful collection of words, authors Marina Calderone and Maggie Lloyd-Williams have amassed an extensive list of verbs that actors can play as actions and tactics using a technique outlined in the Foreword by director Terry Johnson. This approach uses a mad-lib-like blank space between "I (verb) you" as a test of the verb's effectiveness as an action: I challenge you, I embrace you, I humiliate you, and I thank you. This volume's treasure trove of verbs is an excellent starting point for how we can incorporate active energy in every beat or shift in our heightened text. Their extensive list helps actors reinforce the choice they are making and ensuring that it's an active choice by employing this technique.

My approach to this brilliant and efficient way to activate a choice is to take the use of actions and tactics further by asking my students not only to identify a verb that suits the moment, but say the phrase aloud and then play the moment. The verb doesn't just sit idly on the page, but leaps into the scene rehearsal, as an ignition-like burst of energy at the beginning of a beat or shift. The script might be marked with Actions as such:

> **IAGO:** (Attack) How now! (Belittle) What do you here alone?
> **The actor adds this hook-like approach saying the test-phrase aloud before their line:**
> **IAGO:** *I attack you.* How now? *I belittle you.* What do you here alone?
> **EMILIA:** (Challenge) Do not you chide. (Tempt) I have a thing for you.
> **The actor adds the same hook-like approach as well:**
> **EMILIA:** *I challenge you.* Do not you chide. *I tempt you.* I have a thing for you.

The actors are trying out their choices, playing their actions, testing their tactics. It doesn't matter what you call it (an action or a tactic), what matters is that you DO something. The book of verbs certainly helps actors get started (they even have an App!) but there are thousands of other verbs that can be employed (and I've provided an exhaustive list of Action Verbs in the Support Material at www.routledge.com/9781032695297, though it's not categorized like the *Actions Thesaurus*). It's great fun to play Actions and Tactics, and you can try anything to see if it works. It doesn't work if it interferes with the forward action of the story, or if it makes the next line redundant or unable to be spoken.

MARKING UP THE SCRIPT WITH INTENTIONS, ACTIONS, AND TACTICS

In my script, I write the super-objective and intention at the top of the page, or near the scene break, and then my verbs (actions and tactics) in the left-hand margin, serving as prompts for what the character is about to do. My tactics will change based on how my partner responds. In our contemporary money-lending example, it may take you a while to convince someone to give you money, and you may leave empty-handed. Sometimes an action or tactic is reflexive, I do something myself, and I use the phrase "I _____" to engage with what I am saying, such as "I rehearse," "I primp," and "I calm down." What am I doing? That's the question that identifying the action or tactic answers. (The answer is rarely "I'm acting," unless the character themselves is acting!). I want to know what I'm playing – what am I trying to achieve, and how's it going? If I am working on intentions, actions and tactics as part of my homework, I might put some verbs down that I can imagine my scene partner playing, like they avoid me, they distract me, they humiliate me. But when I get into rehearsal, they may have taken a totally different approach, they might console me, support me, and befriend me. Actors have to flexible and fluid in their approach to what they're playing, since not only the other actors, but the director will have very specific ideas that deserve full exploration. When I play a beat change or a shift, or when my partner responds in a way I hadn't predicted, I change gears, find another way to get at the same thing, or change my course entirely.

If we break down the scenario invented earlier, a friend, Noah, needing money in order to leave town in a hurry, turning to an old friend, Blake, it might play out like this:

> **BLAKE:** Hey, Noah – this is a surprise!
> **NOAH:** Blake, I know, it's been a long time.
>   *(Awkward pause)*
> **BLAKE:** Is something wrong?
> **NOAH:** You know what, never mind.
> **BLAKE:** Whoa, hey, what's going on?
> **NOAH:** I don't want to burden you.
> **BLAKE:** Come on, that's what friends are for!
> **NOAH:** Not friends who just show up when they want to borrow some money.

Using our skills in text analysis, even without knowing how the situation is going to resolve, let's hone in on the intentions, actions, and tactics that are possible.

What's Noah's **Super-Objective**? (big picture goal) to leave town in a hurry

What's Noah's **Intention or Objective** in this scene? (immediate goal) to borrow a significant sum of money from Blake

What's Noah's **Primary Action**? (their plan) What are they doing? approaching an old friend for money, heading over to Blake's house

What **Tactics** does Noah employ? (strategy or tangible steps) How do they go about it? Surprise, hide, veil, deflect, and act casual

Did Noah achieve their goal? This short bit of dialogue doesn't play out that far, but imagine that yes, Blake gave Noah the money; **gave** it, not just loaned it, in the end, because Noah broke down and told them the real reason for the visit.

Noah had not planned to do that (reveal) as a strategy, when they thought about how to approach Blake, but it just transpired that way. Noah adapted the tactic to the situation and achieved their objective.

Intentions, actions and tactics are applicable to playing all text, from song lyrics, to Greek plays, to Shakespeare or Moliere, to Ike Holter's *Exit Strategy,* Caryl Churchill's *Top Girls,* and August Wilson's *Fences.* Someone wants something, and they have a specific way to go about trying to get it. The actor has to find what they're doing, what action they're playing, and embody it in an active way to get something from their partner. Whether or not they get the desired result is a matter of text, unless you're in an improvisation group or a devised piece and the end is unknown, making the strongest choice possible is the goal. Strong choices make an actor eminently watchable, with the audience hanging on every word, wondering what will happen next. Finding intentions, then playing actions and tactics means every moment is specific, every change is played with clarity, and the text acted with conviction.

VERBS AND THEIR USES: ALIGNING A CHOICE TO THE MOMENT

Let's use the Iago and Emilia scene as an example of how intentions, actions, and tactics can support making strong choices that are engaging and responsive.

Apply the test about playing the action: say aloud the phrase "I _____ you" or "I _____" with the verbs in parentheses below, and immediately say the line afterwards. This allows the action or tactic choice to support the line like a wind-up for a pitch: "here's what I'm doing." In rehearsal, I think of my action as part of my line (even though, like my hooks, I no longer say them aloud after a certain point). It reinforces that I have a choice for every moment, and that I am adjusting that choice with every beat change or shift.

To begin our work with this scene, Iago's intention when he arrives and sees Emilia alone is to find out what the heck is going on. Why isn't Emilia at Desdemona's side as he had ordered her to be? Emilia's intention (as we noted in her soliloquy) is to take the handkerchief she's found to the embroidery shop to get a copy made and give it to her husband Iago. He's been asking for it (for some unknown reason). She wants to keep him happy, but can't bear how distraught Desdemona will feel when she discovers it's missing.

We pick up the scene at Iago's entrance, during which Emilia's tucked the handkerchief out of his sight. Notice how the action verbs (written in parentheses on the left-hand margin) can help launch the moment by embracing the "I _____ you" method: saying the action aloud and then playing the action fully, as if it's a mantra: "I'm doing this now!" Notice how often things change. Both characters are picking up on what the other one is doing, and both are trying to pursue their own intentions, and realign their strategy (Figure 6.1).

IAGO
(Attack) // How n<u>ow</u>! (Belittle) / What <u>do</u> you here <u>alone</u>?
EMILIA
(Challenge)// Do not you <u>chide</u>. (Tempt) // I have a <u>thing</u> for you -
IAGO
(Mock) / A <u>thing</u> for <u>me</u>? (Lecture) / it is a <u>common</u> thing -
EMILIA
(Interrupt) // <u>Ha</u>?
IAGO (Take Charge)/ To have a <u>foolish</u> wife. *(Iago grabs Emilia's arm to move her along…)*
EMILIA
(Ridicule) // O, is that <u>all</u>? (Taunt) //What will you <u>give</u> me <u>now</u>
For <u>that</u> same <u>handkerchief</u>?

> **IAGO** (Reverse) / What <u>handkerchief</u>?
> **EMILIA** (Mimic)/ <u>What</u> <u>handkerchief</u>?
> (Help) / Why, that the <u>Moor</u> first <u>gave</u> to <u>Desdemona</u>,
> (Boost)/ That which so <u>often</u> you did bid me <u>steal</u>.
> **IAGO** (Celebrate) / Hast <u>stol'n</u> it from her?
> **EMILIA** (Correct) / <u>No</u>, faith, she let it <u>drop</u> by <u>negligence</u>,
> And, to th'<u>advantage</u>, <u>I</u>, <u>being</u> here, took't <u>up</u>.
> (Boast) // <u>Look</u>, here it <u>is</u>.
> **IAGO** (Flatter) A <u>good</u> wench! <u>Give</u> it me. /*Iago reaches for it.*
> **EMILIA** (Halt) / // <u>What</u> will you <u>do</u> with 't, that you have been so <u>earnest</u>
> To have me <u>filch</u> it?
> **IAGO** (Avoid) // <u>Why</u>, what is <u>that</u> to <u>you</u>? //*Iago grabs the handkerchief.*
> **EMILIA** (Re-Evaluate)
> // <u>If</u> it be <u>not</u> for some <u>purpose</u> of <u>import</u>
> <u>Give</u>'t me <u>again</u>. / (Qualify) // <u>Poor</u> lady, she'll run <u>mad</u>
> When she shall <u>lack</u> it.
> **IAGO** (Pacify, externally; Plot, internally) // Be not <u>acknown</u> on't. / I have <u>use</u> for it.

Figure 6.1 Emilia and Iago Scene with Actions, Beats, and Operatives Marked.

Now that's an active scene! Driven by each moment's tactic, both characters/actors are in spontaneous response to what the other character is doing. Iago's not the only one playing tactics, Emilia is, too! Emilia's initial plan is to get the handkerchief copied. She quickly has to change gears. The scene is lifted to new heights as a result of the thorough and detailed homework, and the physical dynamics that hooking brought to the process. I might observe that they are too busy playing their actions to worry about their acting. Once you are in rehearsal, playing intentions, actions, and tactics are essential, and they provide vital energy to what's happening for each character.

TRY IT! FINDING INTENTIONS, ACTIONS, AND TACTICS IN HEIGHTENED TEXT

Here's a short excerpt from *Romeo and Juliet,* in which the character Juliet is trying to convince Friar Laurence to help her get out of being forced to marry Paris, an extraordinary circumstance since she has already secretly wed Romeo.

If you are not familiar with the play and this particular text, begin by reading it aloud, and then doing the basic three steps of homework (scansion, paraphrase/GC's, operative words), look up any words you don't know or are curious about, and mark the beats and shifts. This will give you a bit of practice on putting together the work we've been doing throughout the previous chapters. At this point, seeing the value of taking the time to do each phase of the homework builds a foundation of knowledge that supports this advanced level of engagement. You can also jump right in the deep end and choose intentions, actions and tactics based on your first impressions.

Begin by reading the text aloud a couple of times, then follow the prompts at the end of the speech:

> JULIET
> Tell me not, friar, that thou hear'st of this,
> Unless thou tell me how I may prevent it!
> If, in thy wisdom, thou canst give no help,
> Do thou but call my resolution wise,
> And with this knife I'll help it presently.
> God join'd my heart and Romeo's, thou our hands;
> And ere this hand, by thee to Romeo seal'd,
> Shall be the label to another deed,
> Or my true heart with treacherous revolt
> Turn to another, this shall slay them both:
> Therefore, out of thy long-experienced time,
> Give me some present counsel, or, behold,
> 'Twixt my extremes and me this bloody knife
> Shall play the umpire, arbitrating that
> Which the commission of thy years and art
> Could to no issue of true honour bring.
> Be not so long to speak; I long to die,
> If what thou speaks, speaks not of remedy.
>
> *(Act IV, scene i)*

If you speak Spanish, there's a version that the Chilean poet Pablo Neruda translated in 1964 called *Romeo y Julieta*. Though Neruda was criticized for making substantial cuts to the text, it is widely held that his poetry rivalled Shakespeare's own in this adaptation.

Think for a moment about Juliet's intention. What does she want? Write that down as an "I" statement, to incorporate thinking as the character as you do this work.

- Read the speech aloud again, using what you've learned about punctuation, beats and shifts, to identify the places where an action or tactic could be incorporated.

152 ACTING HEIGHTENED TEXT

- Using either the Actions book or app, or another resource, find an active verb that energizes each change, using the I _____ you test. Consider what response the Friar is having to these words, and the impact of those reactions on Juliet.
- Take your time and think about what tactics she uses, what strategies she employs, and how it ties to her circumstances.
- If you are working on the Neruda version, what differences do you see between the two speeches besides length? What do you appreciate about the Spanish translation?

Homework check-in: What did you discover when completing the homework? How did scansion impact the later steps? What challenges did you encounter in the paraphrase? Were you able to identify operatives that keep the speech nuanced and detailed?

Here's a version of this speech with suggested intentions, actions, and tactics (Figure 6.2).

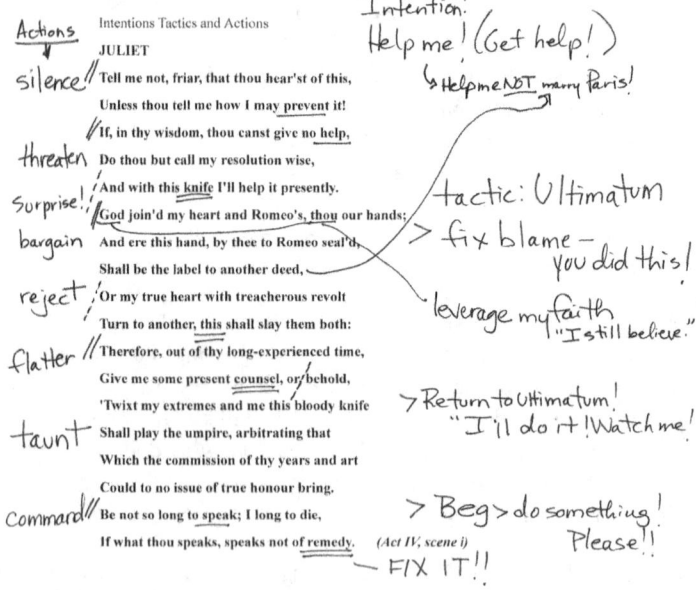

Figure 6.2 Juliet Monologue with Intentions, Actions, and Tactics.

TRY IT! A LIST OF SHORT CONTEMPORARY AND MODERN SCENES FOR PRACTICE

If you're eager to put this skill into practice with contemporary or modern texts, here are some plays with a broad range of roles that can serve as practice for applying actions and tactics to text in order to make strong choices that engage self and partner. All dramatic text is heightened in some way – you can use lyrics from a song, too. This exercise applies to all text, so find a scene or monologue in one of these plays and get started.

In the Red and Brown Water by Tarell Alvin McCraney
The Great God Pan by Amy Herzog
Gloria by Brandon Jacobs-Jenkins
August: Osage County by Tracey Letts
Fun Home by Lisa Kron and Jeanine Tesori (based on the book by Alison Bechdel)
The Inheritance by Matthew Lopez
Top Girls by Caryl Churchill
Other Desert Cities by Jon Robin Baitz
A Streetcar Named Desire by Tennessee Williams
Proof by David Auburn
Exit Strategy by Ike Holter

SUMMARY

In this chapter:

- we discovered the character's intention (what they want);
- we made choices about actions or tactics (how they get what they want);
- we reinforced the value of doing all the homework, and how each step informs the next;
- we made connections to both heightened and contemporary text in applying actions and tactics, saying them aloud, and then making adjustments in the moment.

RESOURCES FOR FURTHER EXPLORATION

The essential pocket-size volume *Actions: The Actor's Thesaurus*, by Maria Calderone and Maggie Lloyd-Williams, contains thousands of verbs that can be used as actions and tactics, with an appendix organizing them in categories for ease of use, and an introduction that provides practical ways to put the verbs into the actor's process. Also available as an app!

Acting Power: The 21st Century Edition, by Robert Cohen, is an updated edition of his book that lays out in clear terms how to play tactics effectively, in addition to offering an accessible approach to learning to act.

The Complete Singer-Actor: Training for Music Theater, by H. Wesley Balk, focuses on the skills needed to sing musical theatre and opera, Balk's work is based in spontaneity and improvisation, and served as ones of the bases for my work in developing the hooking process.

7

ADVANCED SKILLS
Prose, Rhetoric, and Rhyming Couplets

INTRODUCTION

In this penultimate chapter, we will tackle two of the most challenging (and yet common) expressions of language for actors: heightened prose and rhyming couplets. With prose, we will re-visit the lessons learned regarding punctuation and apply a technique called "line-out" or "lining out" prose which breaks up the sentences by thoughts, unpacking the rhetoric, as well as paying attention to operative words and beats and shifts. With rhyming couplets in verse (often also found in song lyrics), we will apply the tools we learned in employing operative words to help us make sense of the lines, while not landing so heavily on the rhyme unless it is called for. Being able to adjust the weight of an operative and continue the connection of the line (and for the actors, this also means using connected speech) is an advanced skill. We will introduce the concept of connected speech to improve clarity of ideas and inhabit the language fully. By now, you've learned new skills, practiced using them, and developed greater ability to read the map and see what the terrain ahead holds. Each of the tools learned in the book thus far (as well as experience and practice in life) builds toward what gets explored in this chapter – like climbing a mountain – all of our experience and skill is called upon in order to serve the actor's goals: to be understood and to convey a richness of character and situation in telling the story.

DOI: 10.4324/9781032695310-8

UNLEASHING THE POWER OF PROSE

The goal of this chapter is to help readers continue to identify and use the right tool for the job, applying new techniques and lessons learned to classical and contemporary prose text, as well as deconstructing how rhyme works effectively in plays and lyrics and can be conveyed without sounding like a nursery rhyme.

Throughout this book thus far, we have focused on **verse** as the primary example of heightened text, with its lines structured by meter and rhythm. Whether it's a play by Shakespeare or musical lyrics by Lin-Manuel Miranda, there is a clear sense that we are no longer having a regular conversation: there are line breaks, rules about syllables (and shortened or extended ones), and so many exceptions to those rules.

With **prose,** which is basically words organized into phrases, sentences, and paragraphs, there is far less structure, with only a few rules that everyone (mostly) agrees upon; so we rely heavily on punctuation (and margins on a page) to provide the structure as we read. Most everything written or spoken in everyday language is essentially prose: the newspaper, websites, novels, textbooks, and emails generally follow the natural way we form thoughts and express them.

Prose can be considered heightened any time the situation is dramatic, not just when it's in a play. In everyday life, we employ heightened text in an effort to be clear and effective. Consider a speaker at a convention is using heightened text, a teacher in a lecture environment, a parent delivering instructions to a babysitter, a maid of honor making a toast at a friend's wedding. All of these situations involve higher stakes, a discrete audience, and a need for clarity in conveying a specific message. Examples of heightened text in writing include a thank-you note, a letter of recommendation, or an essay for a magazine. All of these situations require thoughtful use of language, attention to detail, and perhaps persuasive argument, encouragement, or a message that conveys complex feelings. For actors, the challenge is how to break prose down into manageable chunks of text in order to make specific choices, without the benefit of scansion. The method of the "**line-out**" is a game-changer for navigating prose.

THE LINE-OUT: THE PROSE EQUIVALENT TO SCANSION

If scansion is the secret code of verse, what's the equivalent for prose? How do you begin? For verse, we learned the importance of scansion as a first step, but what do we do when we can't scan? In the same way that scansion provides critical information on an archaeological level for verse, a process called **line-out** is used as the primary investigative step for working with **prose.**

With prose, actors are challenged by the limitations of margins on the page: it's just a big block of text, like Orlando's opening speech from *As You Like It*:

ORLANDO

As I remember, Adam, it was upon this fashion bequeathed me by will but poor a thousand crowns, and as thou sayest, charged my brother, Oliver, on his blessing, to breed me well; and there begins my sadness. My brother Jaques he keeps at school, and report speaks goldenly of his profit: for my part, he keeps me rustically at home, or, to speak more properly, stays me here at home unkept; His horses are bred better; I, his brother, gain nothing under him but growth; and the spirit of my father, which I think is within me, begins to mutiny against this servitude: I will no longer endure it, though yet I know no wise remedy how to avoid it.

Even though we are guided by our good friend Punctuation and aided by the structure of sentences, the text is compacted into a box, so there's little room for marking up the text. The formatting isn't helpful in discovering when to breathe to structure the new thoughts. Let's revisit what I've said above about margins. This is where prose text presents challenges to actors, and the line-out step meets that challenge. As a new thought emerges in the text, it lives on its own new line, just below the previous thought, and tabbed slightly over to the right if the thought is a progression of what came before.

Whether or not there's punctuation, the **length of the thought** is what matters most, rather than the width of the piece of paper.

If there's a beat change, the new line starts all the way over on the left, which requires a new breath as well as a new specific choice. The next paragraph illustrates how text in prose often appears in a printed script and describes the guidelines for lining-out prose:

> Read the text aloud and pause at each punctuation mark. Look for the length of the thought or phrase using punctuation as your guide. Sometimes, there might not be punctuation yet it seems as though the next phrase merits a pause or indicates a shift. If the next phrase or thought continues in the same beat, or is a further progression of what precedes it, set the phrase off by putting it on a "new line" and tabbing it over to the right. If you feel there's a beat or a shift, put the next phrase of text all the way over on the left margin. If necessary, turn your paper sideways or format your text using the "landscape" option on your document, to allow the phrases to use the full width of the page to express the length of thought.

Here's how to format a lined-out version of the same text (you can use a computer or a pencil and paper). Using the guidelines above, let's start a line-out to lay it out thought-by-thought by reading aloud and working with pencil or paper or on your computer. What the first complete thought from this paragraph? Is it:

> **Read the text aloud and pause at each punctuation mark.**

Or is it:

> **Read the text aloud**
>   **and pause at each punctuation mark?**

Either choice is valid and works effectively lined out. The thought maintains its energy if it's all on one line, or if there's a new line without taking much of a pause in between. Let's continue with the rest of the guidelines:

> Read the speech aloud
> > and pause at each punctuation mark.
> Look for the length of the thought or phrase
> > using punctuation as your guide
>
> Sometimes, there might not be punctuation
> > yet it seems as though the next phrase merits a pause or shift.
> If the next phrase or thought continues in the same beat,
> > or is a further progression of what precedes it,
> > > set the phrase off by putting it on a "new line"
> > > and tabbing it over to the right.
>
> If you feel there's a beat or a shift,
> > put the next phrase of text all the way over on the left margin.
> If necessary, turn your paper sideways or format your text using the "landscape" option on your document, to allow the full width of the page to express the length of thought.

After the **line-out process** is completed, review your work **aloud**, continue with your paraphrase, given circumstances and dictionary work, and then add primary and secondary operative marks. The only component of **prose** that's different than verse is **you create a line-out rather than scansion**. This provides a step that is wholly focused on structure prior to thinking about conveying meaning.

Now let's tackle the excerpt from *As You Like It,* applying the guidelines we just learned. Read the speech aloud (as we always do!), using what you've got to work with: essentially, punctuation and your ability to decode the meaning of things on a first reading:

ORLANDO

As I remember, Adam, it was upon this fashion bequeathed me by will but poor a thousand crowns, and as thou sayest, charged my

> brother, Oliver, on his blessing, to breed me well; and there begins my sadness. My brother Jaques he keeps at school, and report speaks goldenly of his profit: for my part, he keeps me rustically at home, or, to speak more properly, stays me here at home unkept; His horses are bred better; I, his brother, gain nothing under him but growth; and the spirit of my father, which I think is within me, begins to mutiny against this servitude: I will no longer endure it, though yet I know no wise remedy how to avoid it.

This is complex stuff: a difficult family history, with serious issues between brothers – and these are the first words spoken in the play! Since we can't scan it, we reformat to essentially "make" separate lines of each thought, literally "delineating" the speaker's various thoughts in the heightened prose text. We need to mind and mine our punctuation for all that it can provide as guideposts as we read. Pay attention to each punctuation mark as you read aloud, perhaps even saying the punctuation aloud as we did in chapter two.

Read aloud, one phrase at a time, or one punctuation mark to the next. What do we have? It might be a word, a phrase, or even a complete thought. Using this logic, when it's something new, we make a new line, to keep the idea flowing until there is a change. If we are working electronically, we use the Enter key to return us to a new line, and then the Tab key to push the text over to the right until there is another logical place for a new line, or significant punctuation. If we're working with pencil and paper, we jot down the next phrase or thought and manage the formatting accordingly on the page, sentence-by-sentence. Every time we have a new thought or phrase, we put it on a **new line**, and if the idea continues, we move it over until we **line-out** the first complete sentence. A new sentence always begins on the far left. If the play is in manuscript form, I use a pencil and write the line-out on the non-printed pages, opposite the text pages on the right. If a script is double-sided or in an acting edition, I write my line-outs in a notebook, or on pages that I can work from instead of the crowded script. Working from the line-out is the key, carrying it with you in rehearsal, making all your notes in it from now on, no longer buried in trying to find your place within the block paragraphs of the original formatting. For visual learners, the line-out process supports being able to visualize the changes, as well as reinforcing the choices of operatives, intentions, actions and tactics.

Say the first part of the lined-out version below aloud, keeping the energy consistent if the line ends with a comma (just like you would with verse) and playing the weight of any full stop (.!?) when appropriate.

> As I remember,
>   Adam,
>   it was upon this fashion bequeathed me by will
>   but poor a thousand crowns,
>   and as thou sayest,
>   charged my brother Oliver,
>   on his blessing,
>   to breed me well;
>   and there begins my sadness.

The line-out helps sort out the beats and shifts in the process. As the shift or beat changes, we tab across the page to indicate the flow of the energy. If the character is talking about the same thing, even if it changes slightly, keep it flowing across the page, with a new line tabbed over for every new thought, shift, or beat, which coincides with needing a new breath.

At this point, go back and work on the paraphrase (and any dictionary work), and then add primary and secondary operatives. Always work aloud to hear the choices you're making, and try alternative ones with full commitment. This is similar to once you've finished scansion if working with verse.

My *paraphrase* for this opening segment – also in prose, but my own version of it – reads like this:

If my memory serves,   (old friend)
there was a certain way my father left things when he died,
                                    I only got a few hundred dollars,
      and like you were just saying,
            he made my older brother Oliver promise
                on his death-bed,
                    to take good care of me;
that's what's making me feel this way.

Here's my finished line-out, marked with operatives, and beats and shifts, now that I have a better idea of what it all means. Please read it aloud, adding emphasis as indicated:

//As I <u>remember</u>, (Adam,)
it was upon <u>this</u> fashion <u>bequeathed-me-by-will</u>
                                but poor a <u>thousand</u> crowns,
    /and as thou <u>sayest</u>,
            charged my <u>brother</u>, <u>Oliver</u>,
      on his <u>blessing</u>,
            to breed me <u>well</u>;
/ and <u>there</u> begins my <u>sadness</u>.

Moving right into the paraphrase step after doing the line-out provides a chance to change things around now that the meaning is abundantly clear. For example, moving "Adam" to be on the same line as "As I remember…" helps keep Orlando's energy flowing. Hyphenating "bequeathed-me-by-will" helps keep that thought all together, as if it were one word. Since no one else ever sees your line-out (or your paraphrase), it creates an invisible but palpable foundation on which your acting choices can confidently reside.

TRY IT! REVIEW THE GUIDELINES FOR LINING-OUT PROSE AND FINISH THE SPEECH

Complete the line-out for Orlando's entire speech and continue with dictionary work, paraphrase, operative words, and beats and shifts.

ORLANDO. As I remember, Adam, it was upon this fashion bequeathed me by will but poor a thousand crowns, and as thou sayest, charged my brother, Oliver, on his blessing, to breed me well; and there begins my sadness. My brother Jaques he keeps at school, and report speaks goldenly of his profit: for my part, he keeps me rustically at home, or, to speak more properly, stays me here at home unkept; His horses are bred better; I, his brother, gain nothing under him but growth; and the spirit of my father, which I think is within me, begins to mutiny against this servitude: I will no longer endure it, though yet I know no wise remedy how to avoid it.

A marked-up lined-out version of this speech is in the Support Material at this link: www.routledge.com/9781032695297, along with additional Shakespeare prose selections for line-out practice from *Hamlet, Henry IV, Part 1,* and *The Merchant of Venice.*

PUTTING THE LINE-OUT ON ITS FEET: WALKING THE LINE-OUT

Entering and establishing the world of the play through heightened language, whether in verse or prose, is a skill. As actors and directors do their text homework, they alter their view of the landscape to see things differently. The line-out process helps free us from the restrictions of standard formatting, margins, and paragraphs but retains punctuation, sentence structure, and, therefore, meaning. The **line-out** organizes the text according to thought, governed by beats and shifts, and can now be further physicalized by putting it on its feet, "**walking the line-out.**" This is similar to how we "**walked the monologue**" in exploring beats and shifts. Apply the same physical rules to moving in one direction, with diagonals in play as needed, to drive the thought in the same direction until there is a full stop and a beat change. Change directions on the change, and begin walking back in the other direction. With every "new line," a slight diagonal manifests the thought continuing, allowing the forward physical and vocal energy to support the length of thought. Using the Orlando line-out as your text, take a walk and experience the way phrasing and breath can fuse with integrity of thought and physical action.

This approach owes a debt of gratitude to notable voice, speech, and text teachers Ellen O'Brien (longtime coach at The Shakespeare Theatre Company in Washington, DC), and Cicely Berry in her book *The Actor and the Text*. Their dedicated work with text and actors reinforces the importance of physicalizing language and identifying rhetoric. The line-out process and eventually "walking it" builds on the road they (and others) paved with their approach to speaking heightened prose with distinction and commitment.

HEIGHTENED TEXT IN CONTEMPORARY PLAYS

Contemporary playwrights use language in thrilling ways, employing prose and other literary devices to elevate the dialogue and the action. Some writers use poetic formatting, which resembles a line-out and adds nuance (and clarity) from the first reading, like Tarell Alvin McCraney's *The Brother/Sister Plays* and Kristin Idaszak's *Second Skin*. In this excerpt from *Angels in America: Pt. 1 Millennium Approaches* by Tony Kushner, the character Belize unleashes a diatribe at his friend Louis. **Read it aloud** in its original format (limited by the margins of the printed page), and then again from the line-out version that follows. Compare the clarity of what you are able to communicate when the thoughts – and subsequently the breaths – are set off with new lines:

> **BELIZE**
>
> You know what your problem is, Louis? Your problem is that you are so full of piping hot crap that the mention of your name draws flies. You don't even know Thing One about this guy, do you? Uh-huh. Well ain't that pathetic. Just so the record's straight: I love Prior but I was never in love with him. I have a man, uptown, and I have since long before I first laid my eyes on the sorry-ass sight of you—No 'cause

you never bothered to ask. Up in the air, just like that angel, too far off the earth to pick out the details. Louis and his Big Ideas. Big Ideas are all you love. "America" is what Louis loves. Well I hate America, Louis. I hate this country. It's just big ideas, and stories, and people dying, and people like you. The white cracker who wrote the National Anthem knew what he was doing. He set the word "free" to a note so high nobody can reach it. That was deliberate. Nothing on earth sounds less like freedom to me. You come with me to room 1013 over at the hospital, I'll show you America. Terminal, crazy and mean. I live in America, Louis, that's hard enough, I don't have to love it. You do that. Everybody's got to love something.

See how this speech gains emphatic power when the line-out, beats and shifts, and operative words are marked:

//You know what your problem is, Louis?
　　Your problem is that you are so full of piping-hot-crap
　　　　that the mention of your name draws flies.
　　/You don't even know Thing One about this guy, do you?
　　　　/Uh-huh.
　　/Well ain't that pathetic.
//Just so the record's straight
　　I love Prior but I was never in love with him.
//I have a man,
　　/uptown,
　　　　/and I have since long before I first laid my eyes
　　　　　　on the sorry-ass sight of you—
　　/No 'cause you never bothered to ask.
//Up in the air,
　　/just like that angel,
　　　　/too far off the earth to pick out the details.
　　　　　　/Louis and his Big Ideas.
　　/Big Ideas are all you love.
　　　　/"America" is what Louis loves.

//Well I <u>hate America</u>, Louis.
　　/I hate this <u>country</u>.
　　　　/It's just <u>big ideas</u>,
　　　　　　and <u>stories</u>,
　　　　　　　　and people <u>dying</u>,
　　/and people like <u>you</u>.
//The white-cracker-who-wrote-the-National-Anthem <u>knew</u> what he was doing.
　　/He set the word <u>"free"</u> to a note <u>so high</u> nobody can <u>reach</u> it.
　　/That was <u>deliberate</u>.
　　/Nothing on <u>earth</u> sounds <u>less</u> like <u>freedom</u> to me.
//You <u>come</u> with me to room <u>1013</u> over at the <u>hospital</u>,
　　I'll <u>show</u> you <u>America</u>.
　　/<u>Terminal</u>,
　　　　<u>crazy</u>
　　　　　　and <u>mean</u>.
//I <u>live</u> in America, <u>Louis</u>,
　　/that's hard <u>enough</u>,
　　　　/I don't have to <u>love</u> it.
　　　　　　/<u>You</u> do that.
　　/<u>Everybody's</u> got to love <u>something</u>.

The process of creating a line-out breaks apart the texts into thoughts, and formats the text into manageable chunks, whether it's on paper or electronically. Sometimes actors see long monologues in a text and anxiety sets in: how will I learn all those lines? How will I be able to mark up the text when there's no room? The best part about lining-out is that it's for the individual actor to determine what makes sense for them. Having a step of homework for prose that's similar to the scansion (and the very first thing you can do with any new text) is essential to demystifying the work and getting to the point where choices grounded in the text can be made.

TRY IT! PRACTICE LINING-OUT PROSE

Use the following two selections from Oscar Wilde's *The Importance of Being Earnest* (written in 1895) as practice for lining-out prose. Copy the text to a blank page line by line as you build your line-out, or enter it into a document on your computer and work electronically. The richness of Wilde's wit requires attention be paid to the length of thought as well as the way he satirizes manners and societal norms. An added challenge with this material is incorporating a British dialect. Begin by reading aloud, and then start to line-out the text based on the narrative logic.

Algernon:
I haven't the smallest intention of doing anything of the kind. To begin with, I dined there on Monday, and once a week is quite enough to dine with one's own relations. In the second place, whenever I do dine there I am always treated as a member of the family, and sent down with either no woman at all, or two. In the third place, I know perfectly well whom she will place me next to, tonight. She will place me next to Mary Farquhar, who always flirts with her own husband across the dinner-table. That is not very pleasant. Indeed, it is not even decent; and that sort of thing is enormously on the increase. The amount of women in London who flirt with their own husbands is perfectly scandalous.

Gwendolyn:
Well, to speak with perfect candor, Cecily, I wish that you were fully forty-two, and more than usually plain for your age. Ernest has a strong upright nature. He is the very soul of truth and honor. Disloyalty would be as impossible to him as deception. But even men of the noblest possible moral character are extremely susceptible to the influence of the physical charms of others. Modern, no less than Ancient History, supplies us with many most painful examples of what I refer to. If it were not so, indeed, History would be quite unreadable.

Versions of these Wilde speeches lined-out, as well as other challenging sections of heightened prose for extra practice, are available in the Support Material online at www.routledge.com/9781032695297.

IDENTIFYING RHETORIC, RHETORICAL HOOKS, AND MAPPING IT OUT

IDENTIFYING RHETORIC: LANGUAGE AS ARGUMENT

If the reason we use language is to communicate, the reason we use rhetoric is to produce an effect. That is, we use rhetoric to make an impression or persuade someone, either in an argument or as part of a conversation. There is a fundamental rhetorical aspect of language that's part of how we form our thoughts, and certainly more so in dramatic works, like plays or songs. Rhetoric is as central to heightened text as it is to our daily language. It's a mode of thought, not simply decorative language, it reveals a rationale, a purpose, and, at times, a strategy. Rhetoric might employ figures of speech like metaphors, similes, and oxymorons; devices such as antithesis, imagery, repetition, and lists; or compositional techniques like narration or exposition; and elegant or blunt persuasive language. Rex Gibson, in his handbook, *Teaching Shakespeare,* writes that "Rhetoric involves all the ways of using language that make it more eloquent and convincing," that we "use rhetoric to gain the confidence of listeners, and appeal to their reason, their emotions, and their imagination."

Imagine you're a parent who has to get your young child in the car to go to a dentist appointment. "Why?" the child responds. Now you have to employ some skill and some rhetoric (persuasive language) to achieve your objective, since they don't like the dentist. You have to make choices about what to say that will help move things along with your end goal in mind: a smooth transition from the house to the car. Now, imagine a few variations of what might come next, each employing rhetoric as well as a different action or tactic:

- (I Remind You) "I told you this morning, we're going to the library to get more books after your dentist appointment."
- (I Sugar Coat It) "It's a beautiful day! There's so much to do!"

- (I Conceal It or I Control You) "Because I said so. Let's go!"
- (I Tease You) "Because the house is on fire!"

In each of these cases you make a rhetorical choice, probably unconsciously, for how to deal with the inquisitive child and what might be a frustrating situation. Everything you say isn't rhetorical. If the house was really on fire, it would be literal. You choose your words carefully, especially if you are trying to be strategic.

Shifting to heightened text, let's take a look at the rhetoric and rationale employed in Iago and Emilia's brief exchange, in which both of them have a stake in the matter at hand, but Emilia is in the dark about Iago's true motive:

EMILIA: If it be not for some purpose of import, give't me again,
Poor lady, she'll go mad when she shall lack it.

IAGO: Be not acknown on't. I have use for it.
Go, leave me!

Emilia's rhetoric qualifies her willingness to give him the handkerchief since it's such an important memento to Desdemona. She has to give a reason to disobey her husband directly – it will cause distress to her friend that isn't necessary if it's only for some trivial purpose.

Iago has to tread carefully here, needing his response to be both firm and dismissive, but not encouraging any further suspicion. He has to lead her on a bit, so she isn't made more suspicious.

Identifying these rhetorical underpinnings like logic, ethics, and emotions, allows actors to wield the rhetoric as a character choice. This enables actors to articulate complex thoughts with clarity and to experience the way these characters think and speak. How a character speaks provides a wealth of information, and ultimately become tools for the character to pursue their objective, as well as the actor.

RHETORICAL PROGRESSIONS AND HOOKS

When one thing leads to another, or when an initial image or metaphor becomes the focus, is further developed and finally arrives at a satisfying conclusion, it is called a **rhetorical progression.** In the

Iago speech that follows, we see that imagery and metaphor can be part of this complexity:

> I will in Cassio's lodging lose this napkin
> And let him find it. Trifles light as air
> Are to the jealous confirmations strong
> As proofs of holy writ. This may do something.
> The Moor already changes with my poison:
> Dangerous conceits are in their natures poisons,
> Which at the first are scarce found to distaste,
> But with a little art upon the blood
> Burn like the mines of sulphur.

The **rhetorical progression** begins with the physical possession of Desdemona's handkerchief, and it becomes a **rhetorical hook** when he finally gets it in his hand: a thin, yet important bit of fabric, which he terms "this napkin," and then continues to tell us that "trifles light as air" – like this handkerchief – are going to be heavy, solid proof, like the Bible, of Desdemona's guilt. As we learned in Chapter 5, **hooks** are what we need from one line to make the next line happen. This points up the **antithesis** (or contrast) – that what seems like an insignificant thing, is actually going to be huge! Iago's "This may do something" is still about the handkerchief, and then he provides the rationale, that Othello is already starting to be poisoned through his "dangerous conceits." Now the metaphor is that the napkin is a poison, and then some detail is provided about how his poison works: one hardly notices it at all, until it's too late.

In song lyrics, the rhetorical progression can be served up as repeated phrases, building dramatic tension up to a reveal, as in these lyrics from the 1927 Cole Porter standard, "*I'm in Love Again*":

> Why am I just as happy as a child?
> Why am I like a racehorse running wild?
> Why am I in a state of ecstasy?
> The reason is 'cause something's happened to me.

The writer poses three rhetorical questions, "Why….? Why…? Why…?" all following a similar structure, all with the same answer, expressed in the fourth line, followed by the chorus of the song: "I'm in love again." The rhetorical build is achieved by the repetition of a question. The first few words are kept the same, but the ending is changed, building to a resolution at the end of the first verse, setting up the expectation for another round (or more) in the same vein. The pattern becomes a method for communicating that is satisfying and effective for the listener, as the musical and rhetorical progression resolves.

Though rhetoric is satisfying and effective for the audience, for the actor, it is a way to go deeper into the actions they are playing by fusing those choices with the power of the language. Here is an example:

Later in the play, **Othello's rhetorical progression builds his argument of Desdemona's guilt** as he strives to shame her by marshaling images in lists, repeating phrases over and over to make his point. In the right margin, as part of creating a paraphrase, I've listed some of the ways he's conjuring up language as rhetorical weapons to cause her harm:

TEXT	Rhetorical Weapons
Had it pleased heaven	*Hypothetical scenario*
To try me with affliction; had they rain'd	*terrible things*
All kinds of sores and shames on my bare head,	*illness, shame*
Steep'd me in poverty to the very lips,	*robbed of livelihood*
Given to captivity me and my utmost hopes,	*slavery and bondage*
I should have found in some place of my soul	*power of redemption*
A drop of patience; but, alas, to make me	*forgiveness*
A fixed figure for the time of scorn	*laughing stock*
To point his slow unmoving finger at!	*public humiliation*
Yet could I bear that too; well, very well:	*persuasive rebuttal*
But there, where I have garner'd up my heart,	*embodiment*
Where either I must live, or bear no life;	*exaggeration*
The fountain from the which my current runs,	*imagery*
Or else dries up; to be discarded thence!	*embellishment*
Or keep it as a cistern for foul toads	*gross simile/metaphor*
To knot and gender in! Turn thy complexion there,	*calling upon a deity*
Patience, thou young and rose-lipp'd cherubin,--	*challenging the gods*
Ay, there, look grim as hell!	*anger/emotion/ giving up*

A moment later this exchange takes place, as Desdemona, exasperated, replies, "**Alas, what ignorant sin have I committed?**" as if she's asked, "What have I done?" Othello misinterprets this line as a confession and shouts back, "**What committed? Committed?**" as if he's saying, "You admit it! You did it!" Her reply was wholly rhetorical, and his response entirely literal.

MAKING A RHETORICAL MAP

To help point up the rhetorical devices in a section of text, we draw **a rhetorical map.** This helps the actor track the images, ideas, and strategies in the playwright having chosen **these particular words** for the character to say at this moment. The rhetorical map uses just the text, without any of the homework like scansion or operatives marked, so that the only thing it points up is how the language is being mustered to make the arguments and points. An actor might make observations about phrases that are repeated, or dramaturgical notes about how a line connects to another event. It might look like a mess, but it'll be your mess.

Making a rhetorical map of your text (or scene) is a visual way of highlighting how the language connects to and clarifies the character's argument. It provides a clear picture of how rhetoric (using language as argument) is integrated into the action. We can mark all kinds of observations when making a rhetorical map, from how many times the character uses a particular word, or how it takes one form of a word and changes it into another, or how images, motifs, and metaphors are employed. Maybe your character says "God" 15 times in 22 lines; maybe they use a flower metaphor and then an insect metaphor. All of these things are worth acknowledging by marking them on a rhetorical map.

To make a rhetorical map, start to circle words and draw arrows to any other words that progress the use of language, metaphor, rhetoric or any other form of connection, like these two examples of the same section of text: (Figure 7.1):

ADVANCED SKILLS: PROSE, RHETORIC, AND RHYMING COUPLETS 173

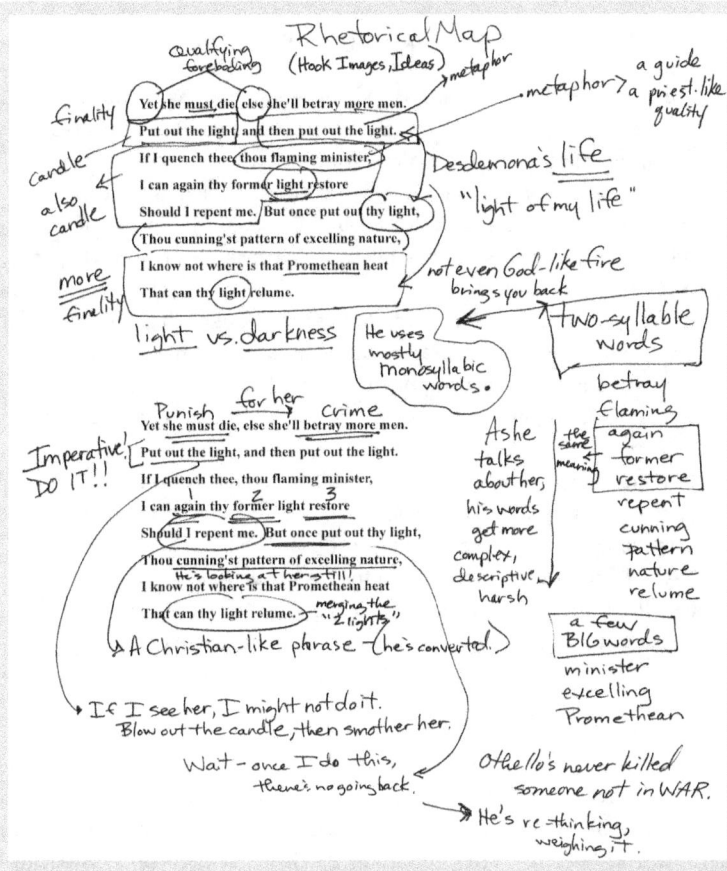

Figure 7.1 Sample Rhetorical Map from *Othello*.

> ### TRY IT! MAKE A RHETORICAL MAP
>
> Use this lively rhetorical exchange between King Richard and Queen Elizabeth from *Richard III* to create a rhetorical map. Read the speech aloud, then begin circling words, drawing arrows of connectivity to images, metaphors, phrases, rhetorical devices, religious references. Anything you notice or observe about the text is valid in a rhetorical map. It can be a mess: no one needs to make sense of it but you, so have fun!
>
> The goal is to see how many connections exist, what those connections are, how the character uses language to make their argument. This isn't about paraphrasing or finding operatives anymore, it's just about experiencing the text through a focus on the rhetoric.
>
> | | |
> |---|---|
> | **KING RICHARD** | Wrong not her birth; she is a royal princess. |
> | **QUEEN ELIZABETH** | To save her life I'll say she is not so. |
> | **KING RICHARD** | Her life is safest only in her birth. |
> | **QUEEN ELIZABETH** | And only in that safety died her brothers. |
> | **KING RICHARD** | Lo, at their birth good stars were opposite. |
> | **QUEEN ELIZABETH** | No, to their lives ill friends were contrary. |

A rhetorical map is like a combination of a Word Find puzzle and "Where's Waldo?" – what can you discover, what rises up, what's in there that you didn't notice before when doing your paraphrase? When I am preparing to direct a play or a musical, I do a few readings of the text aloud, at least one of which is just to dig into the language. I make hundreds of little rhetorical maps on my script – not every single line, perhaps – but wherever I spot something interesting and I think "wow, look what's happening with the text here!"

The Support Material at www.routledge.com/9781032695297 contains a rhetorical map of this brief excerpt and shares examples from an actor's rhetorical map.

HEIGHTENED LANGUAGE AND CONNECTED SPEECH: "THIS IS THE WAY WE TALK"

Arthur Lessac, a pioneer in the training of the human voice as a natural and instinctive instrument, believed in developing skills that energized the text through integrated engagement of the body and voice. One aspect of his work that applies effectively to acting heightened text, whether in verse or prose, is called "linking." The idea behind linking is that we have a normal pace of talking and, more importantly, what I call a **pace of understanding**. I have to speak a line a certain way for you to understand me. I don't have to pronounce every sound and consonant with precision necessarily, since that may not be what I am trying to convey. Being precise or correct isn't always the best way to convey an idea. If your high school language arts teacher told you to pronounce all your consonants, especially the ones at the beginning and the ends of words, then your reply might sound like this: "But I don't talk that way." A high level of precision on all the [t] sounds makes the speaker seem angry, defensive, or both. Without realizing it, most of us employ **connected speech** (which Lessac calls "linking") as a way to communicate effectively without sounding obnoxious or pretentious, and if we're acting, not drawing attention to the sounds over the meaning of the words or the ideas we strive to convey. Connected speech reflects the way we talk. Actors need to ensure that their characters do the same, rather than sound like they are over-articulating or projecting in order to be understood and heard (unless that's the character's intention and tactic!).

Gary Logan, a professor of voice, speech, and text at Carnegie Mellon University, devotes a significant portion of the introduction to his extraordinary book, *The Eloquent Shakespeare: A Pronouncing Dictionary for the Complete Dramatic Works with Notes to Untie the Modern Tongue* to providing an overview of connected speech as it relates to heightened text, with particular attention paid to the letter [t]. Simply pronouncing things properly is not an acceptable way to give voice to a three-dimensional character. People (and therefore characters) use **idiolects** – the specific way particular people sound. Though theatre began with a tradition of elocution, with actors standing at the front of stages pronouncing the text correctly, with modern sensibilities came more and more naturalistic acting. Playwrights followed suit, and now characters speak in regional dialects, far more specific than the broad categories of accents in which many of us were trained. Logan's book, which can be found in many professional and academic rehearsal rooms as a primary reference, provides supportive and clear instruction and guidance about how to navigate text and sounds.

In life, as we speak, we pause for any number of reasons: to think, to breathe, to change our minds, to punctuate our meanings, or for particular emphasis. Words are connected until the stream of sound is broken for any of these reasons. **Connected speech** allows for clarity and precision without sounding too careful or affected, which would only draw attention to how we are speaking rather than to what we are saying. Linking means we connect one sound to the next, which achieves easier and more natural sound progression, and it minimizes wear and tear on the throat and vocal folds. This is true even when speaking in large open spaces without amplification, because the focus is on moving the sound forward (and to the receiver).

This approach, to connect speech, keeps the ideas intact and allows the actor to embody the text as the character, not merely as an actor trying to say things properly. Voice, speech, dialect, and text teachers, like Gary Logan, Catherine Fitzmaurice, Phil Timberlake, David Smukler, Krista Scott, Andrew Wade, Kate Wilson, Ralph Zito, Tim Monich, and Paul Meier, and the remarkable resources they have developed, can support actors who are working to improve their speech, vocal resonance, and eliminate habits such as glottal attacks (landing hard on a vowel sound at the beginning of a word) or upward inflection, and to work with tools such as linking, the International Phonetic Alphabet and dialects. I have provided some recommended titles at the end of this chapter and in the Bibliography as further resources for exploration. Since the focus of this book is on the acting of heightened text, this provides only a distant view of the landscape, hoping that those who desire more knowledge and skill, can pursue the work of the experts in that field.

TACKLING RHYMING COUPLETS

Thinking back to Chapter 1, we identified nursery rhymes as one of the first kinds of heightened text we encountered. A **rhyming couplet** is two consecutive lines that connect to the same idea, or make a particular point, or begin a train of thought that continues for some time, but use a rhyme of final syllables to punch up rhythm and tone. It is the most complex form of heightened text, and it is seen most often in song lyrics, classical plays, and verse poetry. Sonnets usually end with a couplet, serving as a final stamp or flourish. Rhyming couplets often appear at the end of a speech, like putting a literary bow on a package. They may signal that a character is leaving, or that they are finished with this topic or this situation. Rhyming couplets can also pepper an entire soliloquy, either for tragic or comic effect.

Here are a few examples of rhyming couplets at the end of a speech or scene:

From Queen Margaret *Henry VI, Pt. 3:*
Off with the crown, and with the crown his head;
And whilst we breathe, take time to do him dead.

From Isabella *Measure for Measure:*
I'll tell him yet of Angelo's request,
And fit his mind to death, for his soul's rest.

From Claudius *Hamlet:*
My words fly up, my thoughts remain below.
Words without thoughts, never to heaven go.

Entire scenes and plays are composed of rhyming couplets, displaying a level of artfulness in writing that requires a matching level of craft from actors. George T. Wright, in *Shakespeare's Metrical Art,* believed that Elizabethan audiences relished the ways in which the gravity of disciplined meter combined with the pleasure of patterned rhyme in dramatic speeches met the needs of the stage dialogue.

Luciana, in Shakespeare's *The Comedy of Errors,* Act III, scene ii is giving some advice to the man she thinks is her sister's husband. She advises him to be kind to Adriana, using an alternating-line rhyme scheme (ABAB):

> If you did wed my sister for her wealth,
> Then for her wealth's sake use her with more kindness:
> Or if you like elsewhere, do it by stealth;
> Muffle your false love with some show of blindness.

In the opening scene of *King Lear,* the King of France, the noblest suitor to Lear's youngest daughter, Cordelia, takes her hand following Lear's cruel dismissal of her:

> Bid them farewell, Cordelia, though unkind:
> Thou losest here, a better where to find.

Rhymes occur in the middle of verse lines as well (these are called internal rhymes) and can occur at any point, as in this example from Edgar Allan Poe's *The Raven:*

> While I nodded, nearly napping, suddenly there came a tapping,
>   As of someone gently rapping, rapping at my chamber door.
> "'Tis some visitor," I muttered, "tapping at my chamber door—
>   Only this and nothing more."

Contemporary music, from the heightened hip-hop of *Hamilton* to the pop lyrics of The Beatles, uses internal rhymes that highlight the shared sounds without being forced to come to a stop by placing the rhymes at the end. This has the effect of bringing the listener in, since they pick up on the sounds as part of the story.

Perhaps the greatest example of a play made up entirely of rhyming couplets is Richard Wilbur's 1955 translation of Molière's French epic, *The Misanthrope,* which was written in 1666. Wilbur, a future two-time recipient of the Pulitzer Prize, was on a fellowship to Paris in 1948, in the aftermath of World War II, where he happened to attend a performance at the Comédie-Française of the play. At a loss for how to break through a writing block, he decided to work on a translation of the play into English, in iambic pentameter (with some metric variations) and entirely in rhyming couplets.

In Wilbur's introduction to his translation, he offers this advice to readers (and players):

> "In short, trust the words. Trust the words to convey the point and person of the comedy, and trust them to be sufficiently entertaining.
>
> When Molière has a character repeat essentially the same thing in three successive couplets, it will have a very clear dramatic point: it will always have the intention of stabilizing the idea against the movement of the verse – and gives a sort of rhetorical pleasure.
>
> It is a convention of the play that its main characters can express themselves logically, and using the most complex grammar. Molière verse, which is almost wholly free of metaphor, derives much of its richness from argumentative virtuosity."

With most instances of rhyming couplets, especially those at the end of a speech or a scene, the second matched sound leaves an imprint of the character's thought, the scene that's just occurred, or their exit. Kristin Linklater, the esteemed vocal coach and teacher, in her book *Freeing Shakespeare's Verse*, writes:

> "Rules existed about how verse-speakers were supposed to handle rhyme, and for a long time the fashion was not to point up the rhyme, but to do everything one could to disguise them, as if they were embarrassing. Practice with rhyming couplets allows the rhyme to be heard, and sometimes pointed up, but to take a second place to sense. Acknowledging the power of rhyme and mastering it is as an instrument of one's craft removes the fear – *how* to do this is simply, to do it. The SOUND OF THE RHYME must be as effective as the SENSE OF THE WORD. The language is not separate from the story. It IS the story."

To align our work with these passionate, yet practical words of wisdom, we apply the lessons of our work with scansion, punctuation, hooking, and, most importantly, **operative words**. In other words, you already have the skills, just like in outdoor games, when running, stopping, and changing direction are baked in to the rules of most sports. This is a skill.

Most of the lines in Wilbur's translation are regular iambic pentameter. The most common variations from this are weak endings, though many lines have anapest feet [Ap] – those two little unstressed syllables followed by a strong stress – so they clip along at a pace, as in this example:

ALCESTE:

˘ ˘ / Ap ˘ / ˘ / ˘ ˘ / Ap ˘ /

If I <u>caught</u> my<u>self</u> be<u>having</u> in such a <u>way</u>,   12 syllables = Anapest in 1st & 4th foot

˘ / ˘ / ˘ / ˘ / ˘ /

I'd <u>hang</u> myself for <u>shame</u>, without <u>delay</u>.   10 syllables = Regular line

---

Since the lines will always rhyme (or be at least near-rhymes), the final syllables will always be stressed – except for weak endings, when the fifth foot has an extra unstressed syllable.

Pay particular attention to line endings and punctuation in order to discern the length of the thought, the opportunity for breath, and enjambed lines (when one thought continues to the next line without a break).

The same attention must be paid to the level of <u>emphasis</u> you give the rhyming words. This depends on what they require for **clarity of sense**. This is very important. Knowing which are the operative words helps us make choices about how hard we land on (or hit) the rhyme. When actors foster this practice, audiences often don't even realize the play is written entirely in rhyming couplets, they only experience the flourish of when the line, the rhyme, and the laugh land.

Imagine enduring a performance that had the same percussive rhythm hitting the rhyming syllable at the end of every line for over two hours. Imagine if an actor hit the rhyme as an operative word no matter what, as if every line-ending rhyme had to be a direct hit, like a nursery rhyme:

Celimene: Madam, I haven't taken you <u>amiss</u>;
            I'm very much obliged to you for <u>this</u>;
            And I'll at once discharge the <u>obligation</u>
            By telling you about your <u>reputation</u>.

(Please don't be that actor, playing the rhyming couplets as if they're a nursery rhyme!)

The basic discernment for artful work with rhyming couplets is **whether or not the rhyming words are also primary operative words** for the line. This is called a **"Direct Hit"** – or as they say in *Hamlet,* "a palpable hit." Give a <u>primary</u>-operative-word-level of emphasis to these words: the sense of the line depends upon them. If you identify <u>secondary</u> operatives within a Direct Hit on the rhyme, give those slightly less emphasis, as in this example:

Arsinoe: I <u>judge</u>, since you've been so <u>extremely</u> <u>tart</u>,
          That my <u>good counsel</u> <u>pierced</u> you to the <u>heart</u>.

If **the couplet is shared by two characters,** it could also be a **Direct Hit**, if **both rhymes are operatives:**

Philinte: Your <u>hatred's</u> very <u>sweeping</u>, is it <u>not</u>?
Alceste: Quite <u>right</u>, I hate the whole <u>degraded</u> <u>lot</u>.

These two friends trade the lead, the other listening so intently that not only does Philinte hook Alceste's line, they rhyme:

Alceste: How <u>dare</u> you <u>joke</u> about a <u>crime</u> so <u>grave</u>?
Philinte: What <u>crime</u>? How <u>else</u> are people to <u>behave</u>?

The line might contain **an operative word other than the rhyme**. In these instances, called an **"Indirect Hit,"** the rhyming word is treated with the same level of emphasis as any other regular word, or perhaps the rhyming word is given, at the most, a <u>secondary</u> operative level of emphasis. Sometimes, the first line of the couplet holds a direct hit, but the second does not, or vice versa. One character speaks a rhyme that's an operative/direct hit, followed by a line that puts the emphasis somewhere else (or an indirect hit), even though the line still rhymes:

Celimene: Madam, I <u>haven't</u> taken you <u>amiss</u>;
　　　　　　I'm very much <u>obliged</u> to you for this;
　　　　　　And I'll at once <u>discharge</u> the <u>obligation</u>
　　　　　　By <u>telling</u> you about <u>your</u> reputation.

Above, Celimene clarifies that she hasn't misunderstood "amiss," and instead thanks Arsinoe for the advice, with "obliged," only to turn the tables on her and "discharge" the debt by talking about what she's heard about her reputation with the emphasis on "your." The savvy-ness of Celimene must be matched by the level of detail with which the actor distinguishes whether the rhymes are also the operatives, and then makes the best choice accordingly.

Here's an example of **a couplet containing a direct hit, followed by an indirect hit** on the rhymes, because there's another word in the **second** line that's more important than the rhyme:

Philinte: With all <u>respect</u> to your <u>exalted</u> <u>notions</u>,
　　　　　It's often best to <u>veil</u> one's <u>true</u> emotions.

If there's **a weak ending the final syllable is unstressed, but still rhymes**, so that the end of the line has a particular rhythm (da-DUM-da). The final syllable isn't emphasized for the rhyme, since in that line the preceding syllable also carries that responsibility:

Arsinoe: Well, if you'd rather be a <u>dupe</u> than <u>doubt</u> her,
　　　　　That's <u>your</u> affair. I'll say no more <u>about</u> her.

The same is true in this next pleading entreaty for an "end," and perhaps some "leniency." Rather than emphasizing two words because they happen to be at the end of the line, and happen to rhyme, **they remain un-emphasized**:

**Philinte: Let's have an <u>end</u> of <u>rantings</u> and of <u>railings</u>,
　　　　　　And show some <u>leniency</u> toward <u>human</u> failings.**

This high level of attentiveness to operatives and sense-making guides us through the complex territory of rhyming couplets. Think of each operative word as a rung or foothold on a ladder of text you are climbing. These are the words we need most.

SUMMARY

In this chapter, we learned:

- the importance of having the right tool for the right job. With heightened verse, you scan; with heightened prose, you line-out;
- how to line-out prose text by thought, using punctuation as a guide;
- how to identify rhetoric in many forms and clarify its uses;
- how to make a rhetorical map;
- how to navigate rhyming couplets using operative weight to balance the hit on the rhyme.

RESOURCES FOR FURTHER EXPLORATION

Arthur Lessac's *The Use and Training of the Human Voice* provides an in-depth system for connecting the body and voice through textual exploration.

Cicely Berry's *The Actor and the Text* has sections that focus on the specific challenges of prose and rhyming couplets, as well as a significant number of exercises for working with heightened text.

Perhaps the most comprehensive book for actors on voice, speech, and text in English is Edith Skinner's *Speak with Distinction*. Loaded with pages of drills to reduce or eliminate glottal attacks (in words that begin with vowel sounds), learn the International Phonetic Alphabet, and apply skills to acting.

One of Edith Skinner's protégés is voice, speech, and text expert Gary Logan, whose book, *The Eloquent Shakespeare: A Pronouncing Dictionary for the Complete Dramatic Works with Notes to Untie the Modern Tongue*, provides an indispensable guide to speaking the speech.

Phil Timberlake is a voice, speech, and text teacher with experience in helping actors deepen their connection to the text. *https:// www.fitzmauriceinstitute.org/teacher-gallery1/phil-timberlake*

Kristin Linklater's *Freeing Shakespeare's Voice* is one of the few resources with a section on rhyming couplets. Her approach is practical and refreshing and builds on both of her earlier books.

The Importance of Being Earnest, by Oscar Wilde (1895), is available online at Project Gutenberg *https://www.gutenberg.org/files/844/844-h/844-h.htm*.

An excellent supplementary resource for a deep dive into rhetorical structures is *Shakespearean Rhetoric: A Practical Guide for Actors, Directors, Students and Teachers* by Benet Brandreth.

Rex Gibson, author of *Teaching Shakespeare: A Handbook for Teachers*, was an astute teacher of teachers, who knew how to engage them in making classical plays accessible to students. He saw the world reflected in Shakespeare's plays as inherently relevant to young people today. His approach and his exercises are refreshing and practical.

Dramatists Play Service holds the performance rights to Richard Wilbur's verse translation of Molière's *The Misanthrope*. James Magruder's brilliant prose translations by of Molière's *The Imaginary Invalid* and *The Miser* are also available there, as well as his nimble version of *The Triumph of Love* by Pierre Marivaux, which served as the basis for the Broadway musical, *Triumph of Love*, with music by Jeffrey Stock and lyrics by Susan Birkenhead.

HELPFUL ADVICE FOR CALLBACKS, REHEARSAL, AND PERFORMANCE

INTRODUCTION

In this final chapter, we experience how acting heightened text becomes collaborative. All the homework needs to translate effectively into choices in rehearsal, and then remain fresh and alive in performance, whether the run is one night only, a few shows, or an extended run or tour. The level of preparation required for heightened text informs what comes next. Preparation should be helpful but also flexible. Homework isn't about having the right answers, it's about asking great questions. Since expectations vary from one rehearsal room to another, whether the setting is academic or professional, this chapter helps actors navigate the journey from auditions and callbacks to rehearsal and performance with particular attention to ways in which heightened text impacts the process. Preparing sides for a callback, whether in-person or on a self-tape, has challenges and advantages, whether it's written in heightened text or not. Receiving feedback and incorporating it can run parallel to our own ideas and choices, or sometimes in opposite directions, so adjusting the mindset is critical. This chapter provides tangible ways to take a note, ask questions, and make new choices to support the creative process once the homework is completed. Getting from Point A to Point B in heightened text means we have to navigate moments of intimacy, stage violence, or a combination of both.

DOI: 10.4324/9781032695310-9

Learning skills and consent-forward practices means actors have a shared vocabulary that is valuable and applicable across industries of theatre, film, and other media. Everyone should contribute to the positive energy of the rehearsal environment to make it safe and supportive, figuring out how the text and the story can merge with action in repeatable and effective ways.

Whether the run is short or extended, heightened text stays relevant and fresh from continuing to play hooks in performance. Hooks become part of the fabric of playing the scene, even though we aren't saying them aloud anymore. The scansion, paraphrase, and operative work contribute to feeling grounded in something besides an arbitrary choice based on feelings or past experiences. Staying in the here and now is what keeps a performance alive – as if it's happening for the first time today at the matinee, or Sunday night after a long, seven-show week. Just as basketball players play by the same rules every time, actors operate within the boundaries of the text and the space, and with the decisions made over weeks in rehearsal, but remain present in every moment, seizing opportunities and making subtle, grounded choices that deepen over time. If you've ever had the chance to see a play in previews or opening night, and then come back and see it again nearer to closing, you may have observed the ease with which the story unfolded, the way the performances have grown rich and detailed over time.

In getting from the page to the stage, knowing that "possession is nine-tenths of the law," then I would posit that "preparation is nine-tenths of the work" of acting heightened text. On the other hand, homework only gets you so far, or, as I mentioned in the Introduction, you can't learn how to drive a car by reading a book. This chapter is about putting all that preparation, thinking, and hard work into use, starting with auditions and callbacks. Getting up on your feet in rehearsal is a step that leverages all the homework. We manifest the work now, with hard work, humility, and the support of others: the director and other actors, designers, stage managers, and all the artists, technicians and administrative contributors to the production. Everyone has a job to do, and part of that job is to foster an environment where each person can be seen, heard, and valued for their individual contributions to the betterment of the whole.

CRUNCH TIME: WORKING WITH HEIGHTENED TEXT IN AUDITION AND CALLBACK SITUATIONS

In audition and callback situations, actors who navigate heightened text confidently can apply those skills in crunch time using shorthand, rather than skipping steps. Strategies for success with a limited amount of prep time can be implemented from the moment a breakdown gets posted, or when you learn of an opportunity for a general audition by some other means. In today's ever-changing entertainment industry, actors are putting together self-tapes and submitting for all kinds of projects, from independent films to national tours. This may not solve all the access issues for actors, but it does create doors and windows by which the people making the decisions can see who's outside trying to get in. There are a few people in your corner who offer resources to support actors.

Brian O'Neil's landmark book, *Acting as a Business* (and its companion website), helps actors understand how the industry works. O'Neil emphasizes that an actor's skills with heightened text are a signal to agents, casting directors, and directors that the actor has training, focus, and discipline. They can be trusted to show up prepared to make dynamic choices grounded in the text and appropriate to the circumstances.

Jen Waldman, a brilliant acting teacher and life/career coach, believes the purpose of an audition is to book the room, not just the job. What that means is that an actor enters the space and seeks to make an impression, connects with the people on the project, does their best with their material, and leaves them wanting to work with that actor, even if it's not necessarily on this particular show.

Taking this long view – that establishing relationships is as important as booking jobs – can be a relief, and provide some perspective for those who get worked up about this or that audition. It's still exciting to get called back, and it would be nice if every single audition turned into a callback, and every callback turned into booking a gig, but actors quickly learn that is not the reality. Just like in culinary school, it's rare when the souffle turns out perfect on the first day, or every time. As actors, each audition or callback is like making a souffle, we want to get it just right. But changing how we measure success is important. "Booking the room" is one way to re-frame the outcome. This strategy sets actors up for measuring success from the experience, rather than from just the result.

The great acting teacher and mentor **Michael Samuel Kaplan** advises actors to focus on positive self-talk as soon as possible after the audition is over. Ask yourself, "What went well?" and come up with at least two or three things, such as "I met a new casting director, and had a positive interaction with the Artistic Director of the theatre, who I hadn't seen in a few years," "My introduction went smoothly, as well as the transition into the start of my first monologue," or "They had audible responses to some of the more complex moments in the second monologue, so I felt like they were engaged and listening." A little positive self-talk goes a long way. Now you can think of something you could work on for next time, whether it's a callback for this production, or for the next audition. "I rushed through the introductions a bit, and need to make sure I breathe and stay present," or, (a recent example from my own professional experience):

> When there are multiple sides to choose from, I should be sure to prepare a little bit on each one, rather than focus on just one in depth. They asked me to do the side for which I was the least prepared.

Lesson learned! This can become a post-audition ritual, setting aside time to process what happened, and then putting it all behind you whether or not you get a callback.

TRY IT! PREPARING FOR A GENERAL AUDITION (IN-PERSON OR VIA A SELF-SUBMISSION)

Here is a sample breakdown for a general audition specifically requesting heightened text, and some questions and suggestions for how to prioritize the steps to prepare for the audition. Respond to each prompt and get a sense of your readiness for this opportunity:

> *Please prepare one (1) classical monologue, preferably Shakespeare and in verse, and a contemporary monologue of your choosing. Total audition time should not exceed 3 minutes. Please bring your headshot and resume stapled together.*

1. Do you have a go-to Shakespeare or classical monologue in verse?

    Actors should have at least 2 monologues in verse prepared, and preferably already recorded as self-tapes. There is a list in the Support Material of suitable and age-appropriate verse monologues from Shakespeare if you need ideas for material at www.routledge.com/9781032695297. Choose something from a play you know or read the monologues from other plays for one that resonates with you. Select a couple of these monologues (both the classical and the contemporary ones) that, with preparation, will become like your favorite outfits in your closet: ready to wear, fit you well, and make you feel good in them. (You'll be wearing them a lot!) Get started on the homework and allow about a week to get it into audition shape.

2. Do you have a go-to contemporary monologue that serves as a contrast to the classical piece?

    Most actors have 2–3 contemporary monologues that reveal a depth of range in roles for a general audition. Having a piece with some comedic moments is important, as well as having ones written in a dialect if that is a skill you wish to showcase when called for. Collections of contemporary monologues can be a good starting point, but be sure to read the play as part of your homework. Use the line-out process to get things rolling and allow a week to go from preparation to audition-ready.

3. Are they under 3 minutes when performed together?

    Make sure you have timed your pieces and write the run times on your script. Some auditions call for one-minute monologues and others for 90 seconds or two minutes. Have some flexibility in terms of starting or ending points for time, rather than having to make internal cuts. Those cuts go right out the window if you're a little nervous before the audition.

4. Do you have copies of your headshot and resume stapled together?

    If you have your professional materials only in electronic versions, you'll need to print a few high-quality color copies of your headshot and be able to staple it to your resume, cut down to an 8x10 size. Some actors choose to have a mini-version of their headshot on their resume, which can be

> helpful as auditors are passing the materials back and forth during your audition. These tools are essential for them to remember you later, which is why it's important to actually look like your headshot. There are resources listed at the end of this chapter for support in career preparation if you are just getting started.

If the audition is for a self-submission, you will be recording the material and sending in a video file or a link. A helpful strategy in self-tapes is to replicate the energy and presence of being in the room as best you can in your recording, even if it's just in your slate or introduction. **Convey your warmth and essence of who you are before you launch into the material.** Many websites and how-to videos to support creating effective self-tapes are posted on the internet, and a few are listed below in the Resources for Further Exploration section.

Getting a callback is like receiving an invitation to an event, whether it's a pre-screen for a college or other training program or a professional production, they want to see more of you and your work. Though you may be asked to do your own material again, most likely you will be provided with "sides," which are short excerpts from the play to use as audition material. Approaching heightened text in a callback means **the homework has to be done efficiently and on a tight time schedule,** i.e. crunch time! Sometimes, actors get a call for an audition more than a day in advance, but often it can be much less. The amount of time between getting the sides and the callback appointment is crucial. Think about each situation as needing triage, like doctors in an emergency room, and determine how much time you have to prepare, what steps will be most helpful, and if any steps can be combined.

The sides and (hopefully) the full script may be included as an attachment to the callback request email. Always open them before you reply, to ensure that you are able to read and download them. The sides might be performed with a reader or another actor in the room. This is good to know in advance, so you can think about where your focus will be during the callback.

Start with the sides, reading them aloud a few times to get to know them. Double-check the punctuation and look for any cuts as you compare it to a published version of the script (if it wasn't provided). As you read it aloud, **listen for any scansion anomalies** that have significant impact, otherwise, **allow the regularity of the iambic pentameter to do its job**. If there are irregularities, mark them, and use that knowledge as you choose operatives. In this way, you're trusting the scansion, rather than skipping it. If something sounds wonky, scan it and mark it, so you tend to that turn in the road with specificity. Sometimes, sides are chosen because they have a tricky section, or some interesting beat changes, or there's something to respond to in the other character's lines. Casting directors and directors need the opportunity to see how actors handle the text, and also how they interpret the material, and what choices they make based on their level of preparation. **Paraphrasing is critical** here: make sure you know what the lines mean.

Combine the next two steps of homework as you read aloud, by underlining operative words (don't mess with secondary operatives unless you have more time), and marking beats with a double slash mark // and shifts with a single slash mark /. Use a pencil on a hard copy to make it easier to change your choices, and carry along in your hand as you get on your feet.

Enlist a friend in reading through the sides with you the day before the callback, after you've completed your homework (or if they're up for it, to work through the homework with you). If you have time, read through the text for beats and shifts with them, and then start hooking, focusing your energy on what you are hearing and what is happening with your partner. Let the hooking process lead you to make some choices about what you want, and how you might employ tactics to get it. Put these in the left-hand margin of your script and keep them active by using the "I _____ you" or "I _____" phrase to support your next line.

Lastly, now that you have some familiarity with the scene and what's at stake, get on your feet and play. Since you still have the script in your hand, be mindful to use it as a reference rather than reading from it. Keep your partner in front of you and slightly to one side (a typical reader configuration at an audition is seated at a music stand or at the table with script in hand). Strive to interact with them as much as possible, especially when you are listening and they are speaking. Resist the temptation to be "on hold" while they speak, strive to remain an active listener, responding and playing your hooks without saying them aloud.

After the callback, be sure to thank the reader and the team at the table. You can say something like "I hope you have a great rest of your auditions," or "It was wonderful to meet you." Once you're out the door, thank the person who's helping out, and as you're leaving, take a few minutes to run through the Kaplan positive-talk ritual: what went well? and what can I improve next time? Get on with your day and your life (easy to say, harder still to do). If you feel compelled to do so, a short follow-up email to the casting director, thanking them for bringing you in, and perhaps offering to serve as a reader at future auditions that require alacrity with heightened text.

Handling callbacks on short notice is like getting passed the ball in the game when you didn't expect it. There's always an "Oh!" factor to getting a message that you have a callback, and the next step is to assess how much time you have to prepare once you've seen the expectations of the sides. Nerves come with the territory but should not be exacerbated by a lack of preparation. Being nervous means that it matters. Being unprepared means that it doesn't. Prepare as best you can with the time you have. My hands shake a little when I'm nervous, so I print my sides or my music on card stock, or staple it onto a manila folder, so no one can see I'm shaking. A few years ago, I got a callback that required multiple sides, and the casting director told me to put the other folders down on the table where they were sitting while I did my first side. Only after my audition did I realize they were looking at my other sides – all my messy scribbles and notes. I got a call a week later, not to be cast in the role, but to be the text coach on the whole production! A door opened, and I jumped at the opportunity. **Book the room, if not the job.**

MANAGING EXPECTATIONS OF YOURSELF AND OTHERS

Though it may have little to do with heightened text *per se,* the advice that follows applies to how we collaborate and communicate with the creative environment. Rehearsals mark another beginning, when we bring what we know (and don't know) into a room to share with others in the same boat. In Damon Kiely's book *Play Directing: The Basics,* he focuses on the key responsibilities (and authority) of the director, as well as what expectations a director could have about their actors. One of the best tools for being successful is to learn how success will be measured, and what the expectations are for daily and periodic progress.

Here are three ways you can meet most anyone else's expectations in a rehearsal setting and four more practices to demand of yourself:

1. Show up on time. Be there where and when you're supposed to be.
2. Know the text; not just your lines, but the big picture and the nuanced details.
3. Bring ideas and choices, based on your homework, and yet be willing to try new things.
4. Listen to what is happening around you. The work is continuing even when you are not the focus. Stay in the room or on set when you can, or be offstage and remain aware.
5. Respect everyone in the room. Each person has a job to do, so respect their contributions and be gracious when mistakes are made. You will make some too, so be accountable and move on.
6. Respond with a positive word or phrase of acknowledgment every time you get a note. Try "Thank you," "Yes," "Got it," or "Heard." One of my former students enthusiastically said "100%!" every time I gave them a note. It made me want to give them more notes – because they wanted every moment to be better, more specific, more dynamic.
7. Take the note. Just do it. You can talk about it later (or not).

When I'm directing and an actor wants to talk about an idea they have about how to play a certain moment, I say, "Show me what that would look like." Have the courage to play a different choice, rather than spending time asking permission to try something new. That said, if it's the last take of a shot on a film set and they're losing the light, it's not the time to try something new. (See #4 above.) Being sensible and taking risks can happen at the same time – tennis players make great shots, but the ball still has to land **in bounds**.

Getting up on your feet usually occurs after a day or two of table work. On the other hand, some directors like actors to get up on their feet on the first day, getting a sense of the flow, and maybe just about wanting everyone to be active, instead of sitting around a table getting into their heads. Actors get to try their ideas without much pressure to be right or to perform. It allows the nerves to settle and can be a great deal of fun. Directors learn a lot about actors during these sessions, as they do in callbacks and auditions. This is why homework is important: it prepares actors for situations in which they are asked to explore. Preparation is like having a candle in a cave, especially with heightened text. Your ability to navigate the text reveals that you have done your work.

Following table work comes staging, when the director and other actors are figuring out where in the space everyone is at any given moment. Even if you know your lines, it's important to carry your script so you can write things down, so that you will remember your staging, as well as your exits and entrances the next time you work on the scene in rehearsal, which could be days (or weeks) from now. When that time arrives, and the scene is on the call sheet for a working session, that's when you should begin to work without your script in hand. This is no longer the time to be reading your lines. Having done your homework, especially hooking, you will likely know your lines without having had to spend time memorizing them. You have built the bridge you need to start connecting and collaborating with others.

MAKING ADJUSTMENTS AND DISCOVERIES IN FRONT OF OTHERS: EMBRACE A GROWTH MINDSET

One of the most endearing qualities in an actor (or partner, student, or friend) is a growth mindset. To be seen learning in front of others is a generous act. In classes and rehearsals, to listen and adjust in collaboration with others is a gift. Having a sense of humor in situations when things don't go as planned makes the difference between an adventure and an ordeal.

With heightened text, especially, for example, a classical play in the public domain, the director or dramaturg might be making some cuts. Sometimes, this also happens when working on a new play, because the playwright is involved in making revisions based on what they see in rehearsals and previews. Often, lines are cut for the sake of length of the show, and these happen before we've been provided with a script. If there's a section of text that's been cut, and during your homework, you discover something key may have been removed, you might choose to raise it, and propose another section of your text with the same number of words or lines to swap out in exchange for the lines you believe could be necessary. These requests can be made outside of rehearsal time, perhaps prompted by an email with the context for the change and the offer of substitute text. If an actor knows a production is concerned about length, they might propose cuts if a speech seems to repeat something that's already been said. Think of the amount of time of a show (perhaps two hours) as if it were the family budget for groceries. Little things add up. Being an actor who understands the need to make cuts helps the production meet its budget.

A line of iambic pentameter verse spoken at a pace of understanding takes 3 seconds: "The duke is very strangely gone from hence." If I need to cut a minute off a scene, I need to cut the equivalent of 20 lines of text. For two minutes, it's 40 lines, etc. For a production I directed of *A Midsummer Night's Dream,* the audience was middle-school children, and the district required that the show be under 90 minutes in order to get all the kids back on buses in time for lunch at school. Even though I'd cut the text to about 80 pages, I assumed that at 20 lines per page double-spaced, I would be well under the time limit, but this was not the case. There was action, music, and laughs, all of which took up time on stage. After a couple of rehearsal runs, it was still running long, and I had no choice but to cut another 300 lines to shave off 15 minutes, mainly from a few longer scenes. (Yikes! 300 lines that the actors had so carefully prepared! How did the cast members handle it, you might ask?) Let me suggest how to respond if you find yourself in this situation, using how the actors playing Helena and Demetrius responded in this particular moment.

Knowing that the production needed to cut time, these two actors, who may have been sad to lose some of their lines, tried the revised scene back and forth a few times and said, "That's a great cut!" The actors got it: helped me do my job, and adapted. The scene was clearer, accomplished the next step in the storytelling, and shaved a chunk off the overall run time.

TAKE THE NOTE: GIVING AND RECEIVING FEEDBACK WITHOUT BLAME OR SHAME

As mentioned before, part of the growth mindset involves accepting feedback, focus, challenges, withstanding setbacks, and sustained effort. If we can be mindful of how we give and receive feedback, it can help make the rehearsal process be not only efficient and productive but also imaginative and playful. In the midst of rehearsals, and especially at technical rehearsals, there are always delays, setbacks, and moments that need to be run again and again, either for safety reasons, or to get the timing just right. Focusing on what needs to be done, not why, or how, or who is responsible, helps foster a healthy environment. We can model how to respond with our actions, by staying away from the blame-game, which is unnecessary and, most importantly, unhelpful.

When a break in rehearsal happens, either because the stage manager calls it, or the director stops the action, actors can jump too easily to a "what did I do wrong?" shame mentality, dreading the note and interpreting it as criticism. Even though a director might express their feedback sternly, "No, no – let's go back and get it right," getting past the negative is important. If we can get beyond the reflexive negative self-talk, we have a chance to discover the real note. Our goal as actors is always to hear the note, and then incorporate the note.

When I was cast in a production of Noel Coward's *Blithe Spirit* the director said to me, "Catherine, darling, could you take that tray upstage right of the sofa instead of downstage since everyone else is standing over to the left?" What I heard was "Catherine, you silly little girl, why can't you see what's happening and go the other way in order to balance the stage picture?" My interpretation wasn't helpful, and it took me into an even more negative spiral. The role was challenging enough (lots of props), and I felt fortunate just to get the Cockney dialect landing in this scene, much less navigating all the action on stage. What I had missed was that the director was expressing warmth (using "darling" was the signal), they'd realized they had staged the scene badly, and needed me to adjust in order to fix it. It wasn't about me at all.

I share this anecdote to make the point that when some actors get a note from the director, their first response is shame: to go into a negative-self-talk spiral, thinking, "I'm a terrible actor." Their second thought might assign blame: "The director has no idea what they're doing." Both of these reactions are unnecessary, and worse, unhelpful. The third and most helpful response is "What's the note?" If actors can find a way to get through the first two stages in a split second, and get to the third, the process will be less stressful, more productive, and time better spent on improving the work, rather than investing in the judgment of how we feel about the work.

In Timothy Gallwey's book *The Inner Game of Tennis,* he emphasizes adapting the mindset to focus on doing, rather than criticizing:

> Getting it together mentally involves the learning of internal skills: how to get the clearest possible picture of the desired outcomes, how to trust yourself to perform at your best and learn from both successes and failures, and learning to see non-judgementally – that is, to see what is happening rather than merely noticing how well or how badly it is happening.

Applying Gallwey's theory to acting heightened text, as soon as an actor understands the note, it's their job to incorporate it the next time, whether it's in two minutes or two weeks. In working rehearsals, an actor might ask, "If we have time, could we try that moment again?" or "We are getting a little tangled up on this exit, could we go back?" and see what happens.

Regardless of whether there's time to run it again or not, the appropriate response to getting a note from a director, stage manager, or other member of the creative or production team is "Yes, thank you, that's so helpful." Any version of that positive, affirming statement helps keep the process moving forward. I often add, "that's a great note," which helps me reinforce that the goal is making the moment clearer and more specific. This is not about me. If I am the director, whether it's an actor, designer, the sound board op, or stage manager that offers me some feedback, I say exactly the same thing – "that's a great note," and then when I give the note, I credit the source. Good ideas can come from anywhere, and I appreciate when people in the room feel comfortable asking a question or checking in about something they've observed. The comments or questions can be written on a sticky note and handed to an assistant, or stuck on my music stand during a break – I know how scary it can be to think about approaching a director with a question. The important thing is to get the note, and be able to consider and implement it.

In general, a can-do approach is the best thing one might bring to the rehearsal. As the great director Wendy Dann says, "Be part of the focus, not part of the distraction," which I think applies in almost any group situation. Watch and learn. Pay attention to where the focus is in the scene (usually it's where the text is coming from) and gain awareness of how the ground-plan works by coming to earlier rehearsals in order to observe. A beginner's mind is full of curiosity and wonder. If you've seen the costume design in a presentation at first rehearsal, be proactive by wearing similar clothes you may have that support the role, a baggy cardigan, a pair of lace-up black boots, an apron. What can help put you in the physical life and status of the character as soon as possible? Establishing rapport with the other actors is important in building a sense of community in early rehearsals. Arriving on time (which means a few minutes early in order to be ready to work at the start of the call), being prepared for the rehearsal (which means reading the call sheet and reviewing any staging, prop or character notes from last time), and thinking about what tactics, intentions, and actions you might play (similar to an athlete visualizing their actions) are ways actors can energize a room. Making brief and supportive comments to other actors, like "you really went for it," or "I saw that adjustment you made from last time," shows that you are invested in the whole. These aren't notes – that's not your job – but they are a way for you to be helpful as a teammate. Watch the way a team behaves in sports when things go well and when they go awry, in both instances, they come together and support each other, whether it's a missed free throw in basketball, or a corner kick goal in soccer. Theatre is not an individual activity; it takes a lot of people to make it happen. Respect the contributions of everyone in the room and show appreciation and gratitude.

CONSENT-FORWARD ARTISTS: INTIMACY AWARENESS IN PRACTICE

In heightened text and all dramatic works, plays, films, musicals, and operas, there are moments of intimacy that require special awareness and a consent-forward approach. This was not always the practice. When affection, kissing, nudity, or simulated sexual acts were portrayed on stage, there were few, if any guidelines in place. Change was needed, and long-overdue. With the "#Me too" movement, initiated in 2006 by survivor and activist Tarana Burke, the 2017 reckoning in the entertainment industry created a pathway for change. The attention now paid to how moments of intimacy are staged is equivalent to dance and stage combat, with trained professionals present who establish practices and protocols that keep artists safe as they enact truthful behavior in imaginary circumstances. In some productions, the resources may be limited, which means actors, directors, and stage managers need a consent-forward practice. While there are different organizations providing support, training, and resources, many of the guiding principles are shared: grounding the choreography in the context of the text, urging communication at all levels of the process, gaining informed consent from those involved, and finding closure at the end of the work.

Actors need a basic understanding of intimacy protocols in the same ways they need basic stage combat skills and movement training. These come with the territory in acting heightened text. Nuanced and embodied attention to the words is rendered meaningless if the actions and physical movements required in the scene are done recklessly or gingerly. Actors must understand, demonstrate, and practice the way they make contact or create the illusion of it in all of these circumstances, including rehearsals, fight calls, and put-in rehearsals if needed. If a play is being staged in masks, whether it's *Medea* or *The Servant of Two Masters,* the company will likely spend some time with professionals who will share the history, care, and practices of these traditions. If a film or play involves firearms or stunts, there is an expectation that safe and appropriate training will be provided. Ask about these things early on in the process if they are not expressly stated: will there be padding in the costume in order to cushion my fall? May I have knee pads to wear? Is there mouthwash available for those engaging in intimate moments? Is there nudity? Where will the quick changes be happening? You don't have to be a member of a union to earn the right to a safe workplace (though the performing unions have made it exponentially better for all).

SUMMARY

In this final chapter, we learned:

- how to bring the homework effectively into auditions, callbacks, and rehearsals;
- how to prepare sides for a callback, whether in person or a self-tape has challenges and advantages;
- how to keep the material fresh in performance;

- how to manage expectations, and contribute to a creative rehearsal room;
- how to receive feedback and incorporate notes;
- how to foster a safe and collaborative environment with consent-forward practices.

RESOURCES FOR FURTHER EXPLORATION

Books by actors, directors, agents, and casting directors can be tremendous resources about how the business really works, and helpful strategies for success. *Tips for Actors* by Jon Jory is a quick read and chock-full of one-paragraph tidbits that provide sage advice. *Play Directing: The Basics* by Damon Kiely gives actors a chance to walk a mile in the director's shoes and provides some important perspectives to consider. Brian O'Neil's *Acting as a Business* is an eye-opening look at how to get inside information and act on it, taking responsibility for your own career. Brian is an expert in helping actors navigate the business aspects of a career in the arts.

Here are some organizations and websites that provide training and education in stage combat and intimacy:

SAFD: **Society of American Fight Directors**
https://www.safd.org/train/training-with-the-safd/

IDC: **Intimacy Directors and Coordinators**
https://www.idcprofessionals.com/

The IDC mission is "to equip every institution and individual artist in the entertainment industry with the resources and education needed to create a culture of consent in which intimate stories can be told with safety and artistry."

TIE: **Theatrical Intimacy Education** https://www.theatricalintimacyed.com/workshops for "everyone who wants to be better at being in the room."

Cheek to Cheek Intimacy https://www.cheektocheekintimacy.com/

Their motto is: "Set the Container. Transform Stress. Free up Artistry."

More Information on the **#MeToo Movement** can be found at: https://metoomvmt.org/

Jen Waldman Studio offers courses, community, coaching, and podcasts with a positive mindset to the artistry and the industry. https://www.jws.community/podcast

Brian O'Neil, *Acting as a Business* http://www.actingasabusiness.com/

AEA: **Actors Equity Association** is the labor union for actors and stage managers in live theater. Their website contains information about their history and services: https://www.actorsequity.org/resources/

Michael Samuel Kaplan http://michaelsamuelkaplan.com/teaching/ Michael Samuel Kaplan is a coach and teacher based in New York City. His private coaching and classes (some are available online) guide actors to expressive, connected performances.

A FEW FINAL THOUGHTS

All dramatic text is heightened text. The only tools in this book that are unique to verse are those that deal with scansion and rhyming couplets (just as a driving manual is about every vehicle with a steering wheel, brakes and a rear-view mirror, not just how to drive a sports car or a pick-up truck). The same is true for all kinds of text – if spoken aloud it will benefit from analysis, infusion of energy, choosing operative words, and identifying beats and shifts. Playing actions and tactics levels up the engagement by focusing on activating our intention and how it's landing on others. Actors who employ hooking and active listening will seem more grounded in the work, and perhaps more at ease in taking risks and making more specific choices, since they have become so invested in the scene, rather than just their own lines. Classical plays, as they are often called, were once new plays. They remain with us today because the messages are still relevant and have the power to move us, whether it's the sacred power of Sanskrit, the melodic complexity of Sondheim, the depths of the human condition of Shakespeare, the political bite of Moliere, or the chilling reverberations of August Wilson.

Heightened text keeps the stakes high, by requiring levels of precision with regard to the physical, vocal and emotional demands of the material. The actor who can perform heightened text can perform anything. Working with this kind of complexity supports trusting simplicity from the language out.

In acting heightened text, we ride the thoroughbred racehorse of language. As actors, we have a responsibility to understand it, to see what it is capable of, and how it requires us to rise to those challenges. The language is not in the way, the language **is** the way.

SUPPORT MATERIAL AVAILABLE AT: WWW.ROUTLEDGE.COM/9781032695297

- Practice Monologues in Verse and Prose
- Practice Scenes in Verse
- Example of a hooked script of Catesby and Hastings scene from *Richard III*
- Detailed examples of text homework, including Given Circumstances, Paraphrasing, Operatives, Rhetorical Maps
- Line-Out examples from *As You Like It* and *The Importance of Being Earnest*
- A list of action verbs as a starting point for practicing playing actions and tactics

APPENDIX 1: GEEK-OUT ON SCANSION IAMBIC PENTAMETER REVIEW SHEET

Most of Shakespeare's verse is written in **regular iambic pentameter**, which means:

- ten alternating unstressed (light) and stressed (strong) syllables: (˘ /)
- organized in 5 "feet" of two syllables each = ten syllables per line.

A line of **regular** iambic pentameter begins with a weak stress (˘) and ends with a strong stress (/).

One Line = 5 feet of (˘ /), each **foot** has 2 syllables, the first is weak, the second one is usually strong.

      ˘ / ˘ / ˘ / ˘ / ˘ /
   Da dum da dum da dum da dum da dum

OR: ˘ / ˘ / ˘ / ˘ / ˘ /
   The duke is very strangely gone from hence. *Measure for Measure*

APPENDIX 1: GEEK-OUT ON SCANSION IAMBIC PENTAMETER REVIEW SHEET

Iambic = (˘ /)   Light stress followed by strong stress
(Regular foot)

˘ / ˘ / ˘ / ˘ / ˘ /
I never did incense his majesty

˘ / ˘ / ˘ / ˘ / ˘ /
Against the Duke of Clarence, but have been

˘ / ˘ / ˘ / ˘ / ˘ /
An earnest advocate to plead for him.   *Richard III*

VARIATIONS FROM REGULAR IAMBIC

Trochee = (/ ˘) Strong stress followed by light stress
(Reversed foot)

Trochees occur when the strong stress of a word (or its place in the line) requires it:

/ ˘ ˘ / ˘ / ˘ / ˘ /
Justice herself to break her sword. Once more;   *Othello*

The word "justice" scans (/ ˘). It doesn't make sense to scan it as regular (˘ /). This is a **fixed trochee**.

Trochees can also occur by CHOICE – because the MEANING of the line will be clearer by switching the stress of a particular word or part of a word:

˘ / ˘ / / ˘ ˘ / ˘ /
Upon my knees, what does your speech import?   *Othello*

This line might seem fine using regular iambic pentameter, but the switch to a trochee on "what" gives her confusion greater emphasis.

Trochees are very common in the first foot of a line, or after a break or punctuation.

/ ˘ ˘ / ˘ / ˘ / ˘ /
Fixed: Dangerous conceits are in their natures poisons *w* *Othello*

˘ / ˘ / ˘ / / ˘ ˘ / ˘
Choice: To be or not to be, that is the question.   *w* *Hamlet*

Spondee = (/ /) Two strong stresses in the same foot. Both words (or syllables) are EQUALLY important. The character is being very clear, adamant, or angry.

     /   / ˘ / ˘ ˘ /   / ˘   /
<u>Four lag</u>ging winters and <u>four wan</u>ton springs   *Richard II*

The spondees reinforce how long the banishment was and a quality of each season, matching in structure with a stressed first syllable, forming the spondee.

Pyrrhic =   (˘ ˘) Weak even stress on both syllables in the same foot.

  ˘ / ˘   /   ˘ ˘   / ˘ ˘   /
O balmy breath, that doth almost persuade   *Othello*

A pyrrhic foot is often formed by two smaller words, or the weak ending of one word in the same foot with a weak stress of another word. A two-syllable word in itself is rarely pyrrhic.

  ˘ ˘   /   /   / ˘ ˘ /   ˘   /
To be call'd whore? Would it not make one weep?   *Othello*

  ˘   / ˘ / ˘ / ˘ ˘   /   /
When in disgrace with fortune and men's eyes,   *Sonnet 29*

A pyrrhic foot precedes a trochee, spondee or relative-stress foot. If it were followed by a regular foot, you would have three unstressed syllables in a row, leaving nothing for the pyrrhic foot to "set-up."

Relative stress = (\ /) OR **(/ \ )** Two strong stresses, but one is given less emphasis (but still more weight than if it were unstressed)

  ˘ ˘   \   / / ˘   ˘ /   /   \
Yet she must die, else she'll betray more men.   *Othello*

  ˘   / ˘ / ˘ /   ˘   ˘   \ / ˘
Or came it by request, and such fair question, *w* *Othello*

After you decide a foot might be a spondee, it would be worth exploring if one of the syllables seems to carry more (or less) weight in terms of the meaning and change it to a relative foot.

    The **regular** stress mark (/) is always the stronger of the two within the foot. The **relative** stress mark (\ ) is the lighter stress (but still stronger than an unstressed syllable) compared to the stronger stress in the foot.

APPENDIX 1: GEEK-OUT ON SCANSION IAMBIC PENTAMETER REVIEW SHEET   207

A foot of verse would never contain an unstressed mark and a relative stress mark. "Relative" only relates to the stronger stress within the same foot.

VARIATIONS FROM PENTAMETER (MORE OR LESS THAN TEN SYLLABLES)

The most common variation from Pentameter (ten) is the use of 11 syllables in a line.

Weak Ending = (˘ / ˘) An 11-syllable line ENDING in an extra weak syllable.

˘ / ˘ / ˘ / / ˘ ˘ / ˘
To be or not to be, that is <u>the question</u>.   w   *Hamlet*

Elisions =   gen'ral   Using fewer syllables intentionally to say a word

Sometimes the line has more than ten syllables, but clearly the line ends in a strong stress, it requires an elision (smushing or compacting a word, eliminating "extra" syllables), similar to the way we say "I'll" instead of "I will" or "can't" instead of "cannot."

˘ / ˘ / ˘ / ˘ / ˘ /
And cleave the <u>gen'ral</u> ear with horrid speech.   *Hamlet*

"General" could be pronounced with 2 or 3 syllables, and in this instance, because we know that "speech" should be stressed, we elide "general" to 2 – and we MARK the elision by putting a slash mark through the elided syllable.

Names are often elided or lengthened to make the pentameter regular. You may see the same name elided in one line and lengthened in another. "Cassio" and "Iago" could be elided to 2 syllables or lengthened to 3 syllables, depending on the needs of the meter in each line:

˘ / ˘ / ˘ / ˘ / ˘ / ˘
Elided: I will in <u>Cassio</u>'s lodging lose this napkin   w   *Othello*

/ ˘ ˘ / ˘ / ˘ / ˘ / ˘
Lengthened: Now do I see 'tis true; look here, <u>Iago</u>   w   *Othello*

Epic caesura = ˘ᴱᶜ A weak ending foot (˘ / ˘) NOT located at the end of a line, but earlier in the verse line, and ALWAYS followed by any form of punctuation such as (, ; : . ? ! --).

˘ / ˘ / ˘ / ˘ / ˘ /
I can again thy former light restore

˘ / ˘ / ˘   ˘ / ˘ / / \
Should I repent me. ᴱᶜ But once put out thy light   *Othello*

An epic caesura MUST be **followed by punctuation**: full stop (. ! ?), comma, colon, or semi-colon.

Remember:

- When you find 11 syllables in a line, look at the ending syllable first.
- Is it unstressed? It's a **weak ending** (*w*).
- If you think the last syllable should be stressed, the line could require an **elision**.
- If you don't think an elision helps, then look for an **epic caesura (ᴱᶜ)**.

In **rare** instances, if any of those aren't possible, an 11-syllable line with a stressed ending could be an **anapest foot**: three syllables (2 unstressed and 1 stressed) within a foot.

Anapest foot: (˘ ˘ /) Two unstressed followed by one stressed syllable in a foot

˘   /   ˘ / ˘   / ˘ / ˘ ˘ / Anapest
The small'st opinion on my greatest misuse.   *Othello*

˘ / ˘ ˘ /Apst˘   /   \   / ˘ /
You made in a day, my lord, whole towns to fly   *Henry VI, Part 2*

˘ / ˘ / ˘ / ˘ ˘ /Apst˘   /
Herself, the land, and many a Christian soul   *Richard III*

Twelve-syllable lines = (A) or (+2) If the line contains an extra two syllables **in an iambic foot**. Also called "Alexandrine"

/ ˘ ˘ / ˘ / ˘ / ˘ / ˘ /   +2 A
Why should he call her whore? Who keeps her company? *Othello*

A twelve-syllable line may occur because of an **epic caesura AND a weak ending**.

```
           ˘    /  ˘ /  ˘    ˘  /  ˘ /  ˘  /  ˘
+2  The thoughts of people. ᴱᶜ She told her while she kept it
                                                   w        Othello
```

An epic caesura can also occur with two **shared lines**:

```
                       /     ˘  ˘ / ˘
+2  OTHELLO:      Swear thou art honest! ᴱᶜ
                    /  ˘   ˘  /  ˘  /   ˘
    DESDEMONA:  Heaven doth truly know it.   w      Othello
```

Thirteen-syllable lines = (A^f) +3 (˘ / ˘) The 13-syllable line contains an extra foot that is either a weak ending or an epic caesura or has an extra element of emphasis earlier in the line. Long lines are more common in the later plays (post-1604).

```
      ˘    /   ˘ ˘ / ap ˘  ˘ / ap ˘  /    ˘   / ˘
   Some powerful spirit instruct the kites and ravens   w
                                                  The Winter's Tale
   /   ˘/ ˘   /  ˘ /  ˘ /  ˘  /  ˘ /
   Now Ulysses,ᴱᶜ I begin to relish thy advice    +3
                                                  Troilus and Cressida
```

In **rare** occurrences, you may see **14- and 15-syllable lines.** These are simply longer variations of all that we have seen before in 11-, 12-, and 13-syllable lines, with 2 extra feet or two extra feet with a weak ending, anapest or epic caesura.

```
     ˘  ˘    / ap ˘    /  ˘   /   ˘ /  ˘    /  ˘ / ˘  /
   By the way we met my wife, her sister,ᴱᶜ and a rabble more.  15!
                                                  Comedy of Errors
    ˘  /  ˘ /   ˘  / ˘    /   ˘  /   ˘ /  ˘ /   ˘
   I cannot tremble at it. ᴱᶜ Were it toad or adder, spider  w   15!
                                                  Cymbeline
```

In **extra-double-secret-rare occurrences**, you will find strange patterns of scansion with unexplainable regular meter – ten syllables but in an unrecognizable order, or nine syllables. To explain these instances, I quote the great George T. Wright, from his spectacular book: *Shakespeare's Metrical Art* (University of California, Berkeley, 1988):

"The **headless line** – that is, a line with a **missing unstressed syllable before the first stressed one** – appears infrequently but at least once is every play that Shakespeare had a hand in. We mark it with a [^] in the position where the missing syllable occurs. Sometimes authors use this kind of line to convey a speaker's impatient or peremptory tone:

```
      /    ˇ  / ˇ      /   ˇ   /   ˇ  /
```
^Where the devil should this Romeo be?   (9)   *Romeo and Juliet*

```
     /   ˇ  /    ˇ  /  ˇ   /   ˇ  /  ˇ
```
^Set it down. Is ink and paper ready?   (10, but *w*)   *Richard III*

The **broken-backed line lacks an unstressed syllable after a midline pause.** The effect is temporarily trochaic, creating an effect of energetic resumption after a pause. The speaker of such a line often shifts from one kind of syntax to another such as a question to a command, a statement to an exclamation. Here, as in the headless line, the iambic current in the rest of the line is unusually strong."

```
    /   ˇ   ˇ      /    ˇ   /    /   ˇ   /   ˇ
```
Made to write 'whore' upon? ^What committed?
                                        (10, but ends *w*)   *Othello*

```
    ˇ    /   ˇ   /  ˇ   /    /  ˇ   /   ˇ   /
```
Struck Caesar on the neck. ^O you flatterers!
                                        (11, but not *w*)   *Julius Caesar*

```
   ˇ    /   ˇ    /     /  ˇ     /   ˇ   /   ˇ
```
Come hither, Count, ^do you know these women?
                                        (10, but ends *w*)   *All's Well*

Headless and **broken-backed** lines can occur with **shared lines** as well:

Headless:	/
OTHELLO:	^Ay. ˇ / ˇ / ˇ
DESDEMONA:	He will not say so.
	/ ˇ / ˇ /
OTHELLO:	No, his mouth is stopped. (11) *Othello*
Broken-backed:	ˇ / ˇ / ˇ /
ISABELLA:	As frankly as a pin.
	/ ˇ /ˇ /
CLAUDIO:	^Thanks, dear Isabel. (11) *Measure for Measure*

APPENDIX 2: VERSE MONOLOGUES FOR PRACTICE (IAGO, PORTIA, LEONTES)

IAGO *OTHELLO* ACT II, SCENE I

That Cassio loves her, I do well believe it;
That she loves him, 'tis apt and of great credit.
The Moor, howbeit that I endure him not,
Is of a constant, loving, noble nature,
And I dare think he'll prove to Desdemona   5
A most dear husband. Now, I do love her too,
Not out of absolute lust, (though peradventure
I stand accountant for as great a sin),
But partly led to diet my revenge,
For that I do suspect the lusty Moor   10
Hath leapt into my seat – the thought whereof
Doth like a poisonous mineral, gnaw my inwards;
And nothing can or shall content my soul
Till I am even'd with him, wife for wife,
Or failing so, yet that I put the Moor   15
At least into a jealousy so strong
That judgment cannot cure. Which thing to do,
If this poor trash of Venice, whom I trash
For his quick hunting, stand the putting on,
I'll have our Michael Cassio on the hip,   20
Abuse him to the Moor in the rank garb—
For I fear Cassio with my night-cap too –
Make the Moor thank me, love me and reward me

For making him egregiously an ass,
And practicing upon his peace and quiet   25
Even to madness. 'Tis here, but yet confused:
Knavery's plain face is never seen till used.   *Exit*

PORTIA *THE MERCHANT OF VENICE* ACT III, SCENE II

I pray you, tarry: pause a day or two
Before you hazard; for in choosing wrong,
I lose your company: therefore forbear awhile.
There's something tells me, (but it is not love),
I would not lose you; and you know yourself,   5
Hate counsels not in such a quality.
But lest you should not understand me well –
And yet a maiden hath no tongue but thought –
I would detain you here some month or two
Before you venture for me. I could teach you   10
How to choose right, but I am then forsworn;
So will I never be – so may you miss me –
But if you do, you'll make me wish a sin,
That I had been forsworn. Beshrew your eyes,
They have o'erlook'd me and divided me.   15
One half of me is yours, the other half yours,
Mine own, I would say; but if mine, then yours,
And so all yours. O, these naughty times
Put bars between the owners and their rights!
And so, though yours, not yours. Prove it so,   20
Let fortune go to hell for it, not I.
I speak too long; but 'tis to peize the time,
To eke it and to draw it out in length,
To stay you from election.

LEONTES *THE WINTER'S TALE* ACT I, SCENE I

Inch-thick, knee-deep, o'er head and ears a fork'd one! –
Go, play, boy, play: thy mother plays, and I
Play too, but so disgraced a part, whose issue
Will hiss me to my grave: contempt and clamor
Will be my knell. – Go, play, boy, play. – There have been,   5
Or I am much deceived, cuckolds ere now;
And many a man there is, even at this present,
Now while I speak this, holds his wife by the arm,
That little thinks she has been sluiced in's absence
And his pond fish'd by his next neighbor, by   10
Sir Smile, his neighbor. Nay, there's comfort in't
Whiles other men have gates and those gates open'd,
As mine, against their will. Should all despair
That have revolted wives, the tenth of mankind
Would hang themselves. Physic for't there is none;   15
It is a bawdy planet, that will strike
Where 'tis predominant; and 'tis powerful, think it,
From east, west, north and south. Be it concluded,
No barricado for a belly. Know't;
It will let in and out the enemy   20
With bag and baggage. Many thousand of us
Have the disease, and feel't not. – How now, boy!

APPENDIX 3: PARAPHRASE OF EMILIA AND IAGO SCENE

PARAPHRASE

OTHELLO ACT III, SCENE III (LINES 294–333)

TEXT	Paraphrase
EMILIA	Oh! (picks up Desdemona's hankie)
I am glad I have found this napkin;	Thank goodness I saw this handkerchief!
This was her first remembrance from the Moor.	This is the first present Othello gave her.
My wayward husband hath a hundred times	Iago, always up to something, hounds me
Wooed me to steal it; but she so loves the token –	to grab it for him; but she treasures it,
For he conjur'd her she should ever keep it -	apparently Othello said "never lose it!"
That she reserves it evermore about her	so she keeps it close always, like a friend.
To kiss and talk to. I'll have the work ta'en out	I have an idea – I'll get a copy of it made,

APPENDIX 3: PARAPHRASE OF EMILIA AND IAGO SCENE

And give't Iago: what he will do with it		*and give THAT to Iago. God only knows*
Heaven knows, not I,		*what he has in mind.*
I nothing know, but for his fantasy.		*I just want to make him happy.*
Enter IAGO.		*Oh! He's here, I'll hide it! (hides it)*
IAGO		
How now! What do you here alone?		*Why are you here and not with Desdemona?*
EMILIA		
Do not you chide, I have a thing for you		*Stop scolding! I have a present for you…*
IAGO		
A thing for me? it is a common thing –		*A present for me? It's so boring to --*
EMILIA		
Ha?		*Excuse me?*
IAGO		
To have a foolish wife.		*To have an idiot for a wife.*
EMILIA		
O, is that all? What will you give me now		*Oh, really? I wonder what you'll say if*
For that same handkerchief?		*you saw a little piece of fabric I have?*
IAGO	What handkerchief?	*What little piece of fabric?*
EMILIA		
What handkerchief?		*What little piece of fabric?*
Why, that the Moor first gave to Desdemona,		*How about the first gift Othello gave her,*
That which so often you did bid me steal.		*The handkerchief you want me to take.*
IAGO		
Hast stol'n it from her?		*Oh! Excellent, you took it?*

APPENDIX 3: PARAPHRASE OF EMILIA AND IAGO SCENE

EMILIA		
No, faith, she let it drop by negligence,		*Of course not! She dropped it right here,*
And, to th'advantage, I, being here, took't up.		*And since I was nearby, I picked it up.*
Look, here it is.		*See? I've got it right here. (Waving it)*
IAGO	A good wench! Give it me.	*Atta girl! Give it to me – (tries to grab it)*
EMILIA		
What will you do with 't, that you have been so earnest		*Not so fast! Why do you want it?*
To have me filch it?		*Begging me to steal it!*
IAGO	Why, what is that to you?	*Aw, it's a secret, none of your business.*
EMILIA		*(He takes it from her)*
If it be not for some purpose of import		*Whoa! If it's not super important,*
Give't me again. Poor lady, she'll run mad		*I want it back! Poor thing, she'll go crazy*
When she shall lack it.		*when she realizes it's gone.*
IAGO		
Be not acknown on't, I have use for it.		*Oh, it's no big deal. I just need it.*
Go, leave me.	Exit Emilia.	*Seriously, don't worry about it. Off you go!*
I will in Cassio's lodging lose this napkin		*Yes! Now I'll hide this in Cassio's bunk,*
And let him find it. Trifles light as air		*and he'll discover it. This little thing,*
Are to the jealous confirmations strong		*in Othello's jealous mind, will prove*
As proofs of holy writ. This may do something.		*her guilt like it's a Bible. This is progress!*
The Moor already changes with my poison:		*Othello was already taking all my bait.*

Dangerous conceits are in their natures poisons,	*Schemes like mine can seem poisonous,*
Which at the first are scarce found to distaste,	*Even if at first it's not noticeable,*
But with a little art upon the blood	*But eventually, with some treachery I add,*
Burn like the mines of sulphur.	*It will destroy him like acid.*

GLOSSARY[1]

Actions: Specific behaviors or maneuvers actors and characters employ in pursuit of their intentions. Actions are typically described with active verbs, using a test phrase of "I _____ you" or "I _____" to gauge their effectiveness.

Active Listening: A communication technique that involves fully focusing on the speaker, understanding their message, and responding appropriately, enhancing engagement in dialogue.

Alacrity: A readiness and eagerness to engage with the material, characterized by promptness and enthusiasm, allowing actors to approach their craft with confidence.

Anapest: A foot of verse that contains two unstressed syllables and one stressed syllable, resulting in a quickened pace, in order to absorb the extra syllable without adding length.

Antiracism: A commitment to actively opposing racism by actively challenging racist policies, behaviors, and beliefs, promoting a more inclusive and equitable artistic environment, particularly important in interpreting and presenting classical texts; often integrated into the artistic process and decisions when working with heightened texts.

Antithesis: A rhetorical device that contrasts opposing ideas. In heightened text, it helps clarify meaning by presenting related, opposing, different, or similar concepts or words.

Apostrophe: A punctuation mark used to indicate possession or the omission of letters (as in elisions). In heightened text, it may also affect the pronunciation of words to maintain meter.

Beat: A unit of action or a significant change in a scene's direction. It signifies a moment during which a character's primary objective or action changes.

Beat Change: A significant change in a scene in topic, emotion, action, or intention.

Beats: Small units of action or emotional changes within a scene. A beat change signifies a significant change in the scene's direction or focus.

Character Connection: The empathetic and emotional bond that an actor establishes with their character and fellow performers, allowing for authentic interactions on stage.

Character's Goals: The desires or objectives that drive a character's actions and decisions within a scene or play, essential for developing conflict and resolution.

Clarity: The quality of being easily understood. In acting, it refers to the articulation and delivery of lines so that the audience comprehends the character's intentions and emotions.

Colon: A punctuation mark that introduces a list, explanation, or elaboration. It indicates that more information will follow and requires energy by the speaker to set up what comes next.

Comma: A punctuation mark that indicates a pause or separation of ideas within a sentence, helping maintain the flow of speech. A comma might be an opportunity for a breath or a signal to continue the text without a break.

Conflict: A struggle between opposing forces, essential for creating drama. Conflict can be internal (within a character) or external (between characters or against societal norms, nature, or technology).

Connected Speech: A natural way of speaking that flows smoothly, often achieved by linking words and phrases together to convey meaning effectively without excessive enunciation.

Dash (Em Dash, En Dash): A punctuation mark that indicates a break or interruption in thought. The em dash (—) often signifies a more dramatic pause, while the en dash (–) can indicate ranges or connections.

Dynamic Acting: Performance characterized by spontaneous, responsive actions influenced by the moment-to-moment interplay between characters.

Ellipsis: A series of three dots indicating that a thought trails off or is incomplete, suggesting a pause in speech.

Empty Feet: The space and time left open for action or response by actors when a verse line is short by metrical feet. An intentional choice by the author to indicate that something must occur in order for the next line to be spoken.

End Stop: A term used to indicate the end of a verse line, sentence, or thought, which can be signified by the use of a period, question mark, or exclamation point. The voice of the speaker typically brings the idea to a close. The term Full Stop indicates some vehemence at the end of the thought.

Epic Caesura: a three-syllable weak ending foot [˘ / ˘] located anywhere but at the end of a line, followed by any form of punctuation (, ; : . ? ! --) that serves as a pause within a thought or between thoughts.

Flexibility in Performance: The ability of an actor to adapt their approach depending on the style of the text, whether it requires a classical or contemporary interpretation.

Given Circumstances (GC): The facts provided by the text that provide information about the who, what, where, and why of setting, previous action, situation, and relationships.

Heightened Text: Language that differs from everyday speech, designed to express feelings, ideas, and intentions with unique power and energy. Often found in plays, poems, and song lyrics, a style of writing that uses elevated language. It requires actors to explore complex emotions and convey meaning through rhythm and word choice.

Hook: A word, action, or phrase that compels a character to speak or act; it connects dialogue and facilitates smooth transitions within conversation and scene flow; enhancing engagement through active listening and response to impulses.

Hooking: A technique for actors to identify and say aloud hooks that drive the scene forward, used to establish a connection between a character's dialogue and another character's response, enhancing interaction and dynamic acting.

Iambic Pentameter: A specific type of meter in poetry consisting of lines with ten syllables, arranged in five pairs of alternating unstressed and stressed syllables.

Imagery: Descriptive language that appeals to the senses, helping to create vivid pictures in the audience's mind and enhance the emotional resonance of the text.

Intentions: Objectives or goals that a character seeks to achieve in a scene. They guide actions and choices, helping to define the character's motivations.

Line-Out: A technique for breaking prose or dialogue into manageable chunks by creating new lines to delineate thoughts or ideas, facilitating easier understanding and performance.

Listening and Responding: A fundamental acting skill that involves being present in the moment, actively listening to fellow actors, and responding in real-time to create a believable and dynamic performance.

Non-Verbal Action: Physical movements or gestures that accompany dialogue, providing additional context and emotional depth to the spoken lines.

Operative Words: Key words in a text that carry significant weight and meaning, which actors underline and emphasize to clarify and enhance the conveyed message. They are categorized into primary operatives (most emphasized) and secondary operatives (less emphasized).

Paraphrase: Rewriting or saying a line or phrase in one's own words to ensure understanding of its meaning, imagery, and references.

Paraphrasing: The process of restating heightened text in one's own words to clarify meaning and ensure that the actor understands the content of the dialogue, meaning, imagery, and references. This is particularly important for actors working with heightened language.

Parenthetical Phrases: Additional information set off by parentheses or commas that provide context but are generally less critical than the main thought. Vocal delivery typically lowers in pitch during these phrases, with a slight increase in pace.

Prose: The ordinary form of written or spoken language, in sentences and paragraphs without metrical structure. Unlike verse, prose adheres to the natural flow of speech, which can pose different challenges for actors. A line-out is used to organize the text by thoughts and phrases.

Punctuation: Marks used in writing to clarify meaning, structure sentences, and indicate pauses or stops. Understanding punctuation is crucial for actors to deliver lines meaningfully.

Pyrrhic: A name for a foot of verse in which both sounds or syllables are unstressed. This can be two small words of little significance to the main idea, or the unstressed ending of a word combined with an unstressed beginning of another word.

Pyrrhic feet usually occur in the 2nd, 3rd, or 4th foot of an iambic pentameter line and direct focus to the stronger stresses in the line.

Rehearsal Room: The space where actors practice and develop their performances, focusing on both text and staging.

Rhetoric: The art of using language effectively to persuade or convey meaning. It includes the study of figures of speech, rhetorical devices, and arguments within dialogue.

Rhetorical Progression: A sequence in a speech where an idea develops through lists, connected thoughts, or a series of images and metaphors, building in energy or emotion, often culminating in a conclusion or significant expression.

Rhyming Couplets: A pair of consecutive lines of poetry that end with words that rhyme with each other. Typically, both lines have the same meter, which gives the couplet a rhythmic and cohesive sound. Rhyming couplets are commonly used in various poetic forms, including sonnets, and they can serve to create an ending, emphasis, humor, or a particular emotional effect.

Scansion: The process of analyzing the rhythm of a line of verse by marking above syllables if they are stressed or unstressed, providing insights into the emotional and rhythmic structure of the heightened language.

Semi-colon: This blended punctuation merges a comma with a colon [;] and separates two related thoughts, often complete sentences. A semi-colon indicates that a slight pause occurs, a little more than a comma, and a little less than a Full Stop, and a breath is needed to invest in the new but related thought that comes next.

Shared Lines: A verse line that ends without being fully ten syllables, but is formatted in a way that indicates that it shares the meter with the previous or next line. Often shared lines can occur across two or more characters' speeches, or shared between two. No pause is needed beyond the existing weight of any punctuation, making the pace quick and the response immediate. In some printed editions, there are no few indications of short or shared lines.

Shifts: Subtle changes in tactics or focus within a beat. Unlike beat changes, shifts indicate more nuanced transitions in thought or emotion.

Short Lines: A verse line that ends without being fully ten syllables, leaving "empty feet" in which action or response occurs. The space that is left empty in a short line is filled with behavior as part of the story, relevant to the time made available by the missing metrical feet. In some printed editions, there are no few indications of short or shared lines.

Soliloquy: A speech where a character speaks their thoughts aloud, often directly addressing the audience or themselves, revealing inner conflicts and motivations.

Spondee: A foot of iambic pentameter in which both syllables are stressed, often for making particular points, conveying urgency or specificity. These rare instances are often preceded by a Trochee or a Pyrrhic foot, in order to set up the higher level of emphasis.

Stage Directions: Instructions in the script that guide actors on movement, tone, and expression, enhancing the portrayal of characters and story dynamics.

Subtext: The underlying meaning or unspoken ideas within a dialogue that add depth to characters' motivations and interactions. What a character really means is often hidden, not expressed, but played in some way.

Table Work: The initial phase of the play rehearsal process where the director, dramaturg, and actors discuss the script, analyze the text, and make initial choices about character and scene before staging or physical work begins.

Tactic: The approach or strategy a character employs to achieve their specific objectives within a scene. Tactics can change based on responses from scene partners.

Text Analysis: The process of examining a script to understand its structure, themes, character motivations, and the subtext of the language. This analysis helps actors to make informed choices in their performances.

Textual Action: Implicit actions or movements suggested by the dialogue itself, which inform how a scene is staged and performed even without explicit stage directions.

Tone: The attitude expressed through the speaker's choice of words and stylistic elements, which can affect how a line or scene is received by an audience.

Trochee: A common variation in iambic pentameter in which the stress pattern of the metric foot is reversed to be a stressed syllable followed by the unstressed syllable.

Verb: A part of speech describing an action, state, or occurrence; in acting, verbs are central to defining the actions and tactics of a character.

Verbal Stimulus: The words spoken by a character that prompt a reaction or change in behavior from another character.

Vernacular Language: The everyday language and expressions used by contemporary playwrights, reflecting how people really talk in their specific cultural context.

Vocal Emphasis: The use of pitch, volume, and rhythm in spoken language to highlight operative words and enhance meaning.

Verse: A form of writing that has a specific rhythmic and metrical structure, often associated with poetry and certain theatrical works. Actors must learn to navigate the rhythm and pace of heightened language within verse.

Weak Ending (formerly "feminine ending"): A final metric foot in a verse line that ends with an extra unstressed syllable.

Word Association Game: An exercise where participants respond to a prompt with related words, enhancing active listening and impulsive response skills.

World of the Play: The unique setting, time period, and atmosphere created by the playwright and director. Actors must fully inhabit this world to deliver a convincing performance.

Note

1 The Author acknowledges the use of sources including the OED and online dictionaries and ChatGPT (https://chat.openai.com/) in generating and organizing glossary terms found within the manuscript.

BIBLIOGRAPHY

Asimov, Isaac. *Asimov's Guide to Shakespeare*, Volumes 1–2. Avenel Books, 1978.
Balk, H. Wesley. *The Complete Singer Actor: Training for Music Theatre*. University of Minnesota Press, 1977.
Barton, John. *Playing Shakespeare*. Methuen, 1984.
Berry, Cicely. *The Actor and the Text*. Virgin, 1993.
Brandreth, Benet. *Shakespearean Rhetoric: A Practical Guide for Actors, Directors, Students and Teachers*. Bloomsbury, 2021.
Calderone, Maria and Lloyd-Williams, Maggie. *Actions: The Actor's Thesaurus*. Nick Hern Books, 2004.
Cohen, Robert. *Acting Power: The 21st Century Edition*. Routledge, 2013.
Dweck, Carol. *Mindset: The New Psychology of Success*. Ballantine, 2006.
Fuchs, Elinor. "EF's Visit to a Small Planet: Some Questions to Ask a Play." *Theatre* 34, no. 2 (2004): 5–9. https://web.mit.edu/jscheib/Public/foundations_06/ef_smallplanet.pdf
Gallwey, Timothy. *The Inner Game of Tennis*. Random House, 1997.
Gibson, Rex. *Teaching Shakespeare*. Cambridge University Press, 1998.
Hamilton, Anne M. and Walter Byongsok Chon. *Dramaturgy: The Basics*. Routledge, 2022.
Hansberry, Lorraine. *A Raisin in the Sun*. Penguin Random House (originally 1959).
Jory, Jon. *Tips: Ideas for Actors*. Smith & Kraus, 2000.
Kiely, Damon. *Play Directing: The Basics*. Routledge, 2023.
Kijo, Murakami, *First Autumn Morning* (1917). "Haiku Analysis," accessed September 2024, https://poemanalysis.com/murakami-kijo/poems/
Kushner, Tony. *Angels in America: Millennium Approaches*. TCG Books, 1993.
Lessac, Arthur. *The Use and Training of the Human Voice: A Bio-Dynamic Approach to Vocal Life*. McGraw-Hill/Mayfield, 1996.
Linklater, Kristin. *Freeing the Natural Voice*. Drama Book Specialists, 1976.
Linklater, Kristin. *Freeing Shakespeare's Voice: The Actor's Guide to Talking the Text*. Theatre Communications Group, Inc., 1992.
Logan, Gary. *The Eloquent Shakespeare: A Pronouncing Dictionary for the Complete Dramatic Works with Notes to Untie the Modern Tongue*. University of Chicago, 2012.

Magruder, James. *The Triumph of Love by Marivaux*. Dramatists Play Service, 1994.
Magruder, James. *The Miser by Molière*. Dramatists Play Service, 2005.
Magruder, James. *The Imaginary Invalid by Molière*. Dramatists Play Service, 2006.
Meisner, Sanford and Dennis Longwell. *Sanford Meisner on Acting*. Knopf Doubleday Publishing Group, 2012.
Miranda, Lin-Manuel. *Hamilton: An American Musical Original Broadway Cast*. Atlantic Recording, 2016.
Moliere. *The Misanthrope* (translated by Richard Wilbur). Dramatists Play Service/Broadway Licensing, 1955.
Neruda, Pablo. *Romeo y Julieta* (translation). Editorial Losada, 1967.
O'Neil, Brian. *Acting as a Business*. Vintage, 2014.
Rodenburg, Patsy. *Speaking Shakespeare*. Palgrave MacMillan, 2002.
Schoolhouse Rock, *(Animated Video)* "Conjunction Junction, What's Your Function?" Back to Schoolhouse Rock: "Punctuation Junction What's Your Function?" Music & Lyrics: Bob Dorough Performed By: Jack Sheldon & Terry Morrell Animation: Kimmelman and Associates First Aired: 1973. Available online: https://www.youtube.com/watch?v=LjdCFat9rjI
Shakespeare, William. *Measure for Measure*, The Arden Shakespeare edition, edited by J. W. Lever. Routledge, 1965.
Shakespeare, William. *The Complete Pelican Shakespeare*, edited by Alfred Harbage. Pelican, 1971.
Shakespeare, William. *The Arden Shakespeare Complete Works*, edited by Richard Proudfoot, Ann Thompson and David Scott Kastan. Thomson, 2001.
Shakespeare, William. *A New Variorum Edition of Shakespeare: Hamlet*. Legare Street Press, 2022 (Originally published in 1877).
Shakespeare, William. "The Complete Works of William Shakespeare." Updated May 10, 2023. https://shakespeare.mit.edu/.
Skinner, Edith. *Speak with Distinction: The Classic Skinner Method of Speech for the Stage*. Applause, 1990.
Spolin, Viola. *Improvisation for the Theatre* (3rd Edition). Northwestern University Press, 1999.
Stanislavski, Konstantin. *An Actor's Work* (translated by Jean Benedetti). Routledge Classics, 2016.
Toner, Anne. *Ellipsis in English Literature: Signs of Omission*. Cambridge University Press, 2015.
Wilbur, Richard. *Moliere The Misanthrope Comedy in Five Acts, 1666* (Translated into English verse). Dramatists Play Service/Broadway Licensing, 1955.
Wilbur, Richard. *Molière: The Misanthrope*. Dramatists Play Service, 1998.
Wilde, Oscar. *The Importance of Being Earnest*. (1895) Project Gutenberg, available online at https://www.gutenberg.org/files/844/844-h/844-h.htm.
Wright, George T. *Shakespeare's Metrical Art*. University of California Press, 1988.
Young, Harvey. *Theatre and Race*. Macmillan International Higher Education, 2013.

INDEX

A Midsummer Night's Dream (Shakespeare) 102, 195
A Raisin in the Sun (Hansberry, Lorraine) 89, 91–92, 225
actions 6, 8, 34, 60, 80, 88–89, 91–92, 106, 112, 114, 118, 121–122, 130, 135, 143–154, 158, 161, 171, 196, 198–201, 203, 218–220, 223–224
active listening 115–121, 127, 138, 141–143, 201, 218, 220, 224
Actor and the Text, The (Berry) 164, 225
adjustments 30, 153, 196, 198
Alexandrine 31, 208
Angels in America (Kushner, Tony) 2, 164, 225
antiracism (Brewer, Nicole) 61, 64, 218
antithesis 67–69, 86, 168, 170, 218
apostrophe 13, 28, 30, 44, 218
archaic phrases 40, 45, 50–51, 56, 58, 60, 63, 77
Arden 38, 48, 226
arrows 138–139, 172, 174
As You Like It (Shakespeare) 157, 159, 203

Balk, H. Wesley, *The Complete Singer Actor* 142, 154, 225
Barton, John, *Playing Shakespeare* 38, 225
beats/beat changes 8, 15, 88, 95–99, 106–109, 112, 115, 117, 128–130, 135, 145–147, 149, 158–159, 161, 163, 191, 218–219, 222

behavior 2, 46, 95, 114, 116–117, 125–127, 142, 199, 222, 224
Berry, Cicely 38, 113, 164, 183, 225
Brewer, Nicole Anti-Racist Theatre Ethos 61, 63
Broca's Area 66, 71, 87

Calderone, Marina & Lloyd-Williams, Maggie *Actions: The Actor's Thesaurus* 145, 154, 225
circles 138–139, 172, 174
colon 27, 43–44, 208, 219, 222
Comedy of Errors, The (Shakespeare) 60, 178, 209
comma 27, 42–48, 76–77, 80, 86, 99, 161, 208, 219, 221–222
comma exclamation point 47
comma question mark 46
conflict/thematic conflict 88; internal and external 102–105, 112, 115, 219, 223
contemporary playwrights 2, 164, 224
contrast 68, 170, 189, 218

dash em--and en 26–27, 44–45, 219
dictionary work 6–7, 40, 51, 55, 57, 61, 63, 65, 106, 115, 159, 161, 163
direct hit 181–182
directors 3, 11, 187, 200; auditioning for 191, 193–194, 199; working with 163, 184, 200, 223–224
Dweck, Carol 4, 225

elision/elide/eliding 13, 28–30, 44, 207–208, 218
emphasis 3, 7, 14, 18, 26, 41, 46–47, 50, 54, 65–73, 76, 86, 132, 162, 176, 180–182, 191, 205–206, 209, 222–224
empty feet/missing feet 34–37, 54, 56–57, 219, 222
epic caesura 27–28, 30–33, 207–209, 220
exceptions 5, 13, 22–23, 30, 36, 49, 156
exclamation point 27, 46–47, 49, 98, 117, 210, 220
expectations 9, 103–104, 185, 192–193, 199–200

feedback 4, 185, 195–197, 200
Folger 38–39, 64
Folio 32, 47

Gallwey, Timothy, *Inner Game of Tennis* 197, 225
Gibson, Rex 168, 184, 225
given circumstances (GC's) 3, 6–7, 88–89, 93–94, 106, 112, 118, 139, 142, 144, 159, 203, 220
growth mindset (Dweck) 4, 66, 194–195

Haiku 12–14, 225
Hamlet (Shakespeare) 23–24, 26, 30–31, 38, 43–44, 51–52, 59, 67, 73, 90–94, 102, 109–110, 118, 127, 163, 177, 181, 205, 207, 226
heightened text/heightened language 1–13, 19, 22, 29, 37–38, 40–44, 49, 57, 63, 65–66, 68, 73, 76, 86, 88, 97–98, 102–103, 105–106, 112–114, 116–117, 141–145, 153–154, 156, 160, 163–164, 168–169, 175–178, 183, 185–188, 190, 192, 194, 197–199, 201, 218, 221–222
Henry VI, Pt. 2, Henry VI, Pt. 3 (Shakespeare) 177, 208

homework/actor's homework 3, 6–9, 11, 15, 19, 22–23, 37, 40, 42, 49, 52, 55, 65–66, 71, 74, 86, 88, 98, 106–107, 112, 114–115, 118–119, 121, 135, 139, 141, 143, 147, 149–151, 153–154, 163, 166, 172, 185–186, 189–191, 193–194, 199, 203
hook/hooking/hooked 8, 114–119, 121, 123–125, 127–143, 154, 180–181, 191, 194, 201, 203, 220; phases of 127–143; rhetorical hook 170, 180–181, 191, 194, 201, 203, 220

iambic pentameter 2, 5, 6, 13–24, 26–28, 31, 37–38, 67, 69, 179–180, 191, 195, 204–210, 220, 223
images 6, 40, 49, 58–59, 65–66, 82, 84–87, 171–172, 174, 220
impulses 115–117; non-verbal and verbal responses to 121–127, 138, 141, 220
indirect hit 181–182
integrity of thought 40–43, 47, 63, 164
intentions 8, 99, 106, 144–146, 148–149, 152, 154, 167, 175, 179, 201, 219–220
intimacy 185, 199–200; consent-forward practices 186, 198–200
irregular lines 21–23, 37, 78, 191

Julius Caesar (Shakespeare) 11, 27, 91, 119, 148, 210

Kaplan, Michael Samuel 188, 192, 201
Kiely, Damon 192, 200
King John (Shakespeare) 69
King Lear (Shakespeare) 33–36, 48, 54–55, 68, 102, 107, 178
Kushner, Tony 2; *Angels in America: Millennium Approaches* 164

length of thought 158–159, 164, 167
lengthened 29, 207

INDEX 229

Lessac, Arthur *The Use and Training of the Human Voice* 175, 183, 225
line-out/lining out 8, 157–164, 166–167, 183, 189, 203, 221
linking 175–176, 219
Linklater, Kristin 38, 179, 184, 225
Logan, Gary 175–176, 183
lyrics 10–11, 18, 64, 103–104, 112, 137, 148, 153, 155–156, 170, 177–178, 184, 220, 226

Magruder, James 184, 226
main thought 47, 76–82, 86; *see also* integrity of thought
Measure for Measure (Shakespeare) 5, 8, 19, 44, 48, 50, 177, 204, 210, 226
Meisner, Sanford 93, 115–116, 142, 226
memorizing lines 3, 10, 18, 106, 129, 194
Merchant of Venice, The (Shakespeare) 38, 163, 212
metaphor 59, 80, 82–83, 169–172, 179
meter 6, 12–18, 22, 29–30, 38, 44, 156, 178, 207, 209, 218, 220, 222
Miranda, Lin-Manuel: *Hamilton: An American Musical* 103, 156, 226
Misanthrope, The (Moliere, translation by Richard Wilbur) 179–184, 226
moment-to-moment 88, 95, 138, 219; moment before 47, 92–94, 128
monologue 88, 93–94, 105–108, 110, 112–114, 136, 138, 152–153, 163, 166, 188–189, 203, 211; *see also* soliloquy
monosyllabic words 16, 20, 26, 30, 44, 66–67, 70, 72, 120
Much Ado About Nothing (Shakespeare) 60
multisyllabic words 16–17, 20, 25, 69
music 3, 5–6, 10–11, 15, 27, 105–106, 115, 154, 178, 184, 191–192, 195, 197

Neruda, Pablo *Romeo y Julieta* 151–152, 226

O'Neil, Brian *Acting as a Business* 187, 199
objective/super-objective 17, 53, 144, 146, 148, 168–169
opera 1, 11, 142, 154
operative words 5, 7–8, 65–79, 81, 84, 86, 106, 114–116, 132, 150, 153, 155, 159, 161–162, 165, 172, 174, 180–183, 186, 191, 201, 221, 224
Othello (Shakespeare) 1, 29, 31–33, 41, 44–46, 52–53, 55, 59, 61, 78, 80–83, 88, 98, 115, 137, 170, 172–173, 205–210, 214–216
Oxford English Dictionary (OED) 40, 57, 203

paraphrase 5–7, 40, 49–55, 57–61, 63, 65–66, 68, 71–73, 78–79, 82, 101, 106, 114–115, 118–119, 125, 136, 138–139, 150, 153, 159, 161–163, 171, 174, 186, 191, 203, 214, 220–221
parentheses/parenthetical phrases 44, 47, 52, 65–66, 76–82, 84, 86, 149, 221
Pelican 5, 38, 226
period/full stop 27, 42–43, 45–49, 98, 106–107, 161, 163–164, 208, 220, 222, 224
personifications/Fortune 59, 111; Hydra 59; Patience 59, 171
preparation 3, 7, 115, 138, 174, 185–186; for auditions and callbacks 185, 188–192, 194, 199
previous action 92–93, 112, 137, 220
primary action 148
problematic phrases 17, 40, 49, 58, 60
prose 12, 155–156, 160, 168, 203, 221; heightened prose 3, 8, 11, 155, 160, 164, 168, 183
public domain 2, 40–41, 55, 60, 194
punctuation 13, 23, 27–28, 30–31, 40–43, 45–46, 49, 63, 76–77, 87,

98, 106, 152, 155–160, 163, 180, 183, 191, 205, 207–208, 218–219, 221–222, 226
pyrrhic 26, 30, 120, 206, 221–223

Quarto 47
question mark 27, 46, 49, 98, 138, 209, 220
quotation marks 44

reading aloud 4, 18, 37, 42, 50, 57, 71–73, 75, 84, 86, 106, 121, 129, 138–139, 158, 160, 167, 191
regular lines 5–6, 11–12, 16, 19–31, 37, 67, 69, 72, 180, 204–206, 209
rehearsing 3, 7, 9, 11, 45, 74–75, 92, 114–115, 118, 121, 128, 135, 138, 141–143, 146–147, 149, 161, 176, 185–187, 189, 192–200, 222
rhetoric 58–59, 155, 157, 159, 161, 164, 168–169; rhetorical hook 170–175; rhetorical map 172–174, 183–184, 203, 222; rhetorical progression 222; rhetorical weapons 171
rhyme 15; ABAB 155–156, 177–179
rhyming couplets 155–157, 161, 163, 171, 175, 177–178; Molière 179–184, 222
rhythm 5, 11–12, 14, 18–22, 38, 65–66, 86, 156, 177, 181–182, 220, 222, 224
Richard II (Shakespeare) 5, 205
Richard III (Shakespeare) 21, 42–43, 51, 68, 139–140; rhetorical map of 174, 203, 205, 208, 210
Rodenburg, Patsy 38, 226
Rogers, Carl & Gordon, Thomas 115; *12 Roadblocks to Communication* (Gordon) 117
Romeo & Juliet (Shakespeare) 11, 29, 91, 148, 150–152, 210, 226

scan/scansion 4–6, 8, 14–15, 17, 25, 27–30, 32–42, 44, 49, 54–55, 60–61, 65–67, 69–73, 79, 106, 114–115, 119, 125, 150, 153, 156–157, 159–161, 166, 172, 180, 183, 186, 191, 195, 201, 204–209, 222; *see also* stress
Schoolhouse Rock 41, 64, 226
script analysis/text analysis 3, 7–8, 89–90, 92, 102, 113, 147, 223
self-tape 187–188, 190
semi-colon 45–46, 99, 209, 222
Shakespeare, William 2, 5, 10, 12, 14, 25, 27, 29, 32, 46–48, 64, 83, 91, 109–110, 113, 148, 151–152, 156, 163–164, 168, 175, 178, 183–184, 188–189, 201, 204, 210
shared lines 32–33, 35–37, 181, 209–210, 222–223
shifts 46, 93, 95–99, 101, 106–108, 117, 129, 130, 132–133, 135, 145–147, 149, 158–159, 161, 163, 191, 201, 210, 222
short lines 32–37, 54, 219, 222–223
sides 185, 188, 190–192, 199
slash marks 96–98, 191, 207
soliloquy 93–94, 105–108; direct address in 109–112, 114, 136, 138, 152–153, 163, 188–189, 223
Spolin, Viola 116, 226
spondee 26, 30, 120, 205–206, 223
stage combat/stage violence 185, 198–200
stakes 11, 35, 49, 69, 88, 102, 156, 169, 191
Stanislavski, Konstantin: foundations of acting 89, 95, 113, 144, 226
stimulus 117–118, 120–125, 201, 224
stress 15–16, 18, 20, 24, 26–28, 30, 66, 68, 72–74, 180, 200, 204–210, 223; *see also* scansion
subtext 52–54, 129, 136, 223

table work 3, 8, 135, 191–194, 223
tactics 3, 6, 8, 34, 46, 60, 80, 88–89, 91–92, 96–99, 106, 112, 114, 118, 121–122, 130, 135, 143–154, 158, 161, 168, 171, 175, 196, 198–201, 203, 218–220, 223–224
textual action 118–121, 128, 143, 223

textually supported choices 6, 11, 42, 53, 74, 115, 223
translating/translation 24, 40, 151–152, 179–180, 184–185, 226
trochee 16–17, 24–27, 30, 33–34, 38, 67–69, 79, 205–206, 224
Twelfth Night (Shakespeare) 59, 110

underlining/underline 5, 7, 14, 65–66, 68–70, 72, 86, 191, 221

variations 11–12, 14, 19–23, 26–27, 30–31, 36–39, 65, 67, 86, 168, 179–180, 205, 207
Variorum 38, 226
verbs/action verbs 70, 143–149, 154, 203, 218, 224
verse 2–6, 11–16, 20–22, 25–26; auditions in 188–189, 195, 201; blank verse 12–13, 34, 48; glossary of verse terms 218–224; iambic 31–38; Molière 179–184; punctuation in 41–42, 49, 51–52, 66, 70, 115, 119; rhyming couplets 155–157, 161, 163, 171, 175, 177–178; scansion review 204–210

Waldman, Jen 187, 201
walking the monologue 106–108, 110, 119; walking the prose line-out 163–164
weak ending/feminine ending 24–33, 67, 180–182, 206–210, 224
Wilde, Oscar 144; *The Importance of Being Earnest* (Wilde) 167–168, 184, 203, 226
Winter's Tale, The (Shakespeare) 46, 209, 213
Wright, George T. 37–38, 177, 209–210, 226

For Product Safety Concerns and Information please contact our EU
representative GPSR@taylorandfrancis.com
Taylor & Francis Verlag GmbH, Kaufingerstraße 24, 80331 München, Germany

www.ingramcontent.com/pod-product-compliance
Lightning Source LLC
Chambersburg PA
CBHW072232240426
43670CB00040B/2480